TEACHER AUTONOMY

Teacher Autonomy is a compelling exploration of the erosion of teacher independence in an era dominated by high-stakes accountability, rigid educational frameworks and a growing distrust of educators. This thought-provoking book delves into the history of autonomy in primary education, examining how shifts in policy and systems have drained creativity, individuality and meaningful connection from classrooms, leaving educators and learners alike disengaged and unmotivated.

Through the voices of real educators, including teachers, teaching assistants, senior leaders and early years practitioners, this book paints a vivid picture of the challenges faced by those on the frontlines of education. It highlights the far-reaching consequences of reduced autonomy, from teacher attrition and low morale to school refusal, mental health struggles and pupil behaviour issues. In response to this, it offers a call to action and provides practical strategies, moments of reflection and actionable solutions to empower educators and leaders to reclaim their professional independence. Covering key topics such as Ofsted, observation and accountability, planning and assessment, teacher retention, teamwork, and mental health and wellbeing, each chapter ignites vital conversations about the future of education.

This book is a must-read for teachers, school leaders and policymakers at any stage of their career, offering valuable insights into how to rebuild trust, foster creativity and rekindle meaningful connections at the core of teaching, as well as navigate the change in the current educational landscape.

Sophie Smith-Tong has over 15 years' experience as a primary teacher and is the founder of Mindfulness for learning. A passionate advocate for teacher wellbeing, she frequently speaks on the topic, including at the Institute of Education. In addition to her work as an educator, she is a Mental Health and Wellbeing Lead and Early Years Specialist, a family wellbeing consultant and hosts a regular podcast on education and family wellbeing.

"Sophie's book has such powerful possibilities…"

Greg Bottrill, *Author and Childhood Advocate*

"The US and England have experimented recently with top-down, government-mandated control of what teachers and their students can do in the classroom and how both are evaluated. The results have been disastrous. Kids dislike school at record rates, meaningful learning has declined, and mental disorders among kids have skyrocketed. Please read and act on Sophie Smith-Tong's impassioned and practical guide for bringing teacher autonomy and sanity back to schools."

Peter Gray, *Research Professor of Psychology and Neuroscience at Boston College, USA*

"Although teacher autonomy matters a great deal, this book is so much more than this. It is about what education means and how children learn. This is a brilliant book; it is comprehensive, powerfully written with numerous case studies and commentaries. It deserves to be read by everyone who cares about the future of education, our children and their teachers."

Dr Sue Roffey, *Honorary Associate Professor, UCL, Director of Growing Great Schools Worldwide and Author of* ASPIRE to Wellbeing and Learning for All

"You need to read this book. It is thought provoking, relevant and necessary to the conversation around teacher retention and recruitment. What has happened to teacher autonomy? Sophie Smith-Tong examines in detail how we have reached this point, what is happening now and what the future holds. Drawing also on a range of voices across education, Sophie presents the case for our educators to have autonomy and agency, to take responsibility and not to be shoehorned into the narrow confines of faceless, prescribed lesson plans and soulless policies. Autonomy doesn't mean being off the leash, it is about professional progress and professionalism, personal development and personality. Whether teacher or leader, you need to read this book. You won't regret it."

Andrew Cowley, *Wellbeing Consultant, Speaker, Author and Coach*

TEACHER AUTONOMY

Where Has It Gone and Why
We Need It Back

Sophie Smith-Tong

LONDON AND NEW YORK

Designed cover image: © Eliza Fricker

First published 2026
by Routledge
4 Park Square, Milton Park, Abingdon, Oxon OX14 4RN

and by Routledge
605 Third Avenue, New York, NY 10158

Routledge is an imprint of the Taylor & Francis Group, an informa business

© 2026 Sophie Smith-Tong

The right of Sophie Smith-Tong to be identified as author of this work has been asserted in accordance with sections 77 and 78 of the Copyright, Designs and Patents Act 1988.

All rights reserved. No part of this book may be reprinted or reproduced or utilised in any form or by any electronic, mechanical, or other means, now known or hereafter invented, including photocopying and recording, or in any information storage or retrieval system, without permission in writing from the publishers.

For Product Safety Concerns and Information please contact our EU representative GPSR@taylorandfrancis.com. Taylor & Francis Verlag GmbH, Kaufingerstraße 24, 80331 München, Germany.

Trademark notice: Product or corporate names may be trademarks or registered trademarks, and are used only for identification and explanation without intent to infringe.

British Library Cataloguing-in-Publication Data
A catalogue record for this book is available from the British Library

Library of Congress Cataloging-in-Publication Data
Names: Smith-Tong, Sophie author
Title: Teacher autonomy : where has it gone and why we need it back / Sophie Smith-Tong.
Description: Abingdon, Oxon ; New York, NY : Routledge, 2026. | Includes bibliographical references and index.
Identifiers: LCCN 2025036742 (print) | LCCN 2025036743 (ebook) | ISBN 9781032874586 paperback | ISBN 9781032874579 hardback | ISBN 9781003532729 ebook
Subjects: LCSH: Primary school teaching | Teacher effectiveness | Learner autonomy | Educational accountability | Educational change
Classification: LCC LB1555 .S64 2026 (print) | LCC LB1555 (ebook)
LC record available at https://lccn.loc.gov/2025036742
LC ebook record available at https://lccn.loc.gov/2025036743

ISBN: 978-1-032-87457-9 (hbk)
ISBN: 978-1-032-87458-6 (pbk)
ISBN: 978-1-003-53272-9 (ebk)

DOI: 10.4324/9781003532729

Typeset in Interstate
by KnowledgeWorks Global Ltd.

For Leisa, my inspiring drama teacher who has always championed autonomy and Liv, a nursery child who fought for education revolution even at the tender age of 3.

CONTENTS

Acknowledgements	viii
Foreword	xi
List of contributors	xiii

Introduction: This is only the beginning   1

including THE BIG IDEA on autonomy and poor retention by Anon

1 Autonomy and teacher wellbeing   7

including THE BIG IDEA on wellbeing by Adrian Bethune

2 Teaching and learning   32

including THE BIG IDEA on curriculum by Annabelle Kapoor

3 Accountability   55

including THE BIG IDEA on accountability and motivation by Andrew Cowley

4 The children   83

including THE BIG IDEA on impacts on children by Tina Farr

5 Digital autonomy   114

including THE BIG IDEA on digital autonomy by Bukky Yusuf

6 Autonomy in action   133

including THE BIG IDEA on the power of real and human collaboration by Eliza Fricker

The future: The revolution begins here   153

including THE BIG IDEA on autonomy by Leisa Rea

Index   156

ACKNOWLEDGEMENTS

Writing this book has been hard – it broke me a little. Not because I found the topic hard (I could have written and spoken about teacher autonomy forever and still not have covered all of the content that arose) but because for the entire two-year writing process I have been a teacher. Teacher life is extremely busy, and it doesn't leave much space to be an author too.

Being an expert in educator wellbeing I was aware that maintaining my routines and positive habits was of utmost importance; however, I failed to do so (said with the most compassion for myself, I promise). Approximately 18 months into the process many of my positive routines had dissolved – my yoga practice went from every night to once a week (thank you to my inspirational yoga teacher Sarah for maintaining that once a week), my running turned into a quick walk here and there and socialising had died a death. Alongside my diminishing movement opportunities my eating habits were unrecognisable – I began to rely on unhealthy snacking to get me through mammoth writing sessions. Suddenly, I looked up and no longer recognised myself – physically and mentally. I share this with you, not for sympathy (after all, I decided to write a book), but to show you that self-care is hard and especially so as a teacher. This book explores many of the challenges that we teachers face every day – it will be a tough (but enjoyable) read as you take note and seek to find balance, answers and ultimately a revolution. With this in mind, it is important that whilst reading this book you avoid responding with "things should be better by now – why is nothing happening"? but instead with "change takes time, and I'm doing my best. Every small step counts". Without compassion and love for ourselves we have no starting point, no momentum or energy required for change – and change is certainly needed.

In view of this, I would like to thank both my School and Children's Centre headteachers – Sandy and Ciara who gifted me flexible working. Ciara – you have been extremely supportive of the writing process and all that it brought with it – a teacher that asks a lot of questions in the name of book research. Thank you for listening to my ideas.

On top of working as a teacher I run my own business – Mindfulness for learning (which ironically started to take off when I committed to writing a book!). Running your own business is time-consuming and exhausting – switching off from work when it is born from your own hard work, creativity and innovation is almost impossible. For this I want to thank my partner teacher who has shouldered the responsibility when needed and has supported my writing process by listening to and holding me – allowing me to bend her ear when I was exploring ideas and trying to get to the bottom of conundrums. She has enabled me to find balance when it was a challenge and offered me comfort when I felt I could no longer achieve what I set out to do – Beth, I love you so much and thank you from the bottom of my heart for being my inspiration and strength.

When you have a full-time teaching job, run your own business and write a book there is not much time left, and my family has been extremely patient with my lack of time. It has been really difficult as a mother and partner to allow myself the time to write. I want to thank my children and partner for lending me to the writing process, for being proud and supportive when I was tapping away at the keyboard, as I sat next to their bed at bedtime, as I disappeared on weekends and evenings and as I mentally went to another space even when I was physically present. Throughout the process, I kept thinking about the pride they would hopefully feel for their mama/partner who despite the challenges as a female founder, educator and writer has written a book – something that I never would have thought I could achieve. I hope you are proud of me and that it makes you realise that you can do anything you want to do. Be bold, be brave and find joy. I love you Woody, Dylan and Lewis.

Thanks to my pops who is a constant source of emotional support – thank you for listening to me as I cried with the pressure of delivering on my writing deadlines and thanks to my sister, Jessica who partied and relaxed with me when I needed to let loose and find peace in the process. To my mama – she has proofread everything that I have ever written since I was 16 years old. Her patience and interest in whatever project I am working on is something I will try my best to emulate for my own children. Thank you so much, fingers crossed there are no mistakes in here mum!

I want to also thank Routledge and in particular my editors Maddie and Bruce who offered very realistic and enlightening tips, suggestions and adaptations – ideas that have helped me develop as a writer. I want to thank them for their positive feedback that kept me going when I really didn't believe that this book would ever actually happen.

Thank you to my social media buddies who inspire me every day including Andrew Cowley, Adrian Bethune, Greg Bottrill, Ben Levinson, Laura Henry-Allain, Eliza Fricker (who did a marvellous job on the cover!), Tina Farr and Dr Poppy Gibson. A HUGE thank you to all my contributors – this book would not work without your real-life experiences to show how autonomy works and describe what happens when we are failed by a lack of it. Your vulnerable and honest contributions have enabled me to dive deep into the topic and have helped me to challenge my beliefs, understanding and experiences. A sincere thank you to Julia Waters for taking the time and emotional energy to read through the chapter on accountability. I am deeply grateful for your care and generosity in helping ensure that my writing honoured the truth and did justice to Ruth's story.

Thank you to Andy Potts, my A-level English literature teacher who told me that I *could* write despite my lack of confidence and told me not to ramble! Hopefully the word count is reflective of the lesson you taught me Mr Potts!

Leisa Rea was my drama teacher in secondary school and showed me what rebellion and positive disruption could achieve. As a child I was taught to be compliant. When I reached 13, I had no idea who I actually was – I wasn't given the space to find out. Leisa showed me what creativity could do, she gave me the tools to explore freely and enabled me to rediscover a playfulness that would become an invaluable tool, not only as a mother and as a teacher but as a writer and creator. Leisa I will hold what you did for me in my heart forever.

Now the time has come to read the book. I hope you're able to take something valuable from it. If you have any comments or questions, then do get in touch and/or follow me @mforlearning. This conversation is ever evolving, and I hope that it is talked about until we get the change we need. Ask questions, challenge and be bold.

Sophie x

FOREWORD

What if children could leave a Tripadvisor review of their school day? I wonder what they would say?

What would motivate one child to give five stars and another zero? What would prove to be their standout moments, those experiences which create core memories that can be revisited across a lifetime? How many children might say that they feel a joie de vivre about their school day? I think we can probably guess the answers...

Perhaps equally as important, and arguably even more so, what Tripadvisor review might teaching staff write? For it seems that in the modern discourse that swirls around education, the central experiences of the adults are barely acknowledged. Yes, there will be wellbeing days, motivational posters and the occasional box of biscuits in the staffroom, but can we truly say that the inner life of the teacher and support staff is at the top of the priority list?

Progress for children, their outcomes, their health and their social identities seem to dominate policies and planning, yet in doing so, the actual source of all of these is overlooked: the adult, the fountain of joy and magnetism.

We know why, of course. The political dogma – still haunting us with the spectres that stretch right back to Victorian Times – dominates the school day, sitting on it like a great big toad. This dogma, what I refer to as The Adult World, is entombed by "The Free Market", neoliberalism, profit before people and "quiet children are good children", and is incapable of giving us the very thing that is truly needed to connect teacher and child, as well as the teacher to themselves. That thing, as we know, is love.

Really, this book is all about love. And it is love that the education system as it stands is bereft of. It cannot offer love because it is freedom. The moment you are free – to create, play, explore, invent – you place yourself beyond the reach of dogma. It is anti-love that consistently holds children back from who they are and who they can become, replacing play and adventure with the Empty Speak of "life chances" and a world of labels which so quickly diminish children – low ability, anyone?

We look around the educational landscape and look for love. Do we see it? Perhaps a glimmer, but it is lost within the mire of uniform policies, curriculums, schemes and the hours spent dragging children through "learning". As individual educators we love children, that is beyond doubt, but the claustrophobia and drudgery we find ourselves in create within us a painful incongruence – we love, but there is no place for this love to go because the systems will not countenance it. The systems shut it down to protect itself. Suddenly, we see that the system is not there for children; it is not there for teachers – it merely exists for its own self-preservation.

And this is why Sophie's book has such powerful possibilities since it questions all the structures that inhibit who we are and who children can become. I hope as you delve into its pages that you are galvanised to ask your own questions and become yet more determined to advocate not just for childhood but for love itself.

It is my belief that a new world can be brought into life, not by attempting to adjust the old world, but by building a whole new one that is so compelling that the old world has to come and join it. For me, play lies at the heart of this new world. It also holds hands with love, and I hope as you turn each page, you will make that commitment to both so that the new world edges ever closer.

Mors janua vitae…

Greg Bottrill
Author and childhood advocate

LIST OF CONTRIBUTORS

Foreword

Greg Bottrill - Author and Childhood Advocate
Greg Bottrill is a passionate Childhood Advocate and author of *Can I Go And Play Now?*, *School and the Magic of Children* and *Love Letters to Play*. He is also the creator of Drawing Club, Adventure Island and The Curious Quests, all of which aim to reclaim childhood and what he calls "teacherhood", the play-full, creative adult. All his work is centred around his Inner Child Led Pedagogy which explores how the unhealed wounded inner child of the adult and the power structures it finds itself in are the prime mountains facing critical educational change.

Introduction

Anon. Early Years Foundation Stage (EYFS) Specialist. Inner London Primary School

Chapter 1

David Smith. Former Secondary English Teacher. Inner London Secondary
David is a programmer/machine learning engineer based in Canberra, Australia. He is a former English teacher who still takes an interest in education systems, although these days you're more likely to find him teaching colleagues about neural networks than teenagers about Shakespeare. Occasionally he writes stuff under the pen name David Cramer Smith. His novel *Medway* is available to purchase here: https://www.medwayish.com/product/medway-a-novel

Lucy Hevawitharane. Primary Teacher. Inner London Primary
Lucy Hevawitharane has been teaching in state and independent schools across London for over 16 years. She specialises in early years education, where she believes that strong foundations and a lifelong love of learning are built through great teaching and a freedom to play and explore. At home, she enjoys cooking and knitting when she's not too busy chasing her three young boys around.

Jayne Carter. Director of Ignite Education Ltd
Jayne is the Director of Ignite Education Ltd, providing consultancy for practitioners within the Early Years and Primary sector. She uses coaching as a model for change, facilitating

professional conversations which are focused on empowering others and generating growth in knowledge and skills. Jayne is also a project manager at Partnership for Children, a charity who develop programmes to support the mental health of pupils in the UK and internationally.

Kaurice Moran. Year 1 Class Teacher. Inner London Primary School
Kaurice Moran has been a primary school teacher for the past 15 years. She started her career working in special needs settings, primarily working with autistic children. For the majority of her time working within mainstream settings she has specialised in the Early Years Foundation Stage; with her specific interests being in supporting children with additional needs and promoting early reading. Kaurice later trained as a yoga teacher and focused on teaching yoga and meditation to children; with a passion for promoting positive wellbeing and coping strategies to young people.

Adrian Bethune. Founder of Teachappy. Teacher. Author. Speaker
Adrian Bethune is a part-time primary school teacher, associate lecturer at Oxford Brookes University, Deputy Chair of the Well Schools strategic board and the founder of Teachappy. Adrian is the author of the award-winning *Wellbeing In The Primary Classroom: A Practical Guide To Teaching Happiness* (Bloomsbury, 2018 and 2nd Ed. 2023), co-author with Dr Emma Kell of *A Little Guide to Teacher Wellbeing and Self-care* (Sage, 2020) and lead author for the *Oxford International Curriculum for Wellbeing* (Oxford University Press, 2021). He is currently co-editing the book *Questions of Teacher Wellbeing for ECTs* (Routledge) due out in late 2025. www.teachappy.co.uk

Chapter 2

Jess Gosling. International Teacher in British International Schools
Jess Gosling is an experienced international teacher of more than 10 years. She has worked in international schools in several continents, as both teacher and leader, often with a majority of international children where English is a second or additional language. She has a keen interest in a nurturing curriculum, based on play-based learning.

Sarah DeSilva. Year 6 Teacher. Inner London Primary

Anon. Primary School Teacher and EYFS Specialist. Inner London Primary School

Annabelle Kapoor. Head Teacher. Inner London Primary School
Annabelle Kapoor is the Headteacher of Drayton Park, a top-performing primary school in Islington, known for its progressive and inclusive approaches to education and its emphasis on wellbeing and the development of life skills. Annabelle is also a leadership trainer and executive coach, specialising in building motivation and happiness at work, empowering teams and creating a culture of connection, ambition and innovation. Annabelle holds a First-Class Honours Psychology degree from University College London and a PGCE from the Institute of Education. Her passion for education was shaped by many joyful years teaching across the primary key stages. Instagram: @annabellekapoorcoaching/@draytonparksch Website: annabellekapoor.com

Chapter 3

Frances. Former Head Teacher
Frances started teaching in 1977 and retired in 2013 after 18 years as a Headteacher in the Primary sector.

Ben Levinson OBE. Executive Head Teacher
Ben Levinson is a school leader, writer and national advisor passionate about building ambitious, human-centred schools where staff and children thrive. He is Director of School and Trust Improvement at The Tapscott Learning Trust and Executive Headteacher at Kensington Primary School. Ben chairs Well Schools (well-school.org), contributes to national conversations on leadership, wellbeing and teacher autonomy, and is currently writing a book celebrating the profession.

Anon. Primary School Teacher

Kiera Godfrey. Parent. Inner London Primary
Kiera Godfrey is a parent to two primary-age children in London.

Andrew Cowley. Wellbeing Consultant. Speaker. Author. Coach
Andrew Cowley is the author of *The Wellbeing Toolkit*, *The Wellbeing Curriculum* and *The School Mental Health Toolkit*. A former teacher and Deputy Head, Andrew now coaches Senior Mental Health Leaders and mentors schools completing the Mental Health Award with the Carnegie Centre of Excellence in Mental Health at Leeds Beckett University. He is also a regular writer and speaker on a range of topics within the theme of wellbeing.

Chapter 4

Peter Gray. Research Professor of Psychology and Neuroscience at Boston College
Peter Gray is a research professor of psychology and neuroscience at Boston College who has conducted and published research in behavioural biology, developmental psychology, anthropology and education. He is the author of multiple editions of an internationally acclaimed introductory psychology textbook (*Psychology*, Worth Publishers, which views all of psychology from an evolutionary perspective. Most of his research over the past 30 years focuses on the role of play in human evolution and development, and especially on how children educate themselves through self-directed play and exploration, when free to do so. He has expanded on these ideas in his book, *Free to Learn: Why Unleashing the Instinct to Play Will Make Our Children Happier, More Self-Reliant, and Better Students for Life* (Basic Books), which has been translated into 18 languages. He also authors a blog called Freedom to Learn for *Psychology Today* magazine and a Substack series entitled *Play Makes Us Human*. He is one of the founders of the non-profit Let Grow, the mission of which is to renew children's freedom to play and explore independently of adult control. You can follow him on Facebook and find many of his published articles on his website.

Woody. Year 6 Child. Inner London Primary

Livia. Year 11 Child. Inner London Secondary

Berrin S. Bates. Art Teacher and Art Therapist. Inner London Primary
Berrin S. Bates has an MA in art and art therapy. She is passionate about the positive effects of art in education and child development. She practices as an artist, art teacher and an art therapist. Contact Berrin: www.artwithberrin.co.uk.

Tina Farr. Headteacher at St. Ebbes Primary School. Oxford
Tina Farr is a primary school Headteacher with 30 years' experience in education, including two headships. Her driving inspiration was, and always will be, the late Sir Ken Robinson and she is passionate about creating school cultures that maximise the opportunity for creativity to be unleashed in children and adults and where each individual belongs and feels a part of a greater purpose. Find out more about Tina's approach here:www.st-ebbes.oxon.sch.uk, www.joyoverfear.co.uk, https://www.linkedin.com/in/tina-farr-8667952bb/

Chapter 5

Lucy Lewin
Lucy Lewin has been involved in the wonderful world of early years for over two decades (almost three if you count her time as a mother) where her passion for learning, bringing joy to the lives of others and her unwavering positivity united – now as a self-confessed educational rebel Lucy serves the education sector through her innovate software and simple but effective solutions to business – find out more here: www.theprofitablenurseryacademy.com

Lyle Perkins. Artist. London
Lyle has a BA Hons from the University of Brighton and is an Artist who lives and works in London. He has exhibited widely in solo and group exhibitions since 1997, including a performance at the National Theatre and has been a finalist in the John Moores painting. Ambassador for Leadership Matters, a Network Leader for WomenEd London and co-lead for WomenEd Tech. Website: www.lyleaperkins.com. Instagram: @lyleaperkins.

Anon. Secondary School Teacher

Bukky Yusuf. Senior Leader, Educational Consultant and Coach
Bukky Yusuf FCCT FRSA is a senior leader, educational consultant and leadership development coach, working with educators on a national and international basis. She has undertaken several leadership roles within mainstream and special school settings. Beyond the classroom, Bukky is a Thought Leader with a wide variety of Ed(ucation) Tech(nology) experiences and has been co-chair of the EdTech Leadership Group to support the Government's EdTech strategy. Bukky supports the development of educators at all levels and promotes projects that help colleagues to maintain their wellbeing. She is an ambassador for Leadership Matters, a Network Leader for WomenEd London and Co-Lead for WomenEd Tech.

List of Contributors   xvii

Chapter 6

Beth Ewin. ECT Reception Class Teacher. Inner London Primary School

Hannah Grange. Manager of Secondary Training, Inspection and Improvement at Aldar Education HQ
Hannah Grange is an accomplished education professional with over a decade of leadership experience across the UK and international settings. She currently serves as Manager of Secondary Training, Inspection and Improvement at Aldar Education HQ in Abu Dhabi, supporting over 30 schools in areas such as leadership coaching, curriculum development and inspection readiness. Previously, Hannah led university guidance, and non-academic achievement at Nord Anglia's BIS Abu Dhabi and held senior roles in Literacy and English faculties across the UK. She is an NPQ facilitator, school inspector and holds postgraduate qualifications in SEND, educational leadership and an MBA. Her work is grounded in inclusive practice, curriculum innovation and staff development.

Ciara Rush. Head of Children's Centre. Inner London Children's Centre and Primary School
Ciara Rush is a dynamic senior leader with over 15 years of experience, known for her warm and approachable nature and her unwavering commitment to providing high quality, inclusive and creative early childhood education. As Head of EYFS at Ambler Primary School and Children's Centre, Ciara champions professional learning and collaborative leadership within the team. Her open-door approach creates a culture where everyone feels heard, valued and inspired to grow. Outside of the setting, Ciara contributes to local early years networks, delivers professional learning and participates in research projects aimed at improving early years practice and outcomes.

Eva Long. Baby Room Lead. Inner London Children's Centre
With over a decade of experience in early years education, Eva Long leads the baby room at her setting and serves as Equality & Diversity Lead. A passionate advocate for inclusion and anti-racism, she draws on both lived experience and professional insight. Of mixed-race heritage and a mother to a Black child, Eva's commitment to equity is deeply personal. Soon to begin teacher training, she remains dedicated to creating inclusive, meaningful learning environments where all children feel seen, valued and safe.

Eliza Fricker. Author and Illustrator. Advocate and Consultant
Eliza Fricker is an author and illustrator, and an advocate and consultant for Pathological Demand Avoidance, autism and learning. She has published several books, including *A Different Kind of Parenting*, the Sunday Times Bestselling title *Can't Not Won't*, and the acclaimed autobiographical *Thumbsucker*. Eliza offers a range of support for parents and educators on navigating autism and education, including one-to-one consultations, webinars, presentations, a podcast and the enduring original Missing the Mark illustrations and blog.

The Future

Leisa Rea. Creative Producer and Former Secondary Drama Teacher
Leisa Rea is a British director, performer and musician. She's currently the Creative Producer for a small touring orchestra. With a diverse career spanning radio, stage and education, she began by teaching in London secondary schools in the mid-1990s, later expanding her practice to hospitals, museums and a wide range of arts and community settings. Leisa is deeply committed to the belief that sparking creativity in others is a powerful catalyst for growth, connection and transformation.

Introduction
This is only the beginning

Teachers love a silver bullet, but the truth is that there isn't one.
(Lucie Lakin. Square Pegs. 2023)

Autonomy might not be a silver bullet, but it might be the closest thing to it.

"On the 24th November 2023 out of 10,199 responses on Teacher Tapp only 18% of teachers said they strongly agree with the following statement: **I have a great deal of choice and freedom in deciding how I do my work**" (Cumiskey, 2024). Why is this so low?

It's the middle of the summer holidays, and last night I had a dream. I was in perpetual work mode, on a loop. I was given a new classroom that had someone else's displays up. Their classroom was set up just as they had left it, and all of their plans were laid out on the desk for me to follow. I was told to "sort it out" but was not to *change* anything. A sense of disappointment and disconnection ensued. How on earth can I make it work if it doesn't come from me – a lack of personal investment leads to a lack of meaning, and a lack of meaning results in confusion and fragmentation. I spent my entire dream (or nightmare) attempting to find happiness at work without the means to do so. I was at a loss. Deskilled and devalued.

Autonomy is everything. Self-determination theory (SDT) is a theory developed by Edward Deci and Richard Ryan and is the idea that we have three basic psychological needs – competence, relatedness and autonomy. Simply put, when these needs are met, we are motivated, when they are not, we are less productive and unhappy. Autonomy gives us a sense of worth, belonging and connection. It makes us individual but empowers us to work together. It requires us to be creative and promotes self-expression, and by modelling self-expression we are giving those around us the permission to express.

Do you have autonomy in your setting? If you answer "yes", then I ask you to read this book and ask that same question again at the end.

Whenever I come across something in education that causes discomfort and/or frustration – a longer than required meeting, an unreasonable request, a conflicted parent exchange or a statutory assessment – I pause and reflect. As I peel back the layers, I consistently see the same foundational problem – a lack of teacher autonomy. If I could *just* make decisions about my classroom and the children I know so well then my job could be more enjoyable and rewarding. If I could be trusted to choose what work is displayed, if I could cut my carpet times down by half, if I could decide against sending homework or remove the idea of a pen licence, then maybe the kids would be alright. But many feel they can't, and they don't.

The absence of educator autonomy in modern education history is overwhelming. The Hadow Report of 1933 is one of the earliest reviews that considers the importance of educator autonomy, stating that "No teacher can do his best work with a new method until he has welded it on to his educational faith and has coloured it with part of his personality" (The Hadow Report, 1931). Despite this early mention, the increase in policy, curriculum documents and schemes do nothing but remove autonomy even further.

It was back in 2010 that I realised what little autonomy we actually have as teachers. I had just left teacher training at the Institute of Education and embarked on my newly qualified teacher (NQT) year, which is what we now call the early career teacher (ECT) years. I had been given a reception classroom job at the school where I had my longest student placement and was excited to get started. I had noted in my NQT year that the coordinator had an extremely formal approach, one that was at odds with (a) what I had learned at university and (b) how I enjoyed teaching. I was extremely naive to think that when *I* was the class teacher, I wouldn't have to teach in that same formal way and that I would be able to teach my class the way I felt best. Little did I know that the way I taught would be dictated by the senior leadership team (SLT). As I pushed back (which looking back was incredibly brave as an NQT!), it became clear that there was just no space for me or my ideas in my classroom. For an entire year I had to teach in a way that made the children cry and me feel incredibly disheartened – safe to say I left at the end of the academic year. It is quite common when struggling in this way to receive advice such as – find a school that suits you – but *surely* you should be able to be yourself wherever you work?

Our education system in the UK (and in many other countries that adopt similar approaches) isn't working; in fact, it's actively failing. Our workforce is dedicated, but our efforts are aimed at a goal that isn't shared by all: creating cookie-cutter humans. With standardised testing and high-stakes accountability, schools are scared. They are scared that children will not meet the milestones they are supposed to, that children will not have the skills and knowledge to pass tests and fear that Ofsted will visit and judge their work negatively. Fear can drive irrational behaviour, and the loss of trust in teachers is causing catastrophic outcomes.

Over the years, I have become quite accustomed to working around the constraints of the system; the lack of trust and the ever-growing use of schemes and micromanagement in our schools. But just because I have become used to it does not mean it's easy. I still battle with it daily because quite often it feels unnatural, it goes against what I have been taught and what I feel is best for the children. As I have learned to accept this battle as part of my job, I often question how long I can keep it up – educator burnout is real and commonplace. I truly believe that our lack of autonomy is a major contributor to the teacher-retention crisis.

It is from these frustrations that this book is born. I wanted this book to be both honest about the serious problems we are facing and to provide hope for and inspire those still working in schools (and perhaps bring some of you back!). This is a book that explores the idea that we are losing our autonomy but argues that it is worth fighting for. I hope that by gathering stories from those on the ground along with practical tips to work *around* a system that requires change, we can initiate a ripple effect. If we start with setting small boundaries, communicate whispers of "no thank you's" and be curious about the requests that are made of us, we may be able to put our collective foot down. That small stamp that we begin to see in our classrooms may then turn into a giant thud in our school communities, and then next, perhaps a movement towards policy change and a taking back of our profession.

For many of us, staying in the job we love requires constant renewal of our motivation for change. It's about finding a way to stay inspired, even when the path feels hard. The conversations and ideas here are not just for the few - they are for all children, all families, and all settings. Every principle I discuss in this book is something every educator and child should have access to and could benefit from. Everything I mention in this book is also mindful of the need to safeguard our children - when risk taking is mentioned it is never with the idea that we would make mistakes that would be deeply damaging to the wellbeing of the children we care for. It is my belief that the risk taking I ask of educators is only for the *benefit* of the child.

Whilst writing this book, I had extensive conversations with people working in education - people based at the Department for Education (UK), senior leaders, teachers, children, ECTs, parents, teaching assistants, creatives, all of which had a variety of specialisms and that were based all over the world. I have anonymised many of these examples to protect the contributor.

It is at this point that I should offer a note on terminology: throughout this book, the term "parents" is used to refer broadly to all individuals involved in raising children, including biological parents, adoptive parents, stepparents, guardians, foster carers and other primary caregivers. Similarly, the term "educators" is used to describe all professionals working with children and young people across various settings - including teachers, early years practitioners, youth workers and other related professionals.

Over the course of the next 6 chapters, we will explore autonomy from a variety of angles including Teaching and Learning, Accountability, in Practice, the digital world, the Child and Wellbeing. Each chapter will delve deep into a range of topics and provide you with examples of real-life experiences *and* practical ways you can work around the systems in place.

Each chapter will include:

- an outline.
- an introduction to the main topic.
- an exploration of the subtopics.
- reflection prompts.
- a set of practical steps to "Get Autonomy Back" for Classroom Teachers, SLT and Government Officials.
- educator experiences - stories from the ground - an educator sharing an experience linked to the topics discussed in the chapter.

My partner teacher quite often reminds me that I struggle with being told what to do, and it's true, I *really* do. But I am not sorry. It originates from parents who expected me to comply and an education system that dictated what I learned and how I spent my time. I began to rebel at the age of 16. I wore clothes that I knew would upset my mum,

I sat in exam halls leaving the paper blank, missed lessons to do "Geri Yoga" (90s kids will understand) and sit on park benches in the freezing December conditions. I checked out. Anything was better than being met with failure and/or being out of control of my own destiny. Although this rebellion could have been costly, I now believe it has become a strength of mine. Whether it be in supervision meetings, observation feedback or in professional development training – I try to be curious and avoid just doing anything because I am being told to – if it feels wrong or is having damaging consequences for me or my cohort then questions will be asked. I rarely do anything without asking questions and if you would like to see change, then I *urge* you to do the same.

We begin below with an *educator experience* from a teacher who has decided to remain anonymous, someone who left the teaching profession due to a lack of autonomy – a huge loss to the teaching profession and sadly one of many.

In reading this book, I hope you, the reader, can find a way to stay in education – we need you.

THE BIG IDEA – Autonomy and poor retention

Anon. Former Primary Teacher and EYFS Specialist. South London.

Autonomy is the absolute key to teaching, but completely at odds with the system and expectations laid upon teachers.

My out-of-the-box thinking and constant imaginative ideas are great strengths, and what drew me to teaching. I can find ways to engage even the most disillusioned children: maths can transform into a mission from Mars, and science can become interactive art. I have spark and zeal, and when given autonomy, my creativity is infectious.

Some of the best days of my career were spent in Reception, alongside two other passionate teachers. Our Headteachers at the time were, for all their faults, pretty "hands off". We had the Early Years Foundation Stage (EYFS) framework and development matters, and a "mentor" that would pop to see us every few months, but no long-term plan, no scheme (not even for phonics), no EYFS coordinator... And a shed load of autonomy, which bred beautiful, raw teaching.

That first year together, we three created a rich, sparkly bespoke EYFS curriculum that was inclusive and flexible, following the interests of our incredible children (remnants of the curriculum are still floating around that school today). We wrote our own story about a Lego circus, opened a hairdresser's with braiding and beads, celebrated a charity close to a disabled child's heart, got our staff teams to bring in objects from their home countries, held our own Glastonbury festival, had a general election (and Prime Ministers in each class!). We loved books and literacy. Writing and drawings were everywhere – kids would make huge maps on the floor, chalk outside and write secret notes under tables. It was honestly the happiest I have been at work. Until... Until it all fell apart.

You see, we had been so busy teaching the children, playing with them, learning from them and igniting their fires, that we had forgotten about something that didn't seem important at all... league tables. Turns out only 68% of our wonderful, dynamic 4- to 5-year-old children could write sentences. No one had bothered to tell us that that number should have been 80% (pretty much "or else!") until April – a bit late. We had until June to turn it around.

All of a sudden, everything changed. Any freedom and autonomy vanished. The Headteachers were involved now, visiting every day. That sporadic mentor came weekly with an agenda and a serious look on his face. Everyone was mysteriously interested in "examples" against "exemplar", rather than the children's progress and learning.

Our classes were split into groups. We were told to forget about "the lowers" – each of them was "a lost cause". Similarly, the "expecteds" and "exceedings" were apparently no longer a worry of ours – they'd already "made it". It was the six "cuspy" (I wish I could never hear that word again) 4 to 5 year olds from each class that were to be pressurised for weeks. Some of these children had disabilities, some were very young and others disinterested in writing at this stage. However, none of this is considered: each child is a number and each class a percentage.

Our freedom to teach playfully and intuitively was quickly stolen, as we were charged with prioritising formal writing workshops for those six to get the percentages up. In turn, we removed the children from their play, took away their autonomy and forced them to "write", on-demand, multiple times a day. We tried jazzy paper, magic pens, letters from Spiderman, postcards, post boxes, glitter, you name it. But writing a sentence was just not where any of these children were at, developmentally (otherwise they would have been doing it!). They sat there with confused, glazed expressions, trying their best to please us but unable to reach any level of understanding of the task. It all felt wrong. It was clear this was neither "teaching" nor "learning" – "conforming" would be a more accurate adverb (for both us teachers and the children). Nevertheless, we had no choice but to persist.

June came. We were moderated and the borough, moderators, mentor and Headteachers were satisfied that enough 4 to 5 year olds had reached a "Good Level of Development". The pressure on the Heads that had pressured us teachers and trickled down to the children had apparently worked. We were off the hook, and so were they.

A little bit of all three of us Reception Teachers died that summer. Our sparks were trampled upon, our pedagogies flattened and our creativity crumpled. Here began my slow realisation of the damage that the school system is doing to even the youngest of children in our care. I continued teaching but it was never the same – my efforts were no longer for the children, their parents or carers, the community, my fellow teachers or for myself. It was clear now; it was all for "them". And that is a tragedy.

With autonomy, teaching is understanding. Teaching is caring. Teaching is reflecting. Teaching is being. Without autonomy, it's just a job. And I don't think I can do that.

Contributor

1. Anon. Early Years Foundation Stage (EYFS) Specialist. Inner London Primary School.

References

Cumiskey, L. 15 Nov 2024. Schools Week. Are School Teachers Really 'Enslaved'? Here's What the Data Says. https://schoolsweek.co.uk/are-school-teachers-enslaved-heres-what-the-data-says/

Lakin, L. 2023. P. 190. Square Pegs. Crown House.

The Hadow Report. 1931. Report of The Consultative Committee on THE PRIMARY SCHOOL. https://www.education-uk.org/documents/hadow1931/hadow1931.html

1 Autonomy and teacher wellbeing

The 1997 election with the "Education, education, education" soundbite which could translate to "Workload, more workload and even more workload …"

(Andrew Cowley. Mental Health Insights Working Paper. Carnegie School of Education. July 2024)

Chapter 1 outline

In this chapter, we will explore:

- the consequences of a lack of autonomy on our mental health and overall wellbeing.
- professionalism and the lack of trust in teachers as professionals, and what this means for self-esteem.
- how we can be motivated by autonomy.
- how a lack of motivation can be driven by the suppression of individuality.
- the connections between identity and innovation, creativity and teacher wellbeing.
- the links between the retention crisis and the lack of autonomy in teaching.
- practical ways that teachers can take care of their mental health and wellbeing despite the boundaries and barriers outlined.

Wellbeing and autonomy

Along with the words mindfulness, self-care and boundaries, wellbeing has become an incredibly irritating word in the education world. When I deliver staff training on wellbeing, you can see the exasperation and resentment in the teacher's eyes, especially when their session falls on a Friday twilight! I get it, we are talking to them about self-care when the systems in place are creating a space so uninhabitable for self-care, it's laughable.

A primary teacher shared the following anecdote: he had returned to his classroom following a weekend and post-its had been stuck into four of his class literacy books. On the post-its was feedback from one of his senior leaders – written were things to the effect of "love this" and "this child is not ticking their success criteria". Despite some of the comments

8 *Teacher Autonomy*

being positive the teacher was upset and felt that there had been a complete lack of trust in his ability to do his job, as if he had been checked up on. Imagine his scenario, a child had become dysregulated during his lesson, requiring him to pay attention to something other than ticking a success criteria – the professional teacher decided that his priority in that moment was the dysregulated child only to be pulled up on it by the senior leadership team (SLT) who were not present in that lesson. The sudden (and unexpected) appearance of the post its speaks volumes about the lack of trust currently placed in our educators. The National Foundation for Educational Research (NFER) found "… that the average teacher has a lower level of autonomy compared to similar professionals" (Worth and Van den Brande, 2020. P. 2) and it is a common observation amongst us teachers that we are treated like we are not to be trusted.

Isn't it ironic then, that many teachers who find themselves micromanaged to within an inch of their lives are expected to take full responsibility for their self-care. I am repeatedly briefed by heads at schools before training their teams, that their staff do not take enough responsibility for their own wellbeing – the truth is that the education system is not designed

Figure 1.1 Sophie Smith-Tong delivering training to trainee teachers at University College London. June 2024. Photograph belongs to Sophie Smith-Tong

with a wellbeing lens – wellbeing and teaching are at odds and teachers know this. Staff tend to disregard wellbeing initiatives as they understand that developing ways to take care of their wellbeing can feel impossible when they are swimming against the tide. Rough waters are typical in schools, and we are expected to not only learn how to ride them but also take care of our health and happiness whilst we do so.

To support teachers in taking responsibility for their own self-care, SLT and government officials need to take responsibility for *real* change in education. Without revolution, wellbeing will always feel like a sticking plaster, a tick-box exercise and its disingenuous nature will infuriate professionals. It takes a bold leader to question the system, to do things differently, and we can keep hope alive as there are many headteachers out there initiating a revolution including Tina Farr and Ben Levinson, whom I write about in **Chapters 3** and **4**. Whilst we await that revolution (are you coming with us?), let us explore autonomy and wellbeing and how they go hand-in-hand.

The retention crisis

> Those in our schools are voting with their feet. We need teachers that feel more motivated and empowered.
>
> **(Jim Knight. Lords debate. July 2024)**

Jim is not wrong. I kept in touch with five teachers from my training – three of them have left the profession due to frustrations with the system. They are creative people and good at their job – the children adored them, but the system did not. In January 2025, Teacher Tapp ran a survey exploring morale in teaching. One of the top five reasons for teachers saying they are likely to look to leave teaching in 2025 was down to "objections with the education system" including workload and underfunding (Teacher Tapp, 2025). It appears that for many teachers, focusing on their wellbeing means leaving teaching altogether.

If you haven't watched *English Teacher* on Disney Plus yet then I recommend you do so – set in the US, one of the episodes takes place at a teaching and learning conference with the speakers at the conference talking about the depressing decline of the teaching profession with the main character beginning to question his life choices (as many of us have). Teachers are finding it harder to remain in the profession alongside taking care of their wellbeing – it feels like a juxtaposition. An inability to control how we manage and balance our working and personal lives is having a detrimental impact on our ability to stay in education.

In June 2024, the Times Educational Supplement (TES) published an article stating that "Over 12 years, 40,438 state school teachers left within one year of qualifying" (Peirson-Hagger, 2024). The article continues to inform us that the reasons could include a "dissonance" between expectations and reality. The focus on skill and child development is wasted on the reality of teaching (see more on this in my exploration of schemes in **Chapter 2**).

So how can we rethink the education system and establish autonomous working environments that motivate, innovate and respect the professionals in them?

Figure 1.2 Sophie Smith-Tong on strike. March 2023. Photograph belongs to Sophie Smith-Tong

Motivation, innovation and wellbeing

In *Drive: The Surprising Truth About What Motivates Us,* Daniel H. Pink says there are three key factors he believes drive our motivation: autonomy, mastery and purpose.

In education, motivation can be complex and tricky for senior leaders to navigate. Although we can self-motivate (when in a positive state) we cannot work alone. Our workplaces need to provide the space and opportunity for growth and renewal. Our motivation will have ups and downs, peaks and troughs, lose its pace and gain momentum, but in education it is unsupported by the expanding role of standardisation. The more we move towards a uniform approach, a school of thought that is aiming for sameness, the less we need from our professional teachers. As schools become accountable for more, the more we are sent into a state of panic, the more we panic, the more we attempt to tighten the apron strings – a need for control then eliminates the invitation to create, be bold and enthused – we enjoy the job less.

Pink explores extrinsic motivation – schools are big users of extrinsic motivation despite research showing that in the long term it does not create motivated learners or workers. In the same way that some teachers continue to offer out stickers and red cards, staff are threatened with Ofsted inspections (now in the form of a report card), learning walks and observations. If we think about this more deeply, we might begin to see the fault in this approach – if educator motivation is an Ofsted inspection, then when Ofsted leave what replaces that motivation? We run the risk of depriving teachers of motivation every 3-5 years which is never good for retention. In the same way that we should avoid creating a school that acts as a conveyor belt for prizes and stickers, we must avoid making staff believe that extrinsic benefits are the reason for what we do. I am yet to meet a trainee teacher or early career teacher (ECT) that is motivated by Ofsted, money or performance-related pay; teachers are mostly in this for the intrinsic reward – the support and development of the child. We can lose sight of our intrinsic motivations when the pressure is ramped up by hierarchical structures and high-stakes accountability (read **Chapter 3** for more on accountability).

When teachers are not trusted and are asked to prove their worth and verify that the children in their care are "progressing", it ironically takes them away from the children. If teachers are taken away from the children, then they lose their intrinsic motivation, resulting in a decline in job satisfaction – an unwelcoming space for flow, creativity and innovation in the classroom, as evidenced by these teachers on X;

> all teachers in the MAT teaching the same thing at the same time, reading the same books, nothing else.
>
> (@poetiful. 9.14 PM. Sept 16 2024. X)

and

> Yep. Death by PowerPoint and schemes. Constant learning walks where it's expected that parallel classes are doing the same thing at the same time in the same way. No room for independent thought or creativity. Awful. This is why I left this summer.
>
> (@kash645. 6.53 PM. Sept 16 2024. X)

Pink further discusses the variety of situations that require a different combination of reward systems. He describes routine work responsibilities (an example being getting your class to assembly on time) as being enhanced by extrinsic motivations; however, when it comes to more creative tasks, we require something different. Intrinsic motivation provides the perfect foundation for innovation and creativity to flourish. When you have a large task in hand – for example, an art lead exploring ways to exhibit the art of the school community – Pink describes adding an extrinsic reward before they begin this task as "perilous" (Pink, 2011. P. 64). This kind of reward could hamper creative flow as it becomes more about the reward than the task itself. So, back to Ofsted – is an Ofsted "exemplary" badge an extrinsic reward? It's difficult to think of them as a reward, isn't it? But it certainly is used as a motivation tool in schools. I would be surprised if you are a teacher reading this and you hadn't heard the words "If Ofsted saw this we would be failed", or "When Ofsted come they will be looking for this …". For most of the time it feels more like a threat than a reward. So how are teachers rewarded? Extrinsically speaking, we had performance-related pay (PRP), and although the Labour government removed the requirement for PRP, schools can still choose to opt in. There is also promotion, job security, pension pay and recognition in the form of teacher of the year awards, etc. For the most part teachers are driven by the desire to support the child, a sense of purpose, autonomy and developing competence (this one can be upheld with personalised professional learning opportunities – see **Chapter 6**).

Workload and boundaries

Being a teacher feels like you have two or three full-time jobs, and if you have a teaching and learning responsibility (TLR) or are in the SLT, then you can add another full-time role on top of that. Unfortunately, much of the workload is born from the high-stakes accountability pressures. Teachers rarely get to choose how they spend their time at work - timetables are decided for us and the way we plan, assess or now, even how *we teach* can be dictated by others, leaving very little room to take charge. The NFER states that "... nearly half of teachers with the highest autonomy report having a manageable workload compared to less than one in five of those with the lowest autonomy" (Worth and Van den Brande, 2020. P. 15).

Why might this be? Choosing the way you approach your workload is really important for efficiency. Every teacher will have their own ideas as to what will work for them. If you are being asked to use a premade timetable, a list prioritised by someone else, or teach in a way that hasn't been designed by you, then you may not understand the approach which will cause inefficiency. Inefficiency can lead to a backlog of tasks, add in an erosion of self-esteem and you have a recipe fit for failure.

If staff are allowed to have a say in what they deem priority, and are given the space to approach it in a way that they regard as effective, then it makes sense that they will get the job done and done well. When I took 18 months out of the classroom to launch Mindfulness for learning, I very quickly lost touch with what the day of a working-class teacher involved - it became impossible to support those still working in schools when I no longer had an idea as to what the day looked like. When SLT are the ones making the decisions, including timetabling and meeting schedules, it's no wonder we end up creating tension between them and the people working on the ground - there is a pull from what is realistic to the perceived manageable goals created by those at the top of the hierarchy. This is something Dr James Mannion explores in his book *Making Change Stick*. James explores the success of "slice teams" and argues that "When we're dealing with more complex, multi-dimensional issues, top-down change tends to be less effective" (Mannion, 2025. P. 48).

Autonomy takes time, and time is the most precious thing we have as teachers. Where possible decision making on tasking teachers should include the very staff members that are being asked to complete those actions. Additionally, if SLT are requesting something from their team, they should assume that the teacher they are asking is already at capacity and provide them with a space and time to complete the task.

Hours worked in a school are not clear cut - teachers have their working hours, they have tasks in the classroom and then tasks outside of the classroom. They have tasks that are timetabled (which are more straightforward - you can only teach one lesson at a time!), but then you have tasks outside of the timetable. If you aim to leave at 5 pm, this means you have 1.5 hours once the children have gone to complete those tasks. Don't forget to add on meetings, unexpected tasks and impromptu interactions (there are plenty of these) and you are stretched thin. Due to this complex nature unless you have a SLT that assumes you are at capacity, you have placed the responsibility for workload entirely on the teachers and saying no is not easy. Dr Emma Kell shares advice about implementing boundaries saying that "... setting boundaries for your wellbeing and being 'stubbornly determined' to stick to them throughout the year" is vital for wellbeing (Hood, 2023). Despite teachers knowing that saying no is important, most of us find it difficult to do so and overwhelm is widespread. This results in quality suffering which affects job satisfaction and then motivation.

Professionalism

One academic year in the first few weeks of an Autumn term, a teaching assistant (TA) came into my classroom in tears. They were struggling to connect with and take care of a child they were a learning assistant for. This child had unique learning needs, and the teaching assistant shared that they didn't feel they were able to give the specialised care the child needed. They were clearly extremely unsettled and feeling like they were failing at their role. They had been to see the SLT who had in no uncertain terms told them that if this wasn't the role for them then they may need to think about whether they wanted to stay in the school.

This perfectly illustrates a lack of trust and the absence of self-reflection. This senior leader took the teaching assistant's vulnerability as a sign of laziness or an incapability to meet the standards of their role. They failed to reflect upon whether this response signalled a training shortfall. The TA was not provided with the skills and knowledge they needed to meet the expectations of the role. Staff cannot be expected to be autonomous successfully without the personalised and tailored professional learning (see **Chapter 6** for more on professional learning). The issue stemmed from a shortcoming in the senior leader's capabilities rather than those of the teaching assistants, yet the TA was the one suffering.

Let's take a moment to think about inset days, twilight and training sessions where the workshop leader or speaker stops the teachers using a rhythmic clap or "1,2,3, eyes on me". Apart from giving me the ick, it is symbolic of the infantilisation of our workforce. Nothing conveys this more than the treatment teachers receive when taking their sick days or those struggling with punctuality (it wouldn't surprise me if we were given dedicated teacher attendance assemblies to publicly shame us). It is common for teachers to be told they must not text to let their managers know when they are ill but instead call in person. It is often claimed by leadership teams that to know their staff are ok they need to hear their voice. With respect, I find it hard to accept. Calling into work is a practice that most privately run companies got rid of over a decade ago. It is quite obvious that the call is a way to determine the credibility of the sickness and even if it isn't, it feels that way, which is bad enough alone for teacher wellbeing.

When I came back to work following the birth of my second child, a few weeks in, I was asked to go to a senior leader's office. I was told that it had been noted (via the CCTV film footage that is used to keep children and staff safe) that I was leaving at 4.30 pm. I had left at that specific time that week as my partner had been away and I was responsible for childcare (I should also mention that leaving at 4.30 pm every day should be no problem anyway). If the senior leader had trusted me, that week would have passed, my work would have been completed with no need to keep tabs on my attendance. The pressure their shared observations had on my mental and physical health was unnecessary and damaging; it also detached me from my work. My stress levels increased due to not feeling comfortable leaving to collect my children, and I was worried that I would be late (and therefore be charged by my childcare provider). On top of this I felt angry. Persistent feelings like this are no good for wellbeing.

Some may argue that I should have communicated my situation to the SLT and asked to leave at 4.30 pm, but this is where the problem lies – a lack of trust. The question is, do we want educators to be responsible for their wellbeing, or do SLT want to be in control of teacher wellbeing? I often ask myself, what is it about teaching that denies us the professional treatment that other professionals receive?

> ### Educator experience – The retention crisis
>
> **David Smith. Former Secondary Teacher. Inner London Secondary.**
>
> It all seems like a bad dream now, my newly qualified teacher (NQT) year. About halfway through, in early 2013, the school was put into special measures. The most stressful thing I've ever experienced in my working life. There was dysfunction across the entire school, including the English department of which I was a part. Professionally, I felt like I went backwards – I'd finished my PGCE on a high, but I was a worse teacher after a year on the job. I finished that year completely burnt out and knew in my heart that teaching wasn't for me. I emigrated to Australia in October, taught intermittently as a supply teacher for another couple of years or so, but I was already looking for a way out of the profession. I learned how to program in my spare time, eventually making the jump into a new career in IT in 2018. I've spent the last few years as a data analyst, a data scientist and a software engineer, and I haven't looked back.
>
> Of my PGCE cohort, quite a few of us are doing different things now, and of the few that are still teaching, several have expressed to me that they would like to bail. We've all had varied experiences, in different schools each with their own unique philosophies and spanning the full gamut of Ofsted ratings, yet many of us have cited depressingly similar reasons for leaving (or wanting to leave) the profession. The biggest one, unsurprisingly, is the workload. Completely unmanageable and overwhelming. They'd deny it, but the expectation from leadership was that we give up our evenings, weekends and holidays for planning and marking, leaving almost zero time to unwind, or process our experiences, or self-heal. I felt like I was "on" for the entire NQT year; many of my friends in the profession have said the same.
>
> The other major factor is the lack of professional trust and autonomy we were given. On the one hand we were discouraged from teaching to the test. On the other hand, given the outrageous pressure school leaders are under to show progress in examination league tables, any deviation from tried-and-tested, "Ofsted-safe" schemes of work was essentially shut down. The confusing mixed messages I got from my NQT mentor (during the brief, weekly moments I actually got to see her) taught me always to err on the side of caution rather than take any risks. I became an English teacher because I'm a creative person who loves stories, word games, wit and the interplay of complex ideas. I thought I'd be in my element in an English department, but I felt stifled, stressed, and, it pains me to say it, kind of bored.
>
> I still sometimes find myself thinking about a good "starter" for a lesson. I remember some of the brilliant students I taught – their energy and their humour. I miss my clever, kind, hard-working colleagues. But I'll never go back to teaching.

It's time to pause.

Reflection

- How do I feel about the word wellbeing?
- Is there time and space for self-care in school?
- How do I feel about going into work?
- How does my school motivate me?
- What was my motivation for getting into teaching?
- Do I feel able to focus on the children?
- Can I make decisions at work?
- Is there a platform for sharing ideas?
- Am I able to find space for creative flow?
- Can I see myself teaching in 5 years?
- Do I feel comfortable when I need to take sick leave?
- What happens if I am running late?

Get autonomy back

In the classroom:

- Introduce your SLT to "slice teams" and *Making Change Stick* training with Dr James Mannion.
- Prioritise your wellbeing by setting yourself clear boundaries that are easy to stick to such as leaving at 4 pm every Friday or asking for time whenever you are given a task.
- Find joy in experiences outside of work – this will help to maintain perspective.
- Question approaches that you find patronising or demeaning.
- If you do not feel able to speak up then advocate for an anonymous feedback system where you can share your views (speak to your mental health and wellbeing lead).
- If you feel your motivation is declining:
    1. Reflect upon tasks that are eating up your time – are they worth it?
    2. Have a separate list of priorities that are linked to your motivation.
    3. Give yourself space to reflect deeply about what is causing your demotivation or exhaustion.

For senior leaders:

- Remove the hierarchy and introduce a "slice team" ensuring that all staff are being heard. (*Making Change Stick* by Dr James Mannion).
- Listen to your staff – they are the most valuable asset you have and they have the power to create and cultivate a thriving school community.
- Delegate – provide teachers with an opportunity to thrive, share and utilise their passions and skills, you will benefit from this – you can't do everything *and* maintain quality.
- Allow time for the above.
- Develop systems, policies and structures that support the wellbeing of your staff.

- Avoid thinking the above is all you need to do with regard to staff wellbeing - it's a shift in culture, not a tick box exercise. If you don't truly believe in it, then spend your time getting bought into wellbeing, genuinely.
- Have an open mind and think bold.

For government officials:
- Slim down the curriculum (apologies, you may see this repeated throughout the book - read more detail on this in **Chapter 2**).
- Provide training opportunities for schools to implement "slice teams".
- Provide more statutory requirements and protective frameworks for teacher wellbeing (hours worked, mental health support, overhaul of high-stakes accountability systems, protections against burnout dismissal, leadership wellbeing training and promote respect for the profession through public campaigns).

Final thought on teacher retention

Wellbeing is intrinsically linked with autonomy. With more autonomy and less micromanaging teachers can begin to make choices that put themselves first. If teachers are able to put themselves first, then they can give fully to others. It will take systemic change to make autonomy and wellbeing a genuine friend of teaching, but for now we can begin to introduce the idea of change bigger than the odd mindfulness or exercise class. Teachers need to take their working lives back.

Wellbeing in the workplace

Wellbeing isn't "being nice".

(Andrew Cowley. The Wellbeing Toolkit. 2020. P.10)

Back in 2021, I decided to leave teaching due to a toxic work environment - the school that I was working at had adopted a scheme for every subject and the policies and systems created were imposed on staff rather than developed *with* them. The systems and structures were restrictive and prescriptive. My colleagues and I had absolutely no say over what our daily lives in our classrooms looked like. We were detached, disconnected and fragmented. This led to a lot of long-term staff sickness (physical and mental health), an increase in child mental health illness and therefore school family anxiety. The trust was broken. The team's lack of autonomy led to a creativity and motivation block and so the leadership team felt there was further need for schemes, systems and policies, they failed to look more deeply, and so the cycle continued. The staff were not heard or seen. The school community was suffering, and we were firefighting most of the time. The failure to recognise the importance of autonomy in the workplace has a detrimental effect on the wellbeing of school staff.

Connections and relationships

Working environments that value autonomy create the perfect ground for building strong connections and relationships. Autonomy organically fosters collaboration. Feeling safe to share and be vulnerable is an important part of growth and development. This includes having respect for both different and similar approaches - sharing successful practice and critical thinking. Working in a school can sometimes feel isolating - spending time alone in a classroom (especially if you do not allow time for lunch in the staffroom) can lead to individual and isolated thinking which contributes to stagnation. Unfortunately, quite often school environments do not allow for time to *really* get to know the people working in them. I often contemplate how I have worked in many settings for long periods of time and still cannot answer questions about the staff members working with me. This isn't because I haven't *cared* but more to do with the pressure I have felt to deliver on my tasks as a teacher, likely to be a result of high-stakes accountability. Perhaps, over the years, my priorities have changed and as I have learned to manage and let go of certain pressures, I find more time to talk to the staff working with me. However, *even* with this shift, it is still the case that I find it challenging to allow time to be informal with my colleagues. When space is made for this kind of interaction it supports the building of relationships, and with this comes trust, compassion, collaboration and shared purpose. All of these elements are the perfect foundation for autonomous working.

Including *all* staff in professional development, school improvement and decision-making is an important part of valuing autonomy. Listening to those working in all parts of the school and sharing ideas and intentions results in a school community that works effectively for all stakeholders. Just as a member of the staff team at Preston Primary School mentions "Teachers need other teachers. This is not a job that can be done alone. Collaboration and friendship are vital in keeping teachers sane and happy" (Waters, 2021. P. 145).

Self-esteem

So, if connecting as a team creates a comfortable space to share then sharing is the key to building team self-esteem. A top-down micromanagement style is not able to build the self-esteem of its team. When teachers are not heard, when they do not have a choice in what and how they teach, they feel undervalued. This results in persistent frustration and a decrease in self-worth. This type of workplace is a breeding ground for resentment which can very quickly lead to a toxicity - secretive gossip and bad mouthing can fester, become routine and create factions within a team. It is essential that teachers are given the tools to acknowledge and share their strengths but also know that their weaknesses are accepted and held by others. It gives permission for imperfection. Autonomy accepts that we will not know all there is to know but gives us plenty of opportunity for self-growth, individualised learning experiences and builds our confidence to affect change. As a senior leader, delegating tasks to those who have a passion for a specific area is a clever way to achieve a well-balanced and efficient workplace.

> **Educator experience – Self-esteem**
>
> *Lucy Hevawitharane. Primary Teacher. Inner London.*
>
> I trained as a teacher in New Zealand and did a year of cover teaching there and then moved to London. I spent a few months doing supply around London, before landing a job as a planning, preparation and assessment (PPA) teacher and then taking over the reception class teacher position. I completed my qualified teacher status (QTS) and then moved to a new school, taking on the role of reception class teacher.
>
> In this school, I was introduced to the parents during a meet-the-teacher event as an "experienced teacher". I had only been teaching for four years, and two and a half of those years had been in PPA roles. However, I felt empowered by this portrayal and assumed that the school must see something in me and have faith in my ability. How wrong I was. This description was used against me by senior leadership multiple times to belittle me, undermine my judgments and contribute to a decline in my overall well-being. I remember a lesson observation by the head teacher and early years foundation stage (EYFS) lead; I had used a visualiser to display the book I was reading to the class on the board, following advice from my EYFS lead to incorporate more ICT in my teaching. It didn't go well, and I knew it. In my feedback session, instead of allowing me to reflect on the session, I was told that I had failed and asked how I could expect the children to learn anything if I couldn't even read a story to the class properly, the basic bread and butter of teaching. I was demoralised but worked even harder trying to prove them wrong, doing everything that was suggested to improve my teaching. I worked round the clock, following every suggestion that was given to me, allowing other people to step in and do things, even when I knew I was capable myself, and was still told it wasn't enough and I was failing. I started experiencing anxiety, and when I had my first panic attack I went to the deputy head who showed no understanding and told me if I couldn't handle it then perhaps this wasn't the place for me. I started to believe that maybe I wasn't cut out for this and they were right, I was failing. Ten years on from this, I would now call myself an "experienced teacher". I am in a supportive environment with colleagues who lead with kindness and empathy. I am able to thrive. I have been trusted to make my own decisions in the classroom and to build on my knowledge with true autonomy. This is what new teachers need. Not to be bullied or intimidated into submission, but the chance to be supported by those around them, to make mistakes and learn from them, to discover who they truly are as a teacher.

It's time to pause.

Reflection:

- Do I feel confident at work?
- Do I feel valued by my team?
- Do I feel heard by my line manager?

- How have I recently contributed to change in my school?
- Do I feel positively part of a team?

Get autonomy back

In the classroom:

- Have your say – when things are not working in your classroom, make sure you speak up. (Note: this does not need to be in a confrontational way.)
- Try to find solutions or request a team meeting where you have the opportunity to develop a solution together.
- Avoid letting situations fester or join in with gossip – it's better to air the problem with someone who can affect change, otherwise you become part of the problem.

For senior leaders:

- Avoid top-down policy, system and structural change without checking in with your team.
- Allow time and space to discuss and provide feedback on future change and progress with staff teams.
- Be visible and available where possible – teachers need to see that you are there to listen to them.

For government officials:

- Allow funding for regular training from local authorities – this will help to build confidence within teams.
- Offer more training for headteachers on the importance of autonomy in the workplace.
- Remove high-stakes accountability measures that are pressuring SLT into making decisions that do not have staff wellbeing in mind.
- Reduce curriculum content so that time is created to listen and respond to teacher feedback.

Final thought on wellbeing in the workplace

I explore wellbeing in the workplace before autonomy and self-care because that is the order I feel they should be. Structurally, we cannot take care of ourselves if the environment we are working in is not conducive to it. The focus on teacher self-care can sometimes leave leadership teams feeling that wellbeing is out of their hands. But it isn't, and nor should it be. Teachers cannot adopt self-care strategies without a system that can support them. If the wider context is that teaching and wellbeing do not go hand in hand, then self-care becomes futile.

Autonomy and self-care

> *Teaching is a noisy job and a hungry job – one of its unique characteristics is its ability to feel more like a lifestyle than "just" a job.*
>
> **(Adrian Bethune and Dr Emma Kell. 2021. P. 28)**

I wish my staff would take responsibility for their own self-care – they just don't take care of themselves – this is what I regularly hear from senior leaders. It is true, there are many teachers who do not take care of themselves, but I do not believe it comes from a lack of trying or laziness. Very rarely do we find a lazy teacher – it is barely possible. What it can come from is the inability to (a) prioritise (b) maintain perspective (c) manage unreasonable workloads. Humans are not born with the skills to self-maintain in the current school climate – if schools want their staff to look after themselves, they will need to dedicate time to developing supportive school cultures and invest in training. When teachers have autonomy, they can choose to prioritise their wellbeing. Self-care should not be on the outskirts of the school day (like a yoga class or a healthy dinner), and with autonomy teachers could choose the self-care activities they engage in and thread them through their school day. They should also feel comfortable drawing boundaries, saying no and asking for more time.

Mindfulness

You may be wondering why I am exploring mindfulness in a book about autonomy. I genuinely believe that being given autonomy is step one, developing the confidence to leverage autonomy requires you to have a strong sense of self, a clear ethos and direction. It relies on a teacher to reflect upon their core values and beliefs. Mindfulness enables us to pause, reflect and develop oneself.

Mindfulness has the ability to change the way we work together in schools. Regularly practised "Mindfulness promotes the growth of grey matter in many regions of the brain" (Wax, 2016. P. 68) including the Hippocampus (in charge of things like memory recall), the Prefrontal Cortex (the thinking part of the brain) and the Amygdala which will lead to more responsive behaviour rather than reactive. A school day can regularly be back-to-back reacting to situations – stress levels can be high and for sustained periods of time (not great for creative and critical thinking – we will be needing this if we want to be autonomous).

I run an annual 8-week mindfulness course in the school I work in – this is for all staff every January, and the consistent feedback from the delegates is that it enables them to reflect and reinvent how they approach ingrained, negative processes. Imagine if we all chose to follow this path, what would it mean for staff teams and the general overall connections between individuals and team creativity. Could mindfulness be the most straightforward way to seize autonomy?

It is common to hear the word mindfulness in schools nowadays. But as Kamalagita Hughes and I explored in the Mindfulness for learning podcast (Hughes, 2025), the mindfulness that is happening in schools is not always of good quality, practiced regularly or understood. The landscape of mindfulness is changing. The practice of breathing and meditation in schools seems to be dying off and we need to think of new and innovative ways to find time to pause, reflect and develop emotional intelligence in our staff teams. The Mindfulness Initiative, Mindfulness in Schools Project and Esther Ghey's Brianna Ghey Legacy Project are just a few of the organisations that are championing mindfulness in schools, but this is directed more at the children. Staff could really benefit from understanding mindfulness first and foremost; however, it's difficult to get educators to invest when the general feeling is "the system doesn't care about me so why should I?".

Figure 1.3 Staff 8-week mindfulness course. January 2024. Photograph by Sophie Smith-Tong

As Lisa Baylis states in her book *Self-Compassion for Educators* "We all have core values, but often we are not aware of what they are. To be well, it's important that we know what we value most" (Baylis, 2021. P. 24), and for educators we not only have to work out what our personal values are, but we need to find how they fit in with our work values too. It's a complicated job and one that requires the gift of time (something the education system doesn't like to give away too often).

Stress management

> ... teachers are facing burn out with "77% of all staff experienced physical, psychological or behavioural symptoms due to their work".
>
> **(Teacher Wellbeing Index 2024. Education Support)**

Yes, we are stressed; it's far from ideal. With autonomy we can choose the way we manage our workload and also the way we might respond to our stress levels. Stress appears in a variety of different forms and is a personalised journey – what stresses one teacher out will be a breeze for another. Nobody in this scenario is wrong. Stress is stress to the person experiencing it. Often, in education, we tend to make comparisons between staff, with responses such as "well they managed to get that job completed in two days so why is it taking them five days?", or question why one teacher didn't call in sick when they had a cold and another made it in to work, all snotty and coughing on everyone. The truth is that everyone has a different approach, a varied set of priorities and responsibilities. When we are trusted to make decisions using our own set of skills and experiences then we are handed the chance to be present for ourselves, compassionate and sensitive to our individual needs and are not burdened by others' expectations of us.

Educator experience – Autonomy and self-care

Jayne Carter. Director of Ignite Education Ltd.

For me, trust and communication are the same part of a collaborative trajectory. The dynamic between both aspects supports, nourishes and enhances the other. I am fortunate to be part of many teams where this trajectory is not only recognised but is actively implemented. Conversations are grounded in respect, with opportunities to both share and challenge being the norm. There is an awareness of priorities and individual roles within them. There is an ethos of independence alongside the reassurance of support if needed, without opinion.

Any potential hurdles or misunderstandings are approached with clarity and as part of a solution-focused plan. The strength of communication generates trust, with this security subsequently motivating more communication, more solutions, more ideas and more autonomy.

Unfortunately, when autonomy is severely compromised, previous positive experiences acutely highlight the differences, with obvious comparisons being made. Trust and communication were not individually established, which altered the dynamic of both considerably. For example, plans which were agreed as a collective quickly changed with little or no explanation, causing great anxiety, confusion and creating a sense of disassociation. Priorities were not clear and were reported to others, with direct tells, rather than within a shared professional conversation. This directive style of leadership only served to create team members who felt that they had little independence in both ideas and execution, resulting in a poor opinion of individual strengths. Despite being part of a team and our individual best attempts to forge professional/personal relationships to enhance working conditions, even this was not safe from eroding levels of autonomy.

Individual conversations, which had originally been thought to be at least professional if not private, were often used to create difficulties within the team. The intention of "sharing things as a team" resulted in quite the opposite, developing instead a team that eventually worked in isolation, afraid that any sharing of difficulties could result in personal/professional exposure.

Working positively within a team does take a considerable amount of investment by all involved. The continuous nurturing of the balance between individual and shared goals requires that trust remains a constant, supported by empathic yet focused discussions.

It's time to pause.

Reflection

- What self-care routines do I have in place?
- Are they still effective?
- What could my workplace do to support my self-care routines?
- Am I aware of my stress triggers?
- What are my body's signals that I am stressed?
- Am I satisfied with the boundaries I have put in place?

Get autonomy back

In the classroom:

- Learn to say "I need time to complete that job" when delegated a task.
- Write down the hours you would like to work and try to keep to them.
- Dip your toe into mindfulness (I know, I was cynical too, but it works). Check out the Oxford Mindfulness Foundation for ideas on how to get started or download the Headspace App – it's free for educators.
- Learn to respond rather than react (this relies on the above).
- Find what brings you joy and repeat it (whether that is in or out of school).
- Avoid waiting for the weekends/holidays to look after yourself – thread it through your daily life – don't wish your life away!

For senior leaders:

- Speak to your team, what do they want and how can they see it working for them?
- Reflect on your policies and systems as a team – listen to them and make changes where possible.
- Use staff surveys to check in on their level of autonomy and wellbeing status.

For government officials:

- Slim down the curriculum.
- Add a comprehensive teacher wellbeing module to teacher training.
- Place tighter restrictions on workload for teachers – a more detailed look at what teachers should be delegated and how this might fit into their timetable.
- Reduce the high-stakes accountability measures to relieve pressure.

Final thought on autonomy and self-care

Bringing yourself to work and being authentic can only happen when we are feeling refreshed, motivated and well. Be firm, ask for more and have realistic expectations of yourself. Senior leaders will only know what can't be done in the time we have if we do not manage to get it done. If you keep ticking all the boxes at the expense of your wellbeing, then you become part of the problem. Autonomy can only be made possible with colleagues who are in good health, energised and thriving.

Identity

> Keep dreaming as hard as you can, because when you do, not only will childhood burst into life, you'll also continue the Great Unlocking of who you are - a dreamer of limitless wonder and possibilities.
> **(Greg Bottrill. LinkedIn)**

A large part of my teacher training was reflecting on my teacher identity, and I am thankful that I had this space to explore. Becoming a teacher is similar to becoming a parent, very quickly you are aware of the weight of your decision. You understand the responsibility, your position of power and at no point do you take it lightly. Discovering your teacher identity can be hard work - the journey to (a) manifest early traits and (b) develop and hone them, isn't straightforward. Without the autonomy to explore and express our identity freely we can be left feeling unsure as to what we personally bring to our work. What does it mean for teacher wellbeing if we can't be ourselves?

For teachers who have been in this job for a long time, they may find the ever-increasing loss of autonomy extremely hard. Having worked when we were given more freedom to choose what we teach and how we delivered our curriculum can make the loss feel even harder. Many of the ECTs I have spoken to find it difficult to imagine teaching without prescription, and for teachers who have now left the profession due to a lack of autonomy - well, what a loss! Equalities Lead at an inner-city school, Sarah Desilva, states that "... it starts with building that culture of trust and inclusion and belonging and self-expression in your staff and your colleagues to be able to foster that messaging to students - if you can't do it in the staffroom then you can't do it in the classroom" Teacher Talk Radio (TTR) Sarah DeSilva (2024).

What is the connection between our personal identity and autonomy? If we are being invited to bring ourselves to our work how much of ourselves is too much and how can we ensure that this doesn't become partial or inappropriate. There are many parts of our personal life that should not be brought to our roles as teachers and the concern that autonomy leads to chaos may inform the level of control schools attempt to have.

Let's go back to 2019 when there were protests against Andrew Moffat (assistant head teacher at Parkfield Community School in Birmingham). His *No Outsider* programme which he based on the Equality Act 2010 makes use of picture books to explore inclusion and diversity in schools (BBC News, 2019). The backlash that he faced, including children being kept out of school, allows us to see what *can* happen when it is believed that teachers have allowed their personal opinions to inform their teaching - leaders can leave themselves open to abuse and judgement. How does a school protect its community and its educators from this rebuke? With little to no support from the government, it hardly encourages the notion of bringing yourself to school, does it?

Religion

We make ourselves vulnerable when we reveal parts of our identity as we cannot predict how we might be received. This is the case between parents and teachers, but also between staff team members. Teaching brings people from all walks of life – it's what I love about the job but it's also what can stir tensions. You only have to think about the progressive versus traditional teaching debate to understand the potential polarising nature of education. We all work in the same profession but at times we can feel worlds apart. It is important that we do not sit ourselves in echo chambers and learn to get comfortable with reflection and questioning our own beliefs and approaches. I entered the staff training room following an upsetting situation at work and another member of staff approached to comfort me. She asked if it would be ok if she prayed for me in my presence. I didn't understand this as I am not religious but I questioned my own internal reaction – this response was part of that staff member's identity, it was important to her and she deemed *me* important enough to share it with. She felt comfortable enough to be vulnerable and share something special with me. Of course, if I had wanted to say "no" I would have been well within my rights – I am not asking that we all say "yes" despite the discomfort we might feel but pausing and thinking about intention can open up our minds and hearts to real connection, developing an understanding of one another and how we choose to live our lives – a great model for the children we teach.

It can be the case that the strong identity of a school can shut down our own. I worked in a catholic school and during my time there I became pregnant with my first child. During my pregnancy, whilst I was still at work, I was called to a senior leader's office. I was made aware that since I was not married that they would now announce my pregnancy with a double-barrelled surname so no questions would be asked about my pregnancy before marriage. I was also advised to hide this information from the school link priests or Diocese. The rules and policies of the school were taken into account to the detriment of my own – it did not value me or my identity as an individual member of staff.

Finding the balance of sharing religious beliefs with the children in our care is another approach that some SLT may have strict rules on. It's important that staff should (if they wish) be able to share their religious beliefs and identities without attempting to convert others. It is part of our job to develop a sense of curiosity and an understanding of others in the children we teach. Helping them to develop a genuine belief that all can be accepted, unique and loved. I have worked with teaching assistants who go to church every Sunday, and the children really enjoy hearing about their experiences during special times such as Easter and Christmas and we all listen respectfully and intently. It doesn't mean that we have to believe in the same religion – an important lesson. It is also paramount that children can see themselves represented within their schools. The more varied educators we invite to be themselves, the more representatives we have for our young people.

Isolated thinking

Whilst exploring autonomy, I have thought about the prospect of too much autonomy with many mistakenly imagining autonomy as one teacher making all of the decisions all alone in their space. Adrian Bethune states that autonomy "… doesn't necessarily mean acting alone, it means acting with choice", "independently or interdependently" (Bethune, A, 2024. P. 5) I found myself reflecting on the dangers of isolated thinking. Autonomy does not ask for the thinking of one person, it invites the thinking of all. If we bring only our own perspectives to the classroom, we are at risk of teaching with blinkers on and not representing or exploring the diversity in our cohorts. It's especially important to be inclusive in our classrooms and this takes collaboration, reflection and active listening. There is a huge difference to being able to make decisions and feeling in control of your workplace destiny to egocentrism and self-absorbed practice. As educators we need to be open to new ideas and initiatives and be attuned to and listen to our school communities.

Flexible working

The NFER states "... that teachers report a lower level of autonomy over their working hours relative to similar professionals: ..." (Worth and Van den Brande, 2020. P. 8).

Flexible working relies on trust. When it comes to flexible working requests many employers use the "I can't open the floodgates" excuse in fear of encouraging others. Employees can adapt their hours and apply for flexible working from their first day of employment, and there are a number of ways employers can be flexible including where employees work, the days they work and their pattern of hours. Despite flexible working becoming more common, in teaching NFER research shows that "there is considerable demand among teachers for flexible working (ad-hoc and regular working schedule adaptations as well as part-time working), which outstrips the availability of such arrangements in schools" (Harland, Bradley and Worth, 2023; McLean et al., 2024. P. 23).

Vickie Johnson, a deputy headteacher in Greater Manchester was denied flexible working following her maternity leave. As "a deputy headteacher she introduced a policy that meant teachers in her school could work from home for half a day a week to do their lesson planning and marking. But after six months the school phased it out, worried that teachers might be wasting time" (Fazackerley, 2024). Surely a balance can be found between providing flexibility to help retain teachers and managing rotas and costs.

It was in 2013 that I had been back at work for 2 months following 10 months of maternity leave. I was called at work by my doctor (who I had contacted that morning due to my son being poorly in the night) to request I bring him in as he was concerned about what I had told him. I approached a senior leader who rolled their eyes and asked if I could wait and do it another time. I felt my heart sink. I insisted that I leave, and I did. They found cover and the school was fine. The following day I went into school and requested to talk to that same senior leader and calmly and respectfully told them how their reaction had made me feel. They felt I was being unfair. The next thing I know, I am being called into an office with more senior leaders and my contract (with a section highlighted) was laid out on the table in front of them. They believed I had not been meeting the needs of the wider context of the school and said that I may face disciplinary action. I was devastated. I had given this school so much – I worked ridiculous hours and dedicated my life to the job, and now that I had children, this was the appreciation I received. I was so upset. My sense of control stripped away, my autonomy as a parent and as a teacher, gone. I was no longer able to make decisions without shame and guilt, and so I left.

A report by the maternity teacher, paternity teacher (MTPT) reported that "last year in England more than 9,000 women between the ages of 30 and 39 left teaching – many of them feeling unable to juggle parenting with the demands of looking after everyone else's children in school" (Fazackerley, 2024).

Autonomy and Teacher Wellbeing 27

Figure 1.4 Me on maternity leave. 2013. Photograph by Lewis Smith-Tong

Flexible working is a fairly new phenomenon with Anna Whitehouse, founder of Mother Pukka, the face of parents (especially women) facing the motherhood penalty. Anna Whitehouse and her then husband Matt Farquharson co-founded MotherPukka.co.uk to work as a platform for change in flexible working approaches, attitudes and logistics. In the school context, with the seriousness of the retention crisis, flexible working shouldn't be for parents/carers only, with "… 92% of young people wanting flexible working" (Leckie et al., 2021. P. 7) too.

With news of the nine-day fortnight launched by Dixons Academy Trust (they are so proud of it that it pops up as soon as you go to their website!), is it time that education caught up with the Flex Appeal that has been sitting at desks for the last 6 or 7 years? Dixons Academy Trusts say that they have introduced flexible working "to help tackle teacher workload and boost recruitment and retention" (Sparkes, 2024) and that, I am sure, it certainly can do.

Flexible working is not only great for mental health and wellbeing but it's vital for work productivity and retention – a problem we are desperate to solve in education. Dixons also explains that "we want to be bold in our approach. Our ambition is for teachers to be afforded the same flexibility that's available in many other sectors and now even expected in the post pandemic world" (Dixons Academy Trust Website). It may feel that we are not currently set up (mentally and logistically) for this in education but it doesn't mean it cannot work – we just need to work on ways to deliver these options. This takes a bold leader, someone who is willing to make a change.

Clinical psychologist, Dr Naomi Fisher and author and illustrator Eliza Fricker ask "do you feel safest and happiest when you're with a boss who decides what you are meant to do and says 'no exceptions' when you ask for some flexibility about picking your child up from school – and who makes sure there are consequences if you're late to work? Or are you happier when you have a boss you think values you, believes in you and you know will work with you to create a flexible way of working?" (Fisher and Fricker, 2024. P. 78).

I think I can guess your answer.

> ### Educator experience – Identity
>
> **Kaurice Moran. Year 1 Class Teacher. Inner London Primary School.**
>
> For the past seven years I have worked part-time, job sharing and mainly working within the early years foundation stage and key stage one. The original reason that I chose to become part-time was because I decided to train as a yoga teacher (primarily yoga for children). The decision to reduce my days negatively impacted my financial status but the newfound passion and energy that I had for teaching massively outweighed this. For the first time in a long time, I really enjoyed my job and I was motivated. I had that fundamental time and space to now reflect on my practice, have time to think creatively about my planning and to make informed decisions. I could split the planning and resources with my work partner and put more thought and care into it as I had the mental capacity and time. I had someone to discuss the pupils' progress with, converse about pupils' individual needs and next steps.
>
> It felt like the best part of me as a teacher was now resurfacing after years of being burnt out, doing tick box tasks and then having no time or passion for more important tasks such as creative lesson planning and prioritising individual pupil needs. I also felt like the children were getting the best part of me as a teacher, and then when I was starting to feel the toll of the workload, it was time for my job share to take over and inject her positive energy and enthusiasm for the remainder of the week, thus giving the class an overall productive and enjoyable learning experience. I felt so refreshed, and for the first time in a while I felt like I was able to give my all to the class and my job.
>
> On a personal level, my work-life balance was positively impacted. I was able to focus on my mental wellbeing, pursue other interests and passions (such as yoga), eat more mindfully – as opposed to grabbing whatever I could access at the end of a long and exhausting day. I could do more things in the week rather than having to wait for the arrival of half-term holidays.
>
> Now that I have two children, I feel like I can be a good teacher when I'm at work, and then on the days when I'm not teaching, I can dedicate my time to my children's development and wellbeing. This balance is essential to my mental wellbeing, and I know that I am fortunate to be able to work part-time and achieve this. This is not an option for everyone due to issues with childcare and financial impact, so I know that I am blessed, and I would never want to disrupt this equilibrium that I now have. Choosing to work part-time was the best thing I did for my career and my overall wellbeing.

It's time to pause.

Reflection

- Can I be myself at work?
- Do I provide a safe space for others to be themselves?
- Do I model inclusivity and freedom of self-expression?
- Do I feel comfortable in communicating my need or desire for flexible working?
- Can I challenge my own attitudes toward flexible working?
- How might I change my working patterns to benefit me?

Get autonomy back

In the classroom:

- Find your place – if you are feeling like you cannot be yourself at work maybe there's somewhere better out there for you!
- Foster an atmosphere of authenticity in your classroom.
- Find your tribe – connect with your team, both staff members who have similar views and ones that comfortably question them too.
- Speak about your hopes and dreams in your supervision meetings.
- Ask when you need something to support your developing identity.

For senior leaders:

- Question your biases when it comes to responding to flexible working requests and teaching approaches in the classroom.
- Be bold.
- If you value your staff, then make flexible working work.
- Encourage and support self-expression – this can be achieved through up-to-date training and safe spaces to have open and vulnerable conversations.
- Avoid blanket processes – work with individuals, not a cookie-cutter team.

For government officials:

- Support schools in implementing inclusive and progressive processes and learning experiences.
- Avoid blanket statements and try to understand the individual experiences, backgrounds and challenges people may face when working in education systems.
- Make flexible working more appealing for headteachers – support them with funding, policies, sharing good practice and perhaps Artificial Intelligence (AI) (read more on Digital Autonomy in **Chapter 5**).

Final thought on identity

We are vulnerable when we authentically bring ourselves to work each day. It is important that SLT understands this and provides their backing and support. This backing creates a safe space for educators to come forward and share their expertise and passions with their school community. Without sharing who we are as individuals we are unable to genuinely delve deep into learning about values, principles, viewpoints and experiences and this would be a loss to the children we teach and our staff teams.

THE BIG IDEA - Wellbeing

Adrian Bethune. Founder of Teachappy. Teacher, Author, Trainer, Speaker.

We need to view autonomy as a fundamental human need. In the same way that humans need a sense of belonging or feelings of safety to flourish, they also need to feel in control of their lives. Without autonomy, we feel powerless, impotent and the future starts to look bleak. This is true of doctors, or office workers and, of course, it's true of teachers. I have worked in three schools as a teacher and, in two of them, I experienced a strong sense of autonomy. In one of them, I didn't. In the high autonomy schools, I was able to grow and flourish as a teacher. I could take risks, make mistakes and hone my craft. That didn't mean I was left to my own devices. That's not what autonomy means. In those high-autonomy schools, I was part of a team of conscientious professionals that received high-quality CPD and we were trusted to do a good job. Lesson observations felt like a two-way conversation about development rather than judgement. Pupil progress meetings were a celebration of successes as much as a focus on what we could do to help those children struggling. When parents went straight to the head to complain about an everyday grumble, they were always directed back to the class teacher to sort it out in a professional way. Trust, a sense of team, good training and a strong sense of purpose were the hallmarks of these high-autonomy schools.

In the low-autonomy school, I felt micromanaged, and it was a deeply unpleasant experience. Even though I was a senior leader in this school, my work would be regularly checked by the head before it was signed off. If a parent went to the head to grumble about something, the head would step in and immediately apologise to appease the parent rather than check in with me first to find out what the issue was. I regularly felt undermined and not trusted, and so did my colleagues. The staffroom was empty as everyone preferred staying in their classrooms – maybe because that was their safe space and where they felt they had the greatest sense of control. In the end, I started to question everything I did, it chipped away at my confidence and it almost certainly made me a worse teacher.

Thankfully, I now work somewhere that values my experience. I work somewhere where I feel supported and have a sense of being part of a strong team. I am trusted once again to do a good job and because of that, I do.

Contributors

1. David Smith. Secondary English Teacher. Inner London Secondary.
2. Lucy Hevawitharane. Primary Teacher. Inner London.
3. Jayne Carter. Director of Ignite Education Ltd.
4. Kaurice Moran. Year 1 Class Teacher. Inner London Primary School.
5. Adrian Bethune. Founder of Teachappy. Teacher, author, trainer, speaker.

References

@kash645. 6.53 pm 16 Sept 2024. X. https://x.com/kash645/status/1835738781317828910

@poetiful. 9.14 pm 16 Sept 2024. X. https://x.com/poetiful/status/1835774302798655819

Baylis, L. 2021. P. 24. Self-Compassion for Educators. PESI Publishing.

Bottrill, G. May 2025. LinkedIn. https://www.linkedin.com/posts/greg-bottrill-223417159_childhood4neoliberalism0-joy-childhood-activity-7324692108169113600-gsGP/?utm_source=share&utm_medium=member_desktop&rcm=ACoAADSiNDcBj6IHrVTzfMCqIFDtXZiC7GP959s

Bethune, A. 2024. P. 5. Organisation for Economic Co-operation and Development (OECD).

Bethune, A. and Kell, E. 2021. P. 28. Teacher Wellbeing and Self-Care. Corwin.

Birmingham LGBT teaching row: How Did it unfold? BBC. 22 May 2019. https://www.bbc.co.uk/news/uk-england-48351401

Cowley, A. 2020. P. 10. The Wellbeing Toolkit. Bloomsbury Education.

Cowley, A. July 2024. Mental Health Insights Working Paper. Carnegie School of Education.

DeSilva, S. 2024. Nurturing Belonging and Self-expression in Primary School Children. Teacher Talk Radio. https://www.ttradio.org/listenback/episode/49d36ed3/nurturing-belonging-and-self-expression-in-primary-school-children-the-late-late-show-with-sophie-smith-tong

Dixons Trust Website. https://www.joindixonsat.com/641/flexible-working

Education Support. 2024 Teacher Wellbeing Index. https://www.educationsupport.org.uk/media/ftwl04cs/twix-2024.pdf

Fazackerley, A. 2024. https://www.theguardian.com/education/2024/dec/21/we-need-a-total-culture-change-the-uk-teacher-told-to-work-60-hour-week-or-leave-after-having-baby

Fisher, N. and Fricker, E. 2024. P. 78. When the Naughty Step Makes Things Worse. Robinson.

Harland, J. Bradley. E, Worth. J. November 2023. P. 23. Understanding the factors that support the recruitment and retention of teachers – review of flexible working approaches. https://www.nfer.ac.uk/publications/understanding-the-factors-that-support-the-recruitment-and-retention-of-teachers-review-of-flexible-working-approaches/

Hood, N. 2023. New Year, New Boundaries: Self-care for SEND Staff. Twinkl. https://www.twinkl.co.uk/news/new-year-new-boundaries-self-care-for-send-staff

Hughes, K. Jan 2025. Mindfulness for Learning Podcast Episode. The Mindful Teacher's Handbook. https://open.spotify.com/episode/7qyLKZqGiHKobUa7k8g1g7?si=b0c20361fb3349f9

Knight, J. July 2024. Lords debate. https://www.linkedin.com/posts/jimpknight_today-i-enjoyed-taking-part-in-the-lords-activity-7222605013171249154-oTD2/

Leckie, C., Munroe, R. and Pragnell, M. 2021. P. 7. Flexinomics. https://www.motherpukka.co.uk/wp-content/uploads/2021/12/2021-11-12-CONFIDENTIAL-Flexonomics-a-report-by-Pragmatix-Advisory-for-Sir-Robert-McAlpine-and-Mother-Pukka-2.pdf

Mannion, J. 2025. P. 48. Making Change Stick. John Catt.

McLean, D., Worth, J. and Smith, A. 2024. P. 23. Teacher Labour Market in England. National Foundation for Educational Research. https://www.nfer.ac.uk/media/hqdglvra/teacher_labour_market_in_england_annual_report_2024.pdf

Peirson-Hagger, E. 2024. TES. https://www.tes.com/magazine/analysis/general/teacher-retention-scale-crisis-revealed-dfe-data

Pink, D. 2011. P. 64. Drive. Canongate Books.

Sparkes, L. 2024. TES. https://www.tes.com/magazine/leadership/strategy/flexible-working-teachers-schools-nine-day-fortnight-dixons

Teacher Tapp. 7 Jan 2025. New Year, New Job? Plus Morale Tracker and Faith Schools. https://teachertapp.com/uk/articles/new-year-new-job-plus-morale-tracker-and-faith-schools/

Waters, S. 2021. P. 145. Cultures of Staff Wellbeing and Mental Health in Schools. Open University Press.

Wax, R. 2016. P. 68. Frazzled. Penguin.

Worth, J. and Van den Brande, J. 2020. P. 2. Teacher Autonomy: How Does It Relate to Job Satisfaction and Retention?. National Foundation for Educational Research. https://www.nfer.ac.uk/publications/teacher-autonomy-how-does-it-relate-to-job-satisfaction-and-retention/

2 Teaching and learning

Honestly, speaking to people who are being told they have to use specific pedagogical techniques and formats is baffling. These are highly qualified professionals and they should be allowed to apply professional judgement. And people wonder why we have a retention crisis!

(Sue Cowley. 6:37 am 5 Nov 2024. X)

Chapter 2 outline

In this chapter, we will explore:

- curriculum autonomy by exploring the concept of "fidelity to a scheme" and questioning the compatibility of schemes and autonomy.
- how we can use schemes effectively, ensuring they encourage rather than inhibit innovation and autonomy.
- the unfortunate necessity for schemes when managing workload.
- ideas on how to find planning formats and structures that support our individual ideas, creativity and growth.
- how we can tick statutory boxes whilst finding space and time to follow child interest and teacher creativity.
- growing requirements to follow school policy and guidelines with regard to learning environments.
- practical ways that teachers can work with rules and regulations on how to develop classroom environments.

Curriculum and autonomy

The National Curriculum initiated prescription and since its introduction by Margaret Thatcher's Conservative government in 1988 has been left much unchanged (thanks to Gove and Gibb – more on that later).

When I look up the word curriculum, I am interested to see that it originates from the Latin "currere" which means to "run" with the noun curriculum translating as "racehorse". Racing towards an end result, a product, is what us teachers have become experts at. We are

DOI: 10.4324/9781003532729-3

forever racing, hurtling towards a set of expectations, results we like to think we can predict and data that can justify our decisions. This is followed by an inevitable crash, which is what we call "teacher burnout" causing high numbers of professionals leaving the race altogether. In 2024 Education Support's annual wellbeing survey index it stated that "78% of all staff are stressed" (Education Support, 2024), and in 2022 it stated that "59% of staff have considered leaving the sector in the past academic year due to pressures on their mental health and wellbeing". (Education Support, 2022) Surely, if we can see this crisis unfolding, if we know firsthand that stress levels are so high, why do we continue to run?

As we continue to race towards this end product, tiredness inevitably sets in and we begin to look for ways to cut corners. Unfortunately, the hacks that are being sold to us have the potential to quash passion, steal life from classrooms and attempt to build robots rather than inspire children. From the use of images from online publishing houses to paying out thousands of pounds for schemes – addressing the demands of the current curriculum is losing us all – adults and children alike. Teacher personality and individuality have been traded in for display policies, behaviour management scripts and phonics lessons that bore the teachers as much as the children they are supposed to teach.

This paints a bleak picture, but it doesn't need to be. We have an opportunity to be bold and speak up when it comes to curriculum. As Education Consultant Sue Cowley once told me, we (the teachers) are the buffer between children and bad policy and systems. Children cannot speak up for themselves and they *won't* speak up for themselves because they do not know any other way. But *many educators* do. Building a curriculum that encompasses the experiences and opinions of teachers, senior leadership teams (SLT) and children, alongside ticking statutory boxes and staying on the right side of Ofsted, *can* be done. But before we get to the happy ending (and rest assured there is one) let's break down the slow destruction of curriculum autonomy.

A quick note on the curriculum review

As I was writing this book Labour took over the government and a curriculum review was put in place almost immediately. With Becky Francis (Chief Executive Officer of the Education Endowment Foundation) to head the review, educators were asked to contribute to a consultation process through a set of detailed questions and roadshow events with a panel which I attended. The review was introduced as below:

> Curriculum and assessment are inextricably linked to other aspects of the education system, including accountability, inspection, pedagogy and structures. We understand the importance of these interactions. Whilst our primary focus is on curriculum, qualification pathways and assessment, the Review may therefore, for example, offer commentary on the impact of accountability on the curriculum and assessment system. It may wish to recommend how changes to curriculum and assessment should interact with accountability measures.
> (Curriculum and Assessment Review Introduction. September 2024)

There have been numerous ways available for stakeholders to have their say on the curriculum review including in-person, online events and a survey. I attended one of the 11 in-person

34 Teacher Autonomy

Figure 2.1 Becky Francis and Panel at the Curriculum Review Roadshow in London 2024. Photograph by Sophie Smith-Tong

events – the curriculum roadshow was set up for educators to gather, listen to Becky Francis and panel, provide feedback and ask questions as part of the consultation process. My first observation at the London event was the lack of current teachers in attendance (the event was held at an inconvenient time of 4 pm, so many teachers would not have been able to get there on time). There were many former teachers, Trust CEO's and SLT members. There were also many representing companies such as *Into Film* and the *Nutrition Society* with a motive to get more of their content into the curriculum (good luck fitting more in!). There were a variety of views and plenty of heated (but respectful) debate going on. During one conversation I was met with a few sceptics of a broad and balanced curriculum with one history teacher claiming that "what poor kids need is more maths and literacy, not more art, how is that going to help them!?". Fret not, I informed him of what art might do for them. Having experienced firsthand the damage of a heavy focus on maths and literacy, I confidently defended my viewpoint. I left the review feeling both hopeful and frustrated. There was a realisation that (as Becky Francis is eager to repeat) this review "is about evolution rather than revolution", the latter obviously being my preference. Besides budget restraints it was evident that delegates felt revolution was in fact impractical, due to the current intense teacher workload. How on earth could we fit in a revolution alongside everything else we ask of our education workforce? It's a cycle that at some point must be escaped. To gain precious time and reduce workload a revolution may be necessary. Perhaps we are not feeling strong enough yet or potentially if the government had revolution in its plans, we would feel supported to make that big move – who knows?

An employee of the Department for Education (DfE) shared that any curriculum change set to happen will not take place for some time – 2028/29 as an estimate and we must remember that the government may choose to ignore much of the review (we know what happened to Sir Kevan Collins Recovery Curriculum recommendations back in 2021). So, with that in mind, I feel this chapter is still very relevant and if anything *more* so. We can continue to ask ourselves, what *is* it we want from *our* curriculum (and yes, it really should be *ours!*)

My hopes for our curriculum following the review will become clearer after reading this chapter but to sum up in a few bullet points:

- Make it simple.
- Make it relevant.
- Encourage flexibility.
- Allow time for a broad and balanced curriculum.
- Make space for active and experiential learning.
- Give permission for autonomy.

Schemes of work

Mr Bottrill, why are you boring here and when we play you are really good fun?
(Greg Bottrill talking about phonics scheme carpet times on the Mindfulness for learning Podcast. 2023)

Schemes have been among the most problematic introductions to our education system in the last decade, despite the fact that they might reduce workload. There I said it, straight in there. I am not a fan of schemes. Scheme creators might start out with a teacher's best interest at heart, in trying to find an easier way to get stuff done, but ultimately schemes make a lot of money out of schools by capitalising on educator fear – the vulnerable headteachers worrying that they have missed a piece of the curriculum puzzle, the SLT who question their staff capabilities and time-pressured professionals needing a quick fix. With scheme creators providing detailed planning and slides ready to roll, they place their arms around teachers and offer to share the heavy burden of accountability. The unfortunate thing is, schemes come at a cost, both financially (many whole school schemes can cost around £10,000) and developmentally (which we will get to shortly). Schemes end up holding teachers captive – drying up creativity and strapping us firmly in for the ride.

We already spend an average of £10,000 on training UK residents to become teachers (Get into Teaching Website, Dec 2024). Why are we then laying that training to rest and spending more money on pre-made learning experiences? My partner (who is not in education) could teach following a scheme, and yes, I know there is more skill to teaching than just a "plan", but with schemes becoming more and more tight on flexibility you wonder how many of these skills are becoming redundant?

Phonics schemes

One of the most widely used schemes is that of phonics. According to Teacher Tapp "by 2022, 9 out of 10 primary schools were using a validated scheme" to teach phonics, meaning that they were using a scheme authenticated by the DfE (Teacher Tapp, 4 August 2023.) When I asked X if any schools were choosing *not* to use a scheme, consultant Sue Cowley replied, "In theory you can create your own approach but I don't think many schools risk it". You might agree that it would take a bold team to go it alone down the phonics road, surely a map is a must have, for its proof that you are taking the subject seriously, but there are many reasons why a scheme may be damaging to reading development. As a newly qualified teacher I used *Letters and Sounds*. Published in April 2007, it was a "six-phase teaching programme designed to help practitioners and teachers teach children how the alphabet works for reading and spelling" (DfE, 2007). This document provided a lot of space for the teacher to move around within the safety of recommended ideas and was never a statutory document. One of my favourite unplanned phonics lessons was an impromptu outing in the rain, resulting in the introduction of the sound "u" for umbrella. It is a perfect example of what a scheme cannot deliver – in the moment, *with* the children not *to* the children, responsive, interactive and relevant. You cannot get this level of spontaneity and active excitement from a scheme, and I am sure the children will remember this learning as much as I do! You may argue that pre-planned lessons can still exist alongside more active phonics energy bursts, but my argument is that they shouldn't have to coexist in their current state. As of now, the lessons are too long, too scripted and leave many children behind as they refuse to pause for anyone. Phonics already takes up large parts of the day with carpet sessions lasting 30 minutes, not to mention the catch-up sessions. Without a certain level of autonomy, we cannot respond genuinely and creatively to the individuals in our classrooms, and a prescribed plan encourages a reluctance to derail. This can be seen as rebellious behaviour and a waste of school money.

Schemes and disconnect

Learning is not linear (as much as we like to believe it is, for our human need for control). We all learn in different ways and will reach varied outcomes depending on a variety of factors including current circumstances, past experiences, income, diet, sleep and much, much more. A scheme overlooks the professional's knowledge or understanding of learning development and tends to ignore educators' training and connection with those in their care. When a teacher opens a plan that is ready-made they are inherently disconnected from the content and it is potentially meaningless to the children they are teaching.

Many current schemes not only provide an extremely detailed plan but will often lay out comprehensive stage directions. For example, how you place down or shuffle a set of phonics cards. The lessons are designed to be delivered in the way they are directed, in the order they are presented and using the words that are written. How can we possibly have time to go off-piste when a child is getting left behind, noticeably bored or needs the loo! Following an observation, I was once asked why I was not in time with my partner teacher when teaching our phonics scheme lesson. The scheme removes any scope for real life, connection or

Figure 2.2 Experiencing phonics with U for Umbrella. Photograph by Sophie Smith-Tong

experience. We know that finding and feeling connection is vital for wellbeing. Vanessa King (2016) explores the idea of "active listening" in her book, *10 keys to Happier Living* – developing our relationship and communication skills relies on *really* listening and responding to each other. Genuine response comes in the form of planning that has been created by us as professionals for the individuals we teach – like a conversation, it's a back- and-forth interaction. With a scheme it's as though only the teacher is speaking (and not from the heart or soul). Schemes fail to value not only the teacher's knowledge but also what the children bring to the experience of learning.

The hidden identity of schemes

Leaders (and teachers) can understandably become anxious about curriculum coverage and begin to rely on the implementation of schemes. For leaders, schemes can seem like a necessary way to ensure progression and development across the setting with each year doing exactly what the scheme dictates. This leaves less room for error such as doubling up on topics or lessons and establishing clear progression. Error can have catastrophic results as we have seen in the media, with controversial Ofsted visits or "requires improvement" badges that are hard to shake off, resulting in problems with filling school places. Who can blame leaders when their job is so time pressured and with such high-stakes accountability? It's impossible to ignore the desire to seek out pre-made, tried and tested school experience but there is a danger with the reliance on schemes in the stunting of a teacher's professional growth and development. Schemes reduce opportunities to try out new ideas, innovate, get creative and learn from mistakes. We have come to rely so heavily on schemes that we are no longer able to imagine our worlds without them. Reflection has always been a key skill in teaching, but what is there to reflect upon when we believe we can predict what comes next? Schemes make it difficult to stray.

Schemes as support

When speaking to teachers it became clear that ECTs and Postgraduate Certificate in Education (PGCE) students in particular found schemes to be of great support. A scheme can place us in a zone of comfort and ease when we already have so much learning and consolidation to do (and very little time to process). Being given a structure may seem like a blessing but it also fails to recognise the importance of failure and experimentation. Adrian Bethune explores the idea of comfort, stretch and panic zones in his book, *Wellbeing in the Primary Classroom*. Schemes place teachers in the comfort zone (they also put me in a bad mood) but as Adrian Bethune states, "the work is fairly easy and we don't feel stressed because the work isn't challenging". He recognises that it feels nice in the comfort zone, but the problem lies in spending too much time there and so we lose interest. To really challenge and develop our teaching practice we must place ourselves in the stretch zone regularly, an area that Adrian describes as a place you "encounter tricky work" (Bethune, 2018, P. 103), and with persistence you begin to do work that you were unable to do before. These zones are a good example of finding balance. Without challenging ourselves how can we ever begin to grow and develop our individual practice?

Schemes and workload

As I undertook research in the development of this book what became clear is that schemes have become a necessary survival strategy for teachers. With little to no time, space, energy or mental clarity to get creative, schemes can offer us a way out. I use them. There is no judgement of anyone adopting or using a scheme – my problem lies in them having to exist in the first place – there is just too much to navigate and not enough time to do it. Schemes can help with specialised areas of teaching – especially in primary schools where teachers cannot be specialists in all of the subjects they teach. One teacher that I spoke to despises schemes, generally speaking, but in her decade of teaching had come across a great art scheme – an area where she did not feel confident in creating well-rounded learning opportunities for her class. A place where a group of experts has come together to create a set of lessons can only be seen as a helpful tool. It is the extreme use of the scheme that is arguably damaging – what if children loved one of the artists that they had discovered through the scheme – some schools would not allow the flexibility to pause or adapt the scheme to follow the child's interest and head deeper into that topic. Quite often teachers are expected to follow the scheme to complete it in a set time frame. If we deal with workload and free up time, we can get more creative, and with more creativity comes happiness.

Just as artificial intelligence (AI) has the potential to be misused when unregulated or misunderstood (read more on AI and digital autonomy in **Chapter 5**), schemes can harm learning when there is little to no regulation; schemes begin to remove personalisation and autonomy. Without monitoring your own scheme use, they may exacerbate current problems with standardisation and chasing data goals.

Inclusion, child development and schemes

The recognition of time constraints can place schemes into a more positive light. For example, Annabelle Kapoor, headteacher of an Inner London Primary School stated "…teachers also have limited time – with most of their day devoted to the doing, not the planning or reviewing. So ready-made schemes of work have their places as long as they are high-quality, right for the context and ideally linked in with some personalisation". (Kapoor, 2023)

Personalisation is key. We must consider the *individuals* we are teaching to guarantee inclusive practice. There are some schemes that insist on moving forward despite those children you may be leaving behind. "Catch-up" interventions later that same day are indicative of a system too focused on data and numbers and forget about the very fact that children are humans. If the scheme content isn't being absorbed during the lesson, then the scheme probably isn't working in the way it should. Therefore, the child needs fewer schemes and more personalisation, not more schemes in the form of catch-up sessions. Without this personalisation we lack real connection resulting in compromised wellbeing and poor mental health. Andrew Cowley sums it up succinctly in his book, *The Wellbeing Curriculum* – "Every interaction the children have with each other, with their teacher and teaching assistant, with other adults and children at break and dinner time – these all form part of their learning experience" (Cowley, 2021. P. 18). Schemes are unable to recognise the importance of individual learning styles and journeys and can result in children feeling discouraged, disconnected, with a lack of purpose, belonging and trust. They also switch the teacher into robot mode, reeling off insignificant words and offering experiences that are impersonal, devaluing the child and reducing the opportunity for genuine interaction. All of these components lead to problems with retention and absenteeism which I explore in **Chapter 4**.

Educator experience – Schemes

Jess Gosling. International Teacher in British International Schools.

One area in which I have struggled with a lack of autonomy is phonics programs. Often a school will buy in all the resources for one program and teachers are required to follow the prescriptive methods of delivering the sessions. We know as educators that "one size" does not fit all children in terms of teaching methodologies. In these cases, I have supplemented student's learning in different ways, outside of the program.

It's time to pause.

Reflection

- Does my school insist I use schemes?
- If they do, how much flexibility is there within the scheme?
- If there is flexibility, what can I take from the scheme to make it work for me?
- How can I adapt the scheme resources/slides to make them more personalised?
- Do I need to use the slides and worksheets recommended?
- Can I make lessons less "flat" (e.g. reducing use of worksheets) and more active?

Get autonomy back

In the classroom:

- If you must use a scheme, use the scheme as a bank of ideas and avoid relying on its order, resources, slides and planning completely.
- Use the scheme content to inform and begin to develop your own ideas - get yourself in Adrian Bethune's "stretch zone" and have fun! (Bethune, 2018)
- Get excited about and have faith in your own ideas.
- Work with a partner teacher to develop ideas together. This will help you build confidence and save time. Get excited together about the personalised learning opportunities you are creating.
- If you want to personalise learning, you can annotate directly onto the scheme to save time. Print, cut and paste the scheme planning to your own document so as to avoid doubling up on work. Print and adapt/annotate your own ideas onto the plans with a pen.
- Using a pen means you can adapt and annotate your plans easily throughout the week - nothing stays the same, especially in schools.
- Plans are rarely followed to the detail - get comfortable with change and see change as being responsive to your children rather than failure.
- Transform "flat" learning from schemes into learning experiences - up and active! We all know that the more experience the children have, the more the learning is consolidated and embedded.
- Use the scheme slides but adapt the content to ensure you are being responsive to the individuals in your class. For example, changing wording, images or toning it down if you feel the use of colour or images is too overwhelming for learners.
- Avoid relying on the same order and lesson content every year - of course, the lovely thing about repeating years is that you already have so much of the work already done but be prepared to change, adapt and tweak according to the children you have in your new class. Children really feel it when they know something has been created with and for them.
- Avoid expecting that all children will be ready to learn content in the same order - they will not. Learning is not linear.
- Be realistic. Avoid trying to create a bespoke lesson every time but add a sprinkle of them (and you!) into the lessons.

Teaching and Learning

For senior leaders:

- Speak to your team, what do they want and how can they see it working for them?
- It is not a statutory requirement to use a scheme. If it's an option, trust your teachers and avoid using schemes for every single subject, if at all.
- Get excited about and have faith in your staff team's ideas.
- Encourage and give space for collaboration - there will be a variety of strengths across the team - how can you provide time and space for staff to share and learn from one another?
- Ensure your teachers have the resources they need to plan and deliver fun experiences for the children without spending their own money.

For government officials:

- Slim down the curriculum.
- Make the content so relevant and engaging that a worksheet would be unnecessary.
- Support schools' creativity by giving them time and space to move away from prescriptive schemes.
- Change your current view on "evolution rather than revolution" when discussing curriculum change.
- Explore Luke Sparkes' "Aligned Autonomy" and spread the word. (Sparkes, 2020) Autonomy does not mean chaos.
- Replace Ofsted and start afresh. This will remove the immense and unnecessary teams are under.

Final thought on schemes

It is vital to trust teachers and encourage creativity, allowing them to map out a curriculum, avoiding the *scheme-only* approach to deliver National Curriculum content. Schemes are only fully beneficial to one person and that is the founder of the scheme itself; they are making a small fortune when teachers have already paid out a lot of money to train. Instead of using school budgets to buy schemes, ensure you purchase good-quality resources and provide enough planning, preparation and assessment time (PPA) so that teachers have the tools to make the *real* magic happen.

Planning

> *...the teachers who are well prepared, are also the teachers who can take a more flexible approach.*
> **(The Ultimate Guide to Lesson Planning. Carol Thompson et al., 2024)**

If the extensive amount of planning formats available on platforms such as Twinkl and the Times Education Supplement (TES) is anything to go by, it is clear there is high demand for support with finding the *right* planning format. I have tried and tested many in my 15 years of teaching.

I find planning formats baffling. I still haven't found one that has worked for me for a long period of time. I am beginning to explore the idea that this is probably for the best, for no two days, months, years or cohorts are ever the same and require different approaches. Education provides us with a beautiful amount of variety, challenge and change. Depending on the year you teach and where you are in your teaching career, the level of detail in your planning will deviate.

I have worked in schools that have insisted I use their pre-designed format, and I have also worked in schools that are flexible in how I deliver my planning. I have been under senior leaders who have requested that my planning be saved in a specific folder, with a deadline and then consequently checked over and conversely, I have experienced schools where I am trusted that I am planning my lessons carefully without rigorous inspection. The latter is undoubtedly more beneficial.

Safety, time, guidance and space to make mistakes are the most vital components here. The most learning and development takes place when we can have a good balance of support along with the freedom to trial ideas without judgment. One teacher told me that they were expected to hand in their planning to SLT weekly, only to have it returned a day later with annotations and crosses through it. Not only is this incredibly rude and infantilising but it is also not conducive to creating a culture whereby teachers can experiment, improve and most importantly become a responsive practitioner. If our ideas are not valued then how can we develop a sense of purpose and worth at work?

The challenges we face with planning will differ – early career teachers (ECTs) may have trouble envisioning their perfect planning format, and stagnation may take hold for more experienced teachers. The key to successful planning is enabled reflection. Not only in the form of a SLT that is willing to listen but also in the form of collaborative partner teaching. In my personal experience I have found having a partner teacher who has been teaching for only a few years a great way to freshen up ideas that I have used for a long time. On the other hand, she has found my experience helpful when initiating new ideas that she has yet to try.

Legal and policy considerations

There is no legal obligation to plan your lessons and Ofsted state that they will not request to see any planning as part of their inspections. However, planning is encouraged and it is specified in the Teacher Standards that planning will help to deliver well-structured lessons. Many schools will have their own policies around planning and even provide uniformed planning formats for staff to use. I certainly find planning helpful and am yet to find a teacher who would rather not plan at all. I feel it is general consensus that planning can help us think through ideas and develop them further. However, it is important to remember that ideas can come to fruition in the moment and may not always be in the written planning. Being able to respond organically and in the moment happens when we are trusted to follow our professional judgement. For many teachers this may not be a possibility, for fear of perception from SLT and visitors/inspections.

Some settings will require the teacher to plan for their term, their weeks and then their days and depending on the year you teach, the way you plan will look different. A lot of schools will also design their own curriculum progression maps informed *hopefully* by all the staff working in that team and the experiences they are having with teaching in the current context. Any curriculum should allow the freedom to plan according to the individuals they are teaching and utilise the skills of their staff teams.

Teachers may use long, medium and short-term plans which will mean navigating and organising a large amount of information which can be complicated to lay out clearly. It is vital that teachers can do this in a way that is clear to them, rather than completing it with outsiders' viewpoints in mind. Planning is for the teacher and nobody else (apart from the children it is impacting). High-stakes accountability measures can cause teachers to feel pressure to make it fit into a criteria set by SLT. Having trust in your staff teams to plan in a way that suits them will remove this pressure, meaning they are spending less time on concerning themselves with outside perception and more time on the content of the planning itself. It is worth noting that despite planning being complicated, when you are left to do it in a way that suits you, the creativity this freedom encourages results in a state of flow, joy and a feeling of being valued.

Learning objectives and success criteria

In a recent conversation about learning objectives and success criteria, my 7-year-old daughter shared that "sometimes I just colour the ELP (Effort, Learning and Presentation) green because I just don't think about it, because the teachers don't even look at my work and it's meant for me but I don't even think about it so it doesn't really make any sense". In simple terms, she was colouring a version of a success criteria as a tick box exercise; it was a job that needed to be done and did not actually provide a reflective process for her.

Establishing formal processes can help those in education to convey and/or feel a sense of order, especially when we are attempting to prove ourselves to visitors in our classrooms or to those carrying out "book looks". But do these processes actually add anything to our learners' experiences, and are teachers *really* finding them useful? Could it be that we are seeing the product of yet more token system and policy (which is scrutinised through observations, Ofsted visits, book looks and learning walks), rather than developed through collaboration within our professional teams? Teachers are not being asked (or feeling comfortable sharing) what works for them. They are then becoming reliant on these processes and are lacking in time to develop systems and approaches that work more effectively.

This idea is explored in the book, *The Ultimate Guide to Lesson Planning* (Thompson et al., 2024), where a reflection from one of the authors describes a moment when they decide they will *not* use a learning objective for a particular lesson. This approach was met with discomfort from many of the teachers. The lack of a learning objective left them feeling anxious as they were removing part of their routine. Schools can be breeding grounds for inertia. However, if headteachers value and encourage teacher autonomy, this will ensure we are always asking questions about current practice. We may argue that learning objectives can be limiting, inhibiting teacher exploration and narrowing learning possibilities. The use of learning objectives should be a decision for teachers to make at any given moment, not a blanket school rule or expectation.

Timing and pacing

Timetables have been at the heart of school structure since the introduction of the standardised school model in response to the industrial economy. A more structured school day enabled teachers to fit in and organise the subjects that they were required to cover. We have barely moved away from this model in our current systems and find ourselves forcing an extremely old system into our modern day, and guess what? It doesn't fit. The inflexible and tight schedules often mean that teachers are unable to move around within them. It is often the case that the foundation and creative subjects get booted out for more maths and literacy because of the hierarchy of curriculum subjects (remember my colleague from earlier who I met at the curriculum review? He felt that "poor kids" need more maths and literacy, not more art?) Well, surprisingly, there are still many who believe that maths and literacy are the most important subjects. It stems from our early focus on these two areas of learning from our friends all the way back in the Industrial Revolution.

A move to a more flexible and responsive timetable would benefit adults and children alike but would rely heavily on teacher autonomy. Following a scheme and/or squeezing in topics and events results in a lack of time to respond to child interest meaning we are constantly on the move (and not in the physical sense unfortunately). It is common that as soon as a child displays competence in an area, we speed on to the next to provide a challenge. Challenge and progression have become a symbol of teaching success (we have the "gifted and talented" movement to thank for that). On the contrary, when children are finding an area challenging the time pressures can cause teachers frustration, resulting in moving forward and leaving children behind without a moment to repeat areas of learning. Learning experiences become a tick box exercise with minimal learning for children and very little autonomy for both teacher and children (more on our learners in **Chapter 4**).

It can be argued that an agile model will only be made possible with a slimming down of the curriculum content which would free up time and space to make decisions on how our classes use their time. For example, allowing a teacher to remain on a topic such as the Great Fire of London for an extra week in response to a child's interest would result in eager learners and higher engagement. More flexibility and trusting teachers to make decisions on our timetables would ensure that learners are having tailored experiences with positive outcomes for understanding and personal wellbeing (read more on flexible timetables in **Chapter 3**).

Educator experience – Planning content

Sarah DeSilva. KS2 Teacher and Equalities Lead. Inner London Primary.

As a year 6 teacher, I am a firm believer in letting colleagues have more freedom and autonomy in the learning they deliver to pupils. From formulating ideas which are relevant and engaging and having more say over their own topic coverage, teachers value a curriculum which is student-centred and showcases the children's own individual voice. This also ensures the curriculum reflects topics of cultural and contextual relevance to the ever-changing world. Giving teachers more freedom to help build the curriculum they deliver gives them more confidence and ownership in the classroom. Furthermore, it encourages children to also have autonomy and a say in their learning. Our recent curriculum redesign has refocused the learning with a more inclusive and diversity-driven lens. By creating a culture of flexibility and learning that is more student-led, it means children are empowered for their onward personal, social and emotional journeys into adulthood.

It's time to pause.

Reflection

- Do I have a say in the design of my planning format?
- Is my planning format useful and easy to use?
- Do I find planning enjoyable?
- Can I add a sprinkle of myself into my planning?
- Can I get creative in my planning?
- Do I stick rigidly to previous years' planning or am I given time to adapt for individuals/cohorts?
- Am I encouraging learner autonomy through my planning?
- Am I feeling confident to respond to last-minute changes in my planning?
- Do I avoid big ideas due to being under-resourced?
- Am I able to be flexible in my lesson delivery?

Get autonomy back

In the classroom:

- Ask to create your own planning format (with support if required) – it may take time to find what works, but being able to experiment helps work out what is important to you and your cohort.
- If you are unable to create your own format, can you adapt it/collaborate with other teachers to make it more conducive to your aims?
- Allow your planning to reflect your personality, annotate your plans and add in boxes that you feel you need as an individual teacher.
- Make sure that the entirety of your planning format is utilised and nothing is wasteful or goes unused. If it isn't helpful, then get rid of it!
- Reflect on your format – is it still working? It is likely to change over time and with your different cohorts, so try to be open and flexible with this.
- Reflect on your use of Learning Objectives and Success Criteria – do you need them and who are they serving?

For senior leaders:

- Ask your teachers if they would like support with their planning.
- Trust your teachers to create their own planning formats and if you have more than one form in your setting, request that teachers work together to come up with a format that works for all of them so that you have the consistency you feel you need.
- Question if you *really* need consistency in formatting – does it come from a need for control or does it actually *work* better this way? Remember, autonomy doesn't necessarily mean chaos.
- If you find handing over the responsibility of the planning format challenging, then collaborate so that all of your criteria are met.

- Ask your teachers what parts of the format work and which are a waste of time. They are the ones using it, so they will know best.
- Make it well known that Ofsted will not want to see planning. Avoid exacerbating the myth.

For government officials:

- Clarify that planning is for teachers, not for SLT and not for Ofsted.
- Publicise that Ofsted will not want to see planning during their visits.
- Slim down the curriculum, allowing for more streamlined planning and space to get creative.
- Ensure schools have the budget to realise creative and flexible planning ideas.

Final thought on planning

Teachers want to plan in a way that is both efficient and impactful. They can spend a lot of valuable time navigating a planning format that they do not understand, filling in parts that are meaningless to them. They may also find that they are unable to make a change, leaving them feeling frustrated, disconnected and demotivated. The magic comes from the heart of the teacher and connects to the hearts of the children. It derives from a connection formed between teacher and child - the art of active listening and genuine response. Trusting teachers to plan in a way that works for them will help to deliver effective and inspiring lessons that teachers love to teach and that children are enthusiastic about.

The classroom

We aren't robots and actually injecting some of our tastes and preferences and passions into the environment is important too.

(Anon. Early Years Foundation Stage (EYFS) Teacher. Inner London Primary School)

My classroom is my pride and joy and a fruition of my own personal learning, development and experiences alongside guidance and support from my headteacher. I appreciate the trust that my manager places in me to develop my space which I feel is attentive to the individuals in my class, my personality and new research and evidence. My environment changes over the academic year and, year after year, depending on the family that lives in it and what I have learned.

Classroom environment approaches and policies exist on a spectrum ranging from complete freedom, sometimes leaving professionals feeling lost and overwhelmed, to extremely prescriptive, causing frustration and increases in workload and pressure. When it comes to the environment, there are many decisions to make - carpet plan or no carpet plan? Bright-coloured backing paper or muted tones? Pre-formatted online wall decoration or none at all. We all show who we are through the decisions we make about the spaces we work in. Teachers have shared a variety of experiences with me including the ban of certain pre-formatted classroom display resources to a demand for double-backing and specific desk layout. Certain levels of control and expectation for "consistency" throughout a setting run the risk of removing nuance and personality from learning spaces. On the flip side, allowing complete freedom can cause too much overwhelm and change for neurodiverse learners and staff, and also result in spaces that are disorganised and not conducive to learning.

The learning environment

Developing an environment in school and in particular the EYFS could be a full-time job. The EYFS environment acts as a home away from home for the little ones, requiring safe places to change nappies, co-regulate and provide learning opportunities covering all areas of the early years (EY) curriculum. In fact, a huge part of planning for the EYFS comes down to the environment in what is called "continuous provision" (the resources and furniture that are constantly out) and the "enhanced provision" (the added resources and pieces that intend to extend and challenge already existing and developing skills and interests). These elements are carefully considered, requiring professionals to plan and execute this crucial and meticulous task.

Further up the school, it needn't be much different – an environment should feel warm, calm and respond to the family living in it. The space should tell a story and pay homage to the group of individual humans inhabiting it. Adrian Bethune states that "teachers are central to establishing a tribal classroom". Tribal classrooms are our foundations "...as we function best and are at our happiest when we live and work in tribes" (Bethune, 2018. P. 12). It really is clear – the classroom should feel like it belongs to the class, and for those entering the space, it should be clear as to what that particular class is all about.

Micromanagement or support?

Many teachers struggle to find the time to dedicate to what, founder of the Reggio Emilia approach, Loris Malaguzzi states as the "third teacher" – their environment (Bradbury et al., 2022. PP. 74, 75). Being time-poor means we rely heavily on those around us to support our thinking and development around the classroom. Finding the balance between supporting this area of development and micromanaging can be an area many leaders find difficult to navigate. Micromanaging can cause bad feeling, wastes precious time waiting for elements to be "signed off" and an absence of autonomy can result in disengagement, with teachers failing to recognise their purpose within their own spaces. One teacher described an interaction with a leader asking, "would you decorate your house like that?". Negative communication like this leaves teachers feeling devalued with their professional status deemed meaningless.

Again, the time and data pressures on SLT members mean that many leaders are left feeling unable to hand over full responsibility to classroom teachers and support staff. The feeling of losing control results in a tightening of the grip in the form of micromanaging. Dictating how a learning environment looks can limit the ability of teachers to respond to their school families and create a place where they feel a true sense of belonging. When we lose a sense of connection and belonging, we no longer find this space a happy place – maybe where a retention and absenteeism crisis might creep in? As Teacher Transition Coach, Rachel Gibbs

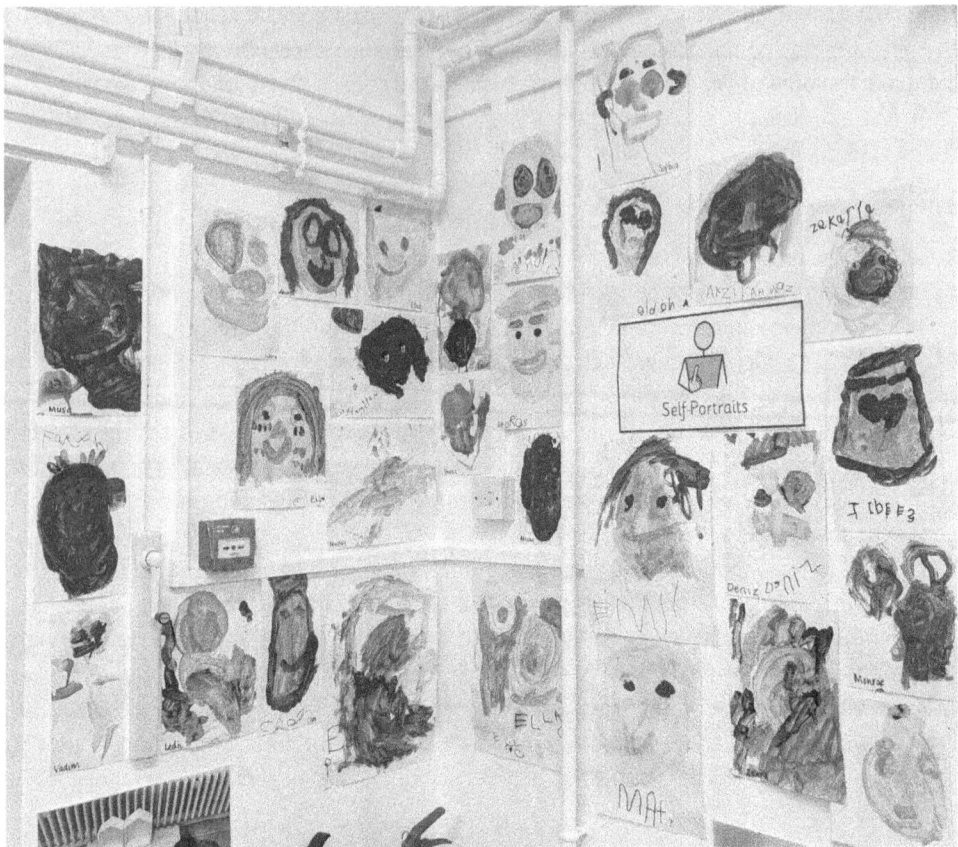

Figure 2.3 The classroom should belong to those inhabiting it. Self-portraits displayed in my classroom in 2024. Photograph by Sophie Smith-Tong

echoed on her Instagram feed – one of the reasons that so many teachers are leaving is due to others not knowing their "true value" (Gibbs, 2023). It is vital in any employment to feel required, needed and relied upon. It is equally important to feel that way as a child in the classroom. We all yearn to be part of the bigger picture.

Environment research and professional development

Of course, our own personal gain is not the sole reason we should be given creative freedoms in our classrooms. A significant factor in decision-making regarding our environments should come from up-to-date research and evidence. Although it is the responsibility of us teachers to keep our finger on the pulse, it is also the job of the SLT to ensure that staff are being provided with new and up-to-date professional learning on developing effective learning environments. This way teachers are able to input what they have learned in a way that reflects their own identity and beliefs. For example, if a behaviour lead believes that muted tones are a plausible way to calm behaviour challenges in the school, then it would make sense to train staff on why they might implement muted tones in all classrooms across the setting. On the other hand, I would strongly suggest that you ask any headteacher demanding you use orange borders on all displays *why* they feel the need to make this request and what they are trying to achieve. A controlling environment is a negative one; a nourishing environment gives good reasons for decisions, requests input from others and allows a team to grow by listening and learning together and from each other.

Being reflective and open to change is an integral part of teacher development but education is full of fads (we are used to seeing initiatives come and go) making educator cynicism commonplace. This can cause resentment toward change, especially when it is unevidenced; it is from here that toxic cultures can evolve. As Alistair Bryce-Clegg said when discussing research on the use of muted tones in the classroom, "...what it doesn't mean is that your whole environment can only be beige..." (Bryce-Clegg, 2023). Leaders must try to recognise the importance of supporting teachers to develop their individual understanding through shared good practice and taking them outside of their four walls to reflect and grow. This can be in the form of borough-wide cluster meetings, in-house exchanges through staff meetings and outsourced training where they can learn about new and exciting ideas and avoid stale practice.

Educator experience – Classroom

Anon. Primary School Teacher and EYFS Specialist. Inner London Primary School.

Standardising classrooms is quite bizarre. I once had a headteacher who was into standardisation – every classroom should have Zones of Regulation, a Numicon number line, an alphabet in cursive writing and photos of children in class. Each board was set out, and each classroom should have a home learning board even though I didn't believe in home learning! Everyone should have a maths and phonics board – it was more to do with what she thought supporting their learning would look like. I would argue that the teachers should have autonomy because the teacher is with the children every day, they are the experts on the children, they are the ones who are going to be supporting their emotions and wellbeing and enabling them to learn.

It's time to pause.

Reflection

- What are my schools requirements when it comes to classroom displays, layout and child-led work presentation?
- Are my experiences of these requirements having a negative impact?
- Do these requirements align with my ethos and understanding?
- What is most important to me in terms of classroom environment?
- Have I shared my time constraints with SLT in terms of any specific requirements such as double backing or borders?
- Am I aware of the evidence/research behind my approach to developing my learning space?

Get autonomy back

In the classroom:

- Be curious about the reasons you are having to develop your classroom in a specific way - asking questions is not rude, it shows you care and are passionate about what you do.
- Ask for space to show leaders your way and do not be afraid to say an idea hasn't worked - we always tell the children mistakes are marvellous, and we should model that too.
- Try to back up what you want to do with research and evidence.
- Try to keep your classroom organised - organisation can be seen as an example of someone who is competent and might allow you more scope to experiment.
- Be bold and innovative - try new ways and share your discoveries with your staff team.
- Be sure that you can talk confidently about the decisions you have made regarding your learning environment (this will be easy if *you* have made the decision - we teachers rarely do anything without thinking about why).
- Ask for training and/or school visits if you feel this is an area you are yet to grow confident in.
- Pick your battles - tick the boxes so that you have scope to get creative.
- Recognise that in some settings you will need to compromise. For example, your school may not be able to budge on their decision that every classroom should have a particular number line visible, but they may be ok with you using your own font style. Small steps.
- Build the environment *with* the children and refer to the displays when talking with them.
- Make the displays child-led - nobody wants to see 30 heavily modelled copies of a piece of work - identity is key.
- Avoid using too many pre-formatted classroom display resources - I know that they can save a lot of time, but a classroom can look amazing and instil a genuine sense of belonging without these cookie-cutter templates.
- Find balance. Avoid becoming obsessed with one new idea so much so that you delete all previous ideas - this is about merging new and old - what works and what doesn't - it's as simple as that.

For senior leaders:

- Ask yourself why you are creating a blanket rule for classrooms - is it a need for control or is there real evidence to back up your decisions? If there is research, then share it with your team.
- Consider workload before putting new rules and boundaries in place when it comes to the class environment.
- Avoid "learning walks" - this can be invasive and judgmental. Why not be a regular and pop into classrooms to genuinely see how things are going and support - this way you can get a feel for your school environments and support your staff at the same time.
- Encourage teachers to showcase their cohort identity through their environments.

For government officials:

- Increase school budgets so that teachers can make their environments innovative, progressive and inclusive.
- Offer up-to-date and well-researched guidance for each age range on what might make an effective learning environment.
- Allow for time to learn about the above.
- Create a role that understands the importance of environments on learning and wellbeing in local authorities to support teachers in developing effective learning environments.

Final thought on the environment

Developing a style in the classroom is lifelong work, changing over time. Not only does it shift as you grow and become more confident, but it also fluctuates with new research and ideas from those around us. It is vital that teachers are given the space to accumulate and formulate their own ideas and approaches with the support of leaders and staff working alongside them. More importantly, the children we work with need to not only *feel* but truly *believe* that their classroom belongs to them, which will be impossible if the truth is – it doesn't. Only the people working in that space will comprehend fully how they need that space to look and feel to be able to fully function and feel safe in there.

THE BIG IDEA – Curriculum

Annabelle Kapoor. Headteacher and Leadership and Well-being Coach. Inner London Primary School.

My school – an inner-city community state primary – has just launched its best curriculum yet. How do I know? Well, first, it was designed collaboratively by 24 brilliant teachers who know their stuff, the context and their pupils, led by our passionate and relentlessly ambitious curriculum leader. Second, it captured the children's voices, telling us of their dreams and identities. And third, like all good plans, it started with the ending.

As a Headteacher, I was involved in the first meeting only, along with my senior leadership team (a brave, creative and altruistic group). In this meeting, we focused on the outcome we wanted, not for the curriculum itself but for the children, our ultimate end product. "When we send them off into the world, at the end of year 6, who do we want them to be?" By asking this question, we ensured that the curriculum that followed was values-driven, future-focused, character-building and full of heart. The ideas that flew around the room that day formed our destination:

- "they will be change-makers, knowing they can make a positive difference to the world";
- "they'll be resilient, knowing how to look after their health and well-being, how to be calm and at their best";

- "and don't forget others, they'll look after others too! The community";
- "they'll know they belong, but also know how to belong...anywhere!";
- "And how to be themselves...and like who they are";
- "they will understand happiness, know how to create it, appreciate it, spread it";
- "they will be inclusive, to understand and welcome all";
- "they will work hard, and enjoy the challenge";
- "they will truly listen and be empathetic, consider new perspectives";
- "How about adventurous, and brave, open to new things and experiences";
- "they'll be inquisitive, critical thinkers, not believe the first thing they read, question the status quo";
- "they will be innovative, creative, think outside the box, problem solvers";
- "they will be excellent communicators, great with people, able to lead and support";
- "they will know how to seek help from others, but also know how to take action to find success on their own";
- "they will understand the value of learning, and understand and enjoy the process of it. Know their own mind and how they learn best".

Our "vision list" left us all smiling, having reminded each of us why we had become teachers in the first place. We always involve our pupils in the big thinking we do and decisions we make and this was no exception. We wanted a curriculum that the children could identify with, feel inspired by and be grateful for. In our school council, which involves every child from years 2 to 6, children were asked these questions:

- What are your dreams and aspirations for your life?
- What knowledge, skills and habits of mind do you need to achieve your dreams?
- Do you feel like you are represented in our curriculum?
- What would you like to see included in the curriculum?

Their responses, along with our vision list and the expectations of the National Curriculum, formed the design brief for our teachers. School leaders stood back and, with trust and confidence in our teachers, allowed the magic to unfold. In a series of design workshops, starting at the finish line with year 6 and working backwards, building each year from the top of our school to the bottom, our teachers carefully and creatively designed our new curriculum. After designing their own section, each year group told the teachers below them what they needed to work towards, giving them their own destination to drive towards. Yes, of course, they mapped subjects to the National Curriculum - it is statutory (and helpful) after all. And of course, year 6 had SATs in mind (whether we agree with the testing process or not, we always want our children to be prepared and successful). But we also made room to realise our "vision list" and the children's views, building in what we knew would add value to the children. With the ambitious brief and a clear framework from our teaching and learning leader, teachers were given autonomy, licence to be creative and to use their professional knowledge and judgement. They were the right people for the job, with vast experience of how children learn at each stage, what engages them and how subjects weave together best and in what sequence. They are also the people who will deliver the curriculum, so their buy-in and passion for it are essential. From year 6 down to the nursery, our teachers produced long-term progression maps for each subject, ensuring there would be no gaps in the knowledge that would be taught.

This comprehensive and sequenced list of knowledge and skills was then drawn together into termly themes designed to encourage deep and critical thinking; themes that inspired curiosity and discussion, like: The Nature of Belief, Conflict in Society, Our Changing Planet. While planning these termly themes, teachers were encouraged to really bring them to life, with expert speakers, educational visits, outdoor learning, drama, debate and high-quality experiential and sensory resources like Lyfta and Now Press Play.

The outcome of all this work is a broad, ambitious, inspiring and memorable curriculum created with, and for, all of the children it will serve, with a focus on the future that stands before them and the paths that they will forge. A curriculum that the teachers who created it are excited to teach. Our best curriculum yet. I trust that the next Ofsted inspectors who visit us will agree.

Contributors

1. Jess Gosling. International Teacher in British International Schools.
2. Sarah DeSilva. KS2 Teacher and Equalities Lead. Inner London Primary.
3. Anon. EYFS Teacher. Inner London Primary School.
4. Anon. EYFS Specialist. Inner London Primary School.
5. Annabelle Kapoor. Headteacher and Leadership and Well-being Coach. Inner London Primary School.

References

Bethune, A. 2018. P. 103. Wellbeing in the Primary Classroom.
Bethune, A. 2018. P. 103. Wellbeing in the Primary Classroom. Bloomsbury.
Bethune, A. 2018. P. 12. Wellbeing in the Primary Classroom. Bloomsbury.
Bottrill, G. Oct 2023. Mindfulness for Learning Podcast Episode. On Top of Nonsense Mountain. https://open.spotify.com/episode/23GU1OGOf6RTIQe65mUdwd?si=f4364fa74aba4d0d
Bradbury, A. et al. 2022. PP. 74, 75. Early Childhood Theories Today. Sage.
Bryce-Clegg, A. Apr 2023. Mindfulness for Learning Podcast Episode. The Early Years Foundation Stage. https://open.spotify.com/episode/0LYRH9RHSjp7moVu4wuf8v?si=d65d9c85ccff427a
Cowley, A. 2021. P. 18. The Wellbeing Curriculum. Bloomsbury.
Cowley, S. X. 17 Oct 2023. Direct Message.
Cowley, S. 6.37 am 5 Nov 2024. X. https://x.com/Sue_Cowley/status/1853687967518191957
Curriculum and Assessment Review Introduction. Sept 2024. https://consult.education.gov.uk/curriculum-and-assessment-team/curriculum-and-assessment-review-call-for-evidence/consultation/subpage.2024-09-19.6878174559/
Department for Education. 2007. Letters and Sounds. https://www.gov.uk/government/publications/letters-and-sounds

Education Support. 2022. Teacher Wellbeing Index. https://www.educationsupport.org.uk/media/zoga2r13/teacher-wellbeing-index-2022.pdf

Education Support. 2024. Teacher Wellbeing Index. https://www.educationsupport.org.uk/media/ftwl04cs/twix-2024.pdf

Get into Teaching. Dec 2024. Tuition Fees. https://getintoteaching.education.gov.uk/funding-and-support/tuition-fees

Gibbs, R. 12 Oct, 2023. Instagram. https://www.instagram.com/reel/CyTmsATrW2I/?utm_source=ig_web_copy_link&igsh=MzRIODBiNWFIZA==

Kapoor, A. 23 Oct 2023. Direct Email.

King, V. 2016. 10 Keys to Happier Living. Headline Home; Illustrated edition.

Sparkes, L. 27 Oct 2020. YouTube clip. Aligned Autonomy. https://www.youtube.com/watch?v=wuclehEjy5U&t=1s

Teacher Tapp. 4 Aug 2023. What Is the Most Popular Validated Phonics Scheme? https://teachertapp.com/uk/articles/what-is-the-most-popular-validated-phonics-scheme/#:~:text=How%20many%20schools%20use%20a,were%20using%20a%20validated%20scheme.

Thompson, C. et al. 2024. P. 2. The Ultimate Guide to Lesson Planning. Routledge.

3 Accountability

...encouraging autonomy doesn't mean discouraging accountability.
(Daniel H. Pink. Drive. The Surprising Truth about What Motivates Us. 2009. P. 106)

This chapter is dedicated to all the headteachers who have been negatively impacted, yet continued to lead with integrity, courage and care. Your contributions to education inspire lasting change, and your resilience in the face of adversity is a testament to the strength and value of your work.

> ### Chapter 3 outline
>
> In this chapter, we will explore:
>
> - how Ofsted contributes to a lack of trust in teachers.
> - the practice of teacher observations and assess their necessity.
> - how observations might hinder teacher autonomy.
> - a school that no longer has teacher observations.
> - the significance of data and evaluate if it is a reliable indicator of teacher ability.
> - how the request for data impacts teacher autonomy.
> - how we might confidently teach without teaching to the test.
> - practical steps to avoid data negatively impacting teaching.
> - satisfying the needs of all stakeholders without diminishing autonomy.

Accountability and autonomy

First and foremost, accountability in education is important; I do not wish for accountability to disappear into thin air. Continuing on from his quote above, Daniel H Pink explains that people wish to be held accountable, as it is part of what motivates them. I hope that accountability measures will begin to *support* educators and help us to develop our reflective processes. We must seek ways to embed formative accountability rather than continue with the current high-stakes approach; however, we need to be mindful of how we go from a high-stakes accountability system to one that is more reliant on self-reflection tools and collaborative working. Accountability plays an important role in ensuring that our education system is fair, and balance will ensure we create a safe space for conversation, exploration and development in our school practices.

I had an interesting conversation with an employee at the Department for Education (DfE) about autonomy and accountability. From their perspective, schools were expected to run things how they saw fit, and they believed that there is a huge element of freedom in terms of how schools are run, with very little being dictated by the DfE. I understand what they are saying - very rarely do we hear the DfE cited as a reason to complete a task in the same way we do with Ofsted, but we cannot ignore the fact that Ofsted and the DfE are intrinsically linked. The DfE is responsible for the introduction and embedding of policies and systems and Ofsted for checking they are being adhered to, thus informing the DfE's future decisions.

From their perspective, the introduction of academies and multi-academy trusts (MATs) has changed the landscape of autonomy in education. They went on to explain that MATs have more freedom than most but ironically choose to run with tighter restrictions, which, in their opinion, was never the intention. Gove and Gibb expanded the academies programme with the idea that it would give teachers more autonomy (or at least this is what they made us believe). With MATs running much more like corporate models, there is a need for larger-scale organisation, causing concern regarding consistency and "sameness". In a bid to compete with the standards of this corporate model, maintained educational settings have followed suit. As a result, schools can feel more like clinical businesses with less autonomy and personality and a steelier and more impersonal feel to them. As mentioned earlier, the irony is that, as it currently stands, academies and MATs are not required to follow the National Curriculum (although this is set to change with the new, reviewed and revised curriculum). MATs actually have the freedom maintained schools do not have, but have had the opposite response with many locking down on policies, systems and schemes. So, how is scaling up and tightening regulations affecting our autonomy and how is watering down the personalities, skills and strengths of our school staff teams impacting the school community? Without high-stakes accountability where would our schools be? In a more autonomy-friendly space is my guess, but let's take a look.

Ofsted

You are trapped by an inhumane, unaccountable inspection system but you don't have to put up with it any more. If you feel despair, you need help and hope, not to think that suicide is a way out. Get help. Talk to those you love. You are not alone.

(Julia Waters, sister of Headteacher, Ruth Perry.
The NEU Conference. 5 April 2024)

When I was 8 years old, John Major decided to introduce a national scheme to inspect schools. Major's government was concerned that the current local inspections were too varied and inconsistent (perhaps they believed there was too much autonomy!?), and so, in 1992, the Office for Standards in Education was born.

Chris Woodhead, who was one of the most controversial chief inspectors from 1994 to 2000 "...challenged the orthodoxy that smaller classes brought better results, and called for a return to whole-class teaching and the abandonment of 'child-centred learning'". He also insisted that phonics, not "learning by discovery", was the best way to teach reading" (The Telegraph, 2015). With what seemed to be an attack on autonomy, Chris was evidently passionate about the results that came with a traditional teaching model. In 1997, he overturned a passing Ofsted inspection at Islington Green school (removing Ofsted inspector autonomy too) and gave them a failing grade despite the pass grade that the visiting Ofsted inspectors had given the school. This was an early example of the ramifications of the high-stakes accountability Ofsted model, with the London Tonight newsroom stating that it "sent the school into a downward spiral" and "ruined careers of some of the staff". It was later in 2005 that the union representative at Islington Green stated that "it was devastating for the teachers, many of whom subsequently resigned from the school and many of them left the profession and some of them were outstanding teachers" (Muller, 2005). This was to become a common theme in education, reaching its darkest point in the year that Ruth Perry took her own life following a damaging Ofsted grade. With Chris accused of starting a "reign of terror", Ofsted seemed to develop further into a monster, one that would stalk teachers and headteachers indefinitely. Tim Brighouse (the then Chief Education Officer for Birmingham) claimed that a headteacher had been "driven to a breakdown by a school inspection" but following this, Chris Woodhead blamed him for using the "distress to discredit Ofsted".

I do not remember Ofsted ever being mentioned in school as a child, but in my working life I have not had the pleasure of teaching *without* the imminent threat of an inspection, unless, that is, when we have just had one. As you may know, an Ofsted recovery can take some time, no matter what the outcome. When you are not immediately due an inspection you are preparing for one in the future – it feels like much of the day-to-day decision-making is considering Ofsted and what their reaction to it would be.

Pre-Ofsted check-ups are prevalent in schools including environment audits, learning walks, book looks and "mocksteds". The invention or use of a "mocksted" is totally bewildering to me – why would you add in more of what causes staff so much stress? Using fear to "get stuff done" in preparation for a *real* Ofsted inspection is a total waste of time – time that could be spent with our children. One of these audits had once taken place without my knowledge and in my absence. This particular consultant had entered my classroom without so much of a warning and had written a list on her clipboard – a list of things I need to do to get "Ofsted ready". Please note, I am always open to reflection and change – it's a vital and inevitable part of working in the education sector. However, the list was read out to me with no chance to talk to this visitor, to explain our working environment or to give her context. There was no opportunity to collaborate on her ideas, to adapt them, to share as to why I feel these may not be in the best interests of the children in my care. I felt devalued and was now having to implement several new approaches in my classroom, approaches that I deemed inappropriate and damaging. When I told my line manager how disappointed and upset I felt about what had happened, they shared that they too were under pressure to "perform" and could not ignore the recommendations but assured me that I was being heard and understood. At least I felt better for speaking up and communicating my dissatisfaction. It's at times like this that we need to ask: who are we doing this for? This top-down instruction does not make for effective or responsive practice.

Following an inspection, at-best staff feel utterly exhausted, depleted and emotionally drained and have received an outstanding badge. At worst, they are "causing concern" and experiencing mental health breakdowns and, in extreme circumstances, suicide. The tragic death of Ruth Perry following an inspection that left her school with an "Inadequate" label is one example of the severity of a high-pressure inspection. It was reported by The Telegraph that "at least 10 other headteachers have been left suicidal in the wake of Ofsted inspections" (Clare-Martin, 2023) and in Professor Sarah Waters' "Written Evidence" drawing upon extensive research into work-related suicide among primary school teachers, she refers to "eight precedent suicide cases where an Ofsted inspection was cited as a factor" (Waters, 2023).

Following a safeguarding concern at Ruth Perry's school, it was graded "Inadequate", having previously received "Good" in a pilot of the new inspection routine in which Amanda Spielman (the Chief Inspector at the time) was present. The pilot inspection led to a highly positive report even stating that Caversham Primary's "staff are vigilant and safeguarding leads are tenacious" (Perry, 2019). It was verified at Ruth Perry's inquest that inspectors agreed the safeguarding concern (which was related to recordkeeping) could be rectified before they published the report. The Lead Inspector even referred to the school's "robust safeguarding culture" when speaking to the Chair of Governors (Connor, 2023).

Ruth was distressed throughout the second inspection, saying that the initial phone conversation was a "car crash" with colleagues noting that she was "flushed, shaky, and unable to speak coherently" (Connor, 2023). She wrote notes about her experiences, writing "I.N.A.D.E.Q.U.A.T.E keeps flashing behind my eyes" and "I do not believe any child has been harmed because I have been negligent in my duties", with Ruth's husband sharing that "she felt powerless" (BBC News, 2023). Feeling powerless in any job, as a professional, is demeaning, inhumane and ineffective. Ofsted failed to respond in a compassionate and individualised way by further writing an insensitive comment about Ruth's death at the bottom of Caversham Primary School's Ofsted report. This comment has since been removed.

The outrage from Ruth Perry's school and family allowed the outside world to see into the worst of teaching, with one parent saying, "these are strong, resilient people who take on the burden of one of society's toughest and most valuable services". "As Caversham parents, Ruth Perry's death has opened our eyes to the realities of Ofsted inspections". It's disconcerting for parents to imagine that these smiling teachers who welcome their children into school could be under so much pressure. It's impossible to see when you are not inside the setting daily, but this tragic incident made it visible. One parent asked, "how can a school be accurately judged based on the events of just one day in its complex life?" (Cutmore, 2023). A question that we are all used to asking regularly in schools, but now it was out in the open for all to see. The whole tragic incident humanised the workforce and unmasked the truth about Ofsted pressures.

Whilst writing this book, Ofsted have confirmed that they will go ahead with their new "reformed" report card system despite negative feedback from the profession – a colour-coded version that exhibits a lack of respect for the maturity and complexity of the individuals it is meant to assess. Simply replacing "outstanding" with "exemplary" and "inadequate" with "cause for concern" is not good enough. With the word exemplary defined as "serving as a desirable model", I give Ofsted a "cause for concern" grade which is colour-coded

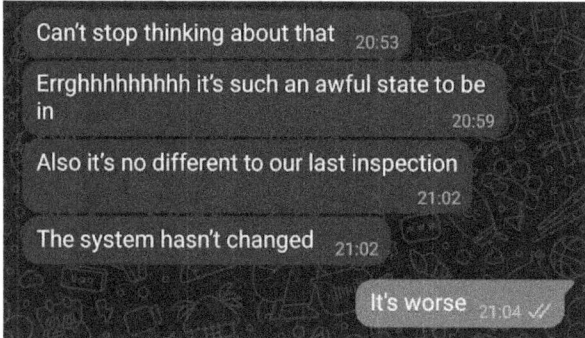

Figure 3.1 WhatsApp message sent during an Ofsted inspection between two teachers discussing the new inspection model. November 2024. Screenshot taken by Anon teacher

red for dramatic and alarming purposes. Headrest, an organisation dedicated to supporting headteachers, responded to the change saying that "This means that the efforts in schools will once again be focused entirely disproportionately on 'preparing for OFSTED' – a practice which we know deflects efforts away from deep and sustained school improvement" (McMullen and Grimshaw, 2025).

The National Foundation for Educational Research (NFER) states that "Teachers in schools with Requires Improvement or Inadequate Ofsted ratings have lower autonomy compared to schools rated Good…" (NFER. Teacher autonomy: how does it relate to job satisfaction and retention?) (Worth and Van den Brande, 2020. P. 13). It is inevitable that fear will shut down the possibility for creative thinking, taking risks and will restrict innovation and prevent teachers from sharing parts of themselves that can enhance school life. The sickly need for consistency, progression and product is hampering our ability to be human, responsive and compassionate. It becomes an impossible environment to provide exciting and tailored learning journeys for the children in schools.

Educator experience – Ofsted

Frances. Former Primary Headteacher.

Prior to 1989, when the National Curriculum (NC) was introduced, schools had a great deal of autonomy over curriculum content and delivery. Teachers could be creative in the classroom, making teaching and learning fun, memorable and relevant.

Administrative tasks were minimal and work-life balance was achievable.

When the NC was introduced very little quality training was provided for experienced teachers, and teacher training focussed heavily on Literacy and Numeracy at Primary level. Tomes of planning pro forma were produced and the baby was thrown out with the bathwater.

In one fell swoop teachers felt deskilled, mistrusted and overwhelmed. Creativity was sacrificed as the curriculum became prescriptive and content driven. At this point, autonomy virtually disappeared as school leaders struggled to manage and deliver the new system in their schools. This situation worsened further when assessment for learning was introduced to support the NC. To say that this had a catastrophic effect on teacher confidence is an understatement. It was chaotic and teachers had to spend hours every week completing tick lists for every statement for every subject. The curriculum was so bulky that there was no time for deep learning in any area, as the focus was on coverage. It was at this point that I decided that the only way I could stay true to my vocation, values and philosophy of what good education should look like was to pursue promotion to Headship.

Fast-forward to 1992 and the birth of OFSTED, we were told that inspections would be supportive, focussing on what schools did well and highlighting areas for development. I experienced seven inspections in total, and not one of them stuck to the brief. They were destructive – even if successful. All focussed on finding fault. Teachers were left demoralised, exhausted and, in some cases, looking for a new career. Schools became puppets to the system and did whatever needed to be done to survive.

Education is now results and data driven. If you want a good OFSTED outcome, your results must be unrealistically above average. Teaching used to be a vocational occupation. A teacher could take initiative and teach to the needs of pupils, whilst at the same time making learning fun, memorable and exciting! Teachers were trusted and respected. Now they are constantly challenged by parents and local authorities.

Many teachers are demotivated and have lost their passion for the job. Workload, pressure to get pupils to meet unrealistic targets and constantly changing curriculum models are forcing many of them to seek new careers that have job satisfaction and a work-life balance.

If school leaders had the confidence and courage to band together and say "enough is enough! We want a greater say in education policy at every level" then we might have a chance to reintroduce a little autonomy. More autonomy to breed more trust in our teachers; reduce the bureaucratic workload and bring some joy back into what was once and can still be one of the best, and most rewarding professions.

It's time to pause.

Reflection

- How do I feel about Ofsted inspections?
- How much extra work does an imminent Ofsted inspection cause me?
- Do I have to change the way I would normally teach for Ofsted?
- Is Ofsted good for my wellbeing?
- Do I feel Ofsted are motivating me?
- How do I feel following an Ofsted inspection?

- How might I approach an Ofsted inspection with my own wellbeing in the foreground?
- Can I speak up about any excess work that Ofsted is unnecessarily causing me?

Get autonomy back

In the classroom:

- Be honest with your senior leadership team (SLT) about what is achievable in the time that you have.
- Do not be afraid to question the necessity of a task if you feel it is solely for inspection purposes.
- Avoid Ofsted being your biggest motivation – when they leave you will feel at a loss.
- Try not to do anything special for those visiting your classroom – it is important people see the results of what is humanly possible, otherwise we become part of the problem.

For senior leaders:

- Do not work for Ofsted. Make a stand and change will come.
- Begin to get into the habit of **not mentioning Ofsted**. If we talk about them, then we embed the idea that they are our motivating force.
- Avoid making your Ofsted outcome important, whether you are exemplary *or* causing concern. You can celebrate what you achieve without Ofsted validation.
- Avoid requesting tasks to be completed by your teachers that are solely for Ofsted – teachers have enough to do.
- Believe in your teachers and their ability to successfully plan for and teach their classes.
- Have faith in your school community.
- Develop opportunities for teachers to share their good practice.
- Provide quality professional learning opportunities to ensure the development of staff skills and knowledge and therefore school improvement.

For government officials:

- Let's talk about saying goodbye to Ofsted and hello to a new formative and collaborative accountability model.
- Keep an eye on the new DfE, "RISE improvement advisors" ensuring they are not providing additional "Ofsted" experiences but more supportive mentoring. For more on RISE advisors, see here: https://schoolsweek.co.uk/rise-improvement-advisers-best-of-the-best-or-clipboard-carrying-bureaucrats/
- Build this new supportive model by working with those on the ground to find ways to support school development collaboratively.
- Utilise local authority (LA) formative accountability and support. LAs are best placed as they are aware of the contexts and challenges that individual schools are experiencing.
- Provide time and space to share good practice within local authorities.
- Slim down the curriculum so that teachers do not feel they need to meet unrealistic demands, adding to the pressure during visits.

Final thought on Ofsted

How can we begin to move around freely when we are too scared of the consequences? With falling birth rates, the stakes have never been higher – it has been estimated that an expected "12% drop in the number of pupil rolls, as it is known, from 2023/24 to 2028/29 – a reduction of 26,836 places needed by 2028/29" (Ford and Warren, 2025). Making mistakes could be catastrophic to the future of a school staff team and its community. Trying out new ideas is an important part of allowing the children and teachers to explore learning openly and with curiosity but impossible with such high stakes. Ofsted will always be Ofsted as long as they exist – it is only with a new formative accountability system that teachers can believe that they are trusted to bring themselves to work.

Observations

> Progress…? When I started teaching, no Ofsted; no retention & recruitment crisis - 65 applicants for my job. No observations, book scrutinies, planning checks…
>
> (Steve Waters. 16:49 pm 18 Jul 2023. X)

In my experience, observations tend to happen too often, are rarely processes that are designed *with* staff, and feedback can be scarce if at all provided. Observations leave us open to criticism, for example, for those who have to strictly follow schemes choosing to go off script in an observation (down to professional judgment) means SLT will see this in all its glory. It can put creativity barriers in place and keep them there. They are sold as a check-in, but in reality, are a check-up. Observations provide little insight into what life is *really* like for a classroom teacher. When working in certain parts of the school (ahem, Early Years Foundation Stage) you are rarely observed by someone who knows their stuff, so it can seem trite when you are given feedback (if at all). Teacher Tapp's data show that the team members who think that observations are most effective are mainly SLT stating that "Senior leaders and headteachers are more likely to feel that feedback they have from observations are helping them improve when compared to classroom teachers (50% vs 42%), and middle leaders are the least likely to find the process helpful (34%)" (Teacher Tapp, 2025). This says a lot about the whole process – shouldn't teachers be getting more out of observation processes than anyone else? Who are observations *really* for?

When I heard that Ben Levinson OBE had done away with observations in his primary school in Newham, I wanted to learn more – we need observations, don't we? How can this work? Does it work? What are the benefits, and do they outweigh the negatives? Are there any negatives? What does it mean for SLT who are supposed to be "keeping an eye" on things?

A school without observations

I arrive at Kensington Primary School in the borough of Newham at 10 am. I can hear the children in the playground as I arrive. The school is hidden amongst many houses, a residential haven in the deep east end of London. As I walk to the office, I pass many signs including a nod to their Times Educational Supplement (TES) Wellbeing and Mental Health School of the

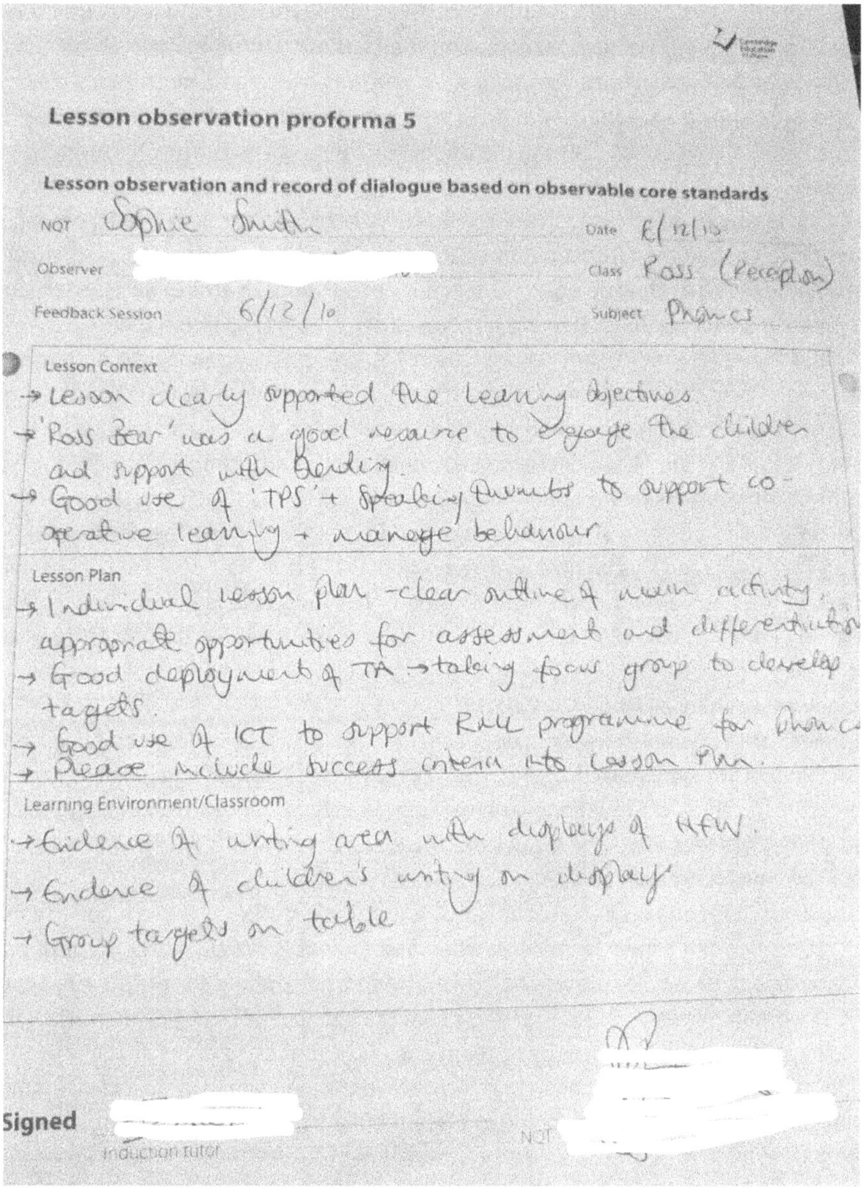

Figure 3.2 One of my early observation reports. December 2010. Photograph taken by Sophie Smith-Tong

Year Award. As I enter the reception area, there are too many awards to list, and they range from ParentGym and the Pearson Teaching Awards to awards for Geography and exceptional outcomes. I am met by a warm person behind the desk, and as I wait for Ben to come and meet me, I overhear her support a parent, "I don't wish to cause you stress", she says as she takes the parent through attendance challenges. There is nothing but love and support in her tone as she navigates a hot and debated topic in education right now.

As Ben approaches, I see he is wearing one of his famous suits (I have previously seen him in a sparkly, gold one!). He says that wearing the suits is "getting harder" as he is now an Executive Head and doesn't see the children as much as he used to, much to his disappointment. He is beginning to wonder who he is wearing the suit for. I beg him not to get rid of the suits - I feel that it sends a strong message - we do things differently here, and we don't take ourselves too seriously. Ben invites me into his office for a cuppa, as he makes the tea he talks me briefly through his journey in education. His experiences as a teacher instigated his passion to change the landscape for educators - and he has undoubtedly achieved that. At Kensington Primary, they do not have teacher observations, learning walks, book looks or weekly planning expectations. They do not have a set of rules regarding their class environments, and they certainly do not have assessment weeks. They rely solely on assessment for learning - formative and entrusted to the team. They have a flexible timetable giving the teacher full discretion over when they teach each subject and it can change daily, if the teacher wants it to. They have decreased the amount of maths and literacy in their school week - 4 hours of maths and 5 hours of literacy, and the rest is filled up with physical activity, foundation and creative subjects. Kensington Primary is part of The Tapscott Learning Trust, so I ask Ben - can this be achieved in a school that is not part of a trust? "Absolutely", he cries! As long as you are covering the content, the timetable is yours to play with, and he certainly knows how to play. It is important to mention, however, that this is no game to Ben; he takes his job seriously. It is clear that his success is down to his relentless reflection, constantly asking himself - does this work?

I ask him - with this much freedom do teachers "slack off"? He smiles, "the honest answer is, I don't know". We explore this further - he talks of the reduction in meaningless admin jobs and pressures such as observations and marking - staff are handed back time so that they can do "the things that matter". He goes on to ask, "do they use this time to do those things? I don't know and I have no idea how I might measure that".

So how does Ben and his senior team ensure that their staff are having a positive impact on the children in the school, especially when assessment is usually in the form of end-of-term assessment data? He admits that it isn't the easier option; for SLT, it can be much harder to work in this way as they have to prove their model works much more than if they were using "traditional" methods. Ben's team is in and out of classrooms all the time - either in the form of support or dropping in to really see what is happening in their classrooms - he describes how this consistent dropping in gives them a better picture of what is happening in their setting instead of unreliable, half-termly 40-minute observations. He believes one-off observations cause unnecessary pressure and provide minimal and inaccurate information about the activity in their classrooms. A lot of work for not much benefit.

As we move around the school, it is calm. Each classroom has its own identity and feel, with the teacher (and their cohort) very much in control of their learning experiences. As we walk around, SLT are very visible with one being situated on the floor, working with the children. I ask Ben if this will have been a scheduled drop-in - he told me that they have timetabled SLT support and also unannounced drop-ins. It seems that a regular drip-drip approach desensitises what might seem to other teachers as a high-stress process. The hierarchy has been dismantled here, and the results are positive - the trust and happiness levels are high.

Figure 3.3 Ben Levinson OBE and Sophie Smith-Tong at Kensington Primary School, Newham. 2024. Photograph by Sophie Smith-Tong

Performance reviews

I love my meetings with my line manager – they are regular, supportive, and a safe space for me to be honest with how I am finding the workload, the cohort and team. Together we find solutions and also design my professional development and support strategies moving forward. I have autonomy over my direction but with the support required to do so. As it currently stands, performance reviews are a legal requirement in the workplace. Maintained schools and LAs must adhere to appraisal arrangements in the Education Regulations 2012 (the Appraisal Regulations). The government guidance for the appraisal cycle promisingly states the following (I have highlighted keywords that I think make this an optimistic read):

> The appraisals process should be intrinsically supportive and developmental, conducted within a school culture that **values openness and fairness**. Appraisal should be a **non-bureaucratic process** that recognises, encourages and **validates a teacher's commitment to professional development**, pedagogical excellence and effective performance. It should offer a **supportive and safe environment** where individual teachers and their line managers can have **open and honest conversations** about successes and areas for improvement. It should also **address the support that will be provided** to enable

all teachers to achieve their objectives and continue to meet the teacher's standards. **Reducing unnecessary workload** should be at the forefront of any considerations around implementing appraisal processes.

(Teacher Appraisal - Guidance for Schools. 2024. P. 3)

Despite this encouraging guidance, the appraisal cycle can sometimes be used as a tool to pressurise teachers into accepting large workloads and adopting a bureaucratic process in spite of the advice saying to avoid it. For those lucky enough to work in a school that upholds the guidance above, please know that this is not the case in all schools - in one school I worked at (when performance-related pay (PRP) was first introduced in 2014) I had to create and present a physical folder at the end of the year - I was required to add printed feedback emails, parent feedback, a detailed form on what I had achieved throughout the academic year and proof that I had fulfilled the actions I had promised. Producing a performance review file is not an easy task, especially alongside an already unreasonable workload. There is a reason that the National Education Union (NEU) has created an "appraisal and accountability bargaining toolkit". The NEU states that "in too many cases, appraisal has been reduced to a tool used to suppress pay, drive up workload, and push many good educators out of the profession" (Appraisal and Accountability Bargaining Toolkit, NEU). A response, perhaps, to an influx of teachers needing support with the previous appraisal processes in their schools.

In 2014, the PRP system was appointed with some schools using it to keep budgets down and add to workloads as opposed to the automatic rise of teacher pay year on year. The current Labour government has now removed the requirement for PRP, but unfortunately, it is still sadly an option that many schools are using. The unions are pressing schools to get rid of it with Teacher Tapp data showing that "10 per cent of the 9,321 teachers surveyed said they still had PRP" (Cumiskey, 2024. Schools Week). PRP is not good for autonomy, and here is why:

- Teachers may feel afraid to open up about challenges they are facing due to fear of not receiving their pay increase.
- It encourages an individual journey rather than working as a staff team to develop a setting.
- It certainly doesn't help our retention crisis - the automatic rise in pay is one of the few perks in teaching and recognises the work that teachers do.
- It can allow systemic inequalities to persist in schools - pay progressions can be denied or awarded with unconscious biases in mind.
- In terms of creative thinking and bringing your passions to your staff teams, it can reduce risk taking for fear of mistakes informing pay pauses.
- Finally, the NEU states that "There is no evidence that PRP improves educational outcomes" (NEU, 2022).

With the PRP changes announced close to the start of a new academic year, we can hope that this time next-year PRP will be a thing of the past and begin to work collaboratively for school improvement in a way that encourages risk taking, innovation and creativity.

Sickness and absence

The *Burgundy Book*: the book that no teacher (that I have met) knows about, let alone has read. If you have no idea what the *Burgundy Book* is, then I shall explain – it's a book that runs alongside teacher contracts that explains the rights and responses to a variety of situations you might find yourself in when employed by schools including sickness, maternity pay and retirement. Nowadays, you will find that the book is no longer a physical book but an electronic document that is shared. I would not be surprised if some schools still have a book – we love a physical copy of most things in schools!

Taking sick days in education is a battle with several outcomes to consider. Going to school when sick means

- spreading the germs.
- prolonging the agony, recovery is harder when working.
- you cannot do your job at full capacity – behaviour can worsen and you are inefficient.
- poor overall wellbeing.

On the other hand, not going in means

- dysregulated children.
- pressure on the rest of the team.
- to do lists getting longer.
- lessons not getting taught.
- class environments not being taken care of due to supply teachers not knowing organisational structures.
- missed meetings and rescheduling taking up future time.
- having to call your line manager.

It is never easy to call in sick even if you have the most supportive line managers. Many teachers still have to make a phone call and also complete a back-to-work form following an absence adding to the weight that teachers naturally carry when they are off sick – they also know the huge impact on all who are left picking up the pieces.

If staff begin to feel that they are being judged for calling in sick, then they are unable to choose to prioritise their own wellbeing – they lack a sense of control. This has an impact on how they perform at work and can rock their sense of belonging in their setting. It is pivotal for autonomy to thrive (as we have discussed in **Chapter 1**) that staff feel safe, secure and acknowledged no matter what life throws at them. If we say we trust that staff will make the right decision, then we must genuinely do that. Saying that you are a trusting leader and then adopting a judgemental tone over the phone when a teacher calls in sick for a third time in a term is not an authentic conveying of trust. I would advise choosing love – trusting who you have hired and supporting those who are finding attendance challenging by giving them space to share and reflect on their current school and home life. I would also suggest broadening perspectives and allowing a text message as an acceptable communication method for staff who are unwell – expecting a call when someone is feeling poorly is impractical and unreasonable and is not how modern workplaces operate.

68 *Teacher Autonomy*

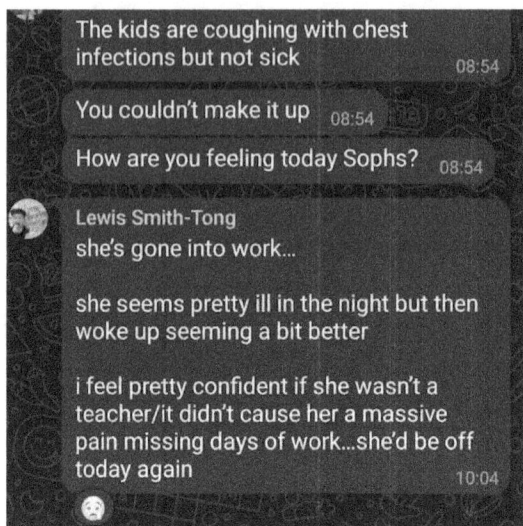

Figure 3.4 WhatsApp Message. February 2025. Screenshot taken by Sophie Smith-Tong of her WhatsApp messages

Teacher Tapp found that in primary schools, "80% call a line manager. Whereas in secondaries most are calling an absence line (91%) and a hefty number are ringing their line manager too (61%)" (Teacher Tapp, 2025). We must remember, separate from the actual process of calling in sick, there is so much more for teachers to fret over including providing plans and work from afar which can feel more difficult than just showing up. Avoiding adding to this load is preferable, treating teachers as the professionals that they are.

Educator experience – Observations

Ben Levinson OBE. School Leader, Writer, National Advisor, Director for School and Trust Development and Executive Headteacher. Kensington Primary School. Newham. London.

When I first arrived at Kensington, the observation record form was seven pages long. A list of arbitrary lesson elements, each one to be graded: Outstanding, Good, Requires Improvement, Inadequate, before the final, overall grade. It was worse than useless; it was deeply damaging.

Developing teacher autonomy has been a mission since my first day. We know the power of autonomy for our wellbeing, but also to maximise our performance. Too often, teachers are constrained by overly didactic policies and approaches, all tightly controlled by monitoring schedules timetabled to the last second.

I quickly jettisoned the observation form. Then observations themselves – performative nonsense that did nothing to help me or anyone understand what teaching and learning was like for the children. Some teachers loved to perform, others hated it.

Either way, it was a diagnostic of how they responded in these situations, when what was important was what was happening day-in, day-out and how we could work collaboratively to develop this.

We looked at different models to try and identify the best way to achieve this. We wanted it to be low threat – we did not want people feeling like someone was constantly looking over their shoulder. We wanted it to be reflective of the challenges of teaching – we all have good lessons and bad lessons; we all make mistakes; the technology will often fail us. We wanted it to support development – teaching is hard, and stepping back when you are mid-flow with 30 children is impossible; we needed a way to support our teachers to reflect and grow. Most of all, we wanted it rooted in trust, enabling teachers to feel free to take risks, teach in the way that suited them and their children and be the professionals they are.

Our model remains imperfect, but it is transformatively better than one-off observations. We prioritise being in classrooms, alongside teachers, as often as possible. We provide another pair of eyes. This allows for professional discussions about learning and how different children are progressing. These discussions support adaptation of learning, considerations around lesson design and approaches to teaching. Everyone works together in year group teams to discuss challenges and ways forward. We invest heavily in professional development to improve mastery of pedagogy and subject knowledge.

These changes have created a culture of collaboration where everyone is open to asking for advice and help. No one is living in fear of the next book look or planning scrutiny, wondering whether they are going to be pulled up because they forgot to fill in a box or they'd missed a child who hadn't responded to feedback. They are certainly not investing precious time and energy in preparing for, worrying about and delivering a one-off lesson. Then more time and energy worrying about the feedback and either feeling the pressure of continuing to be "outstanding" or the kick in the gut of working every hour to be told you "require improvement." Even when feedback is more constructive and developmental, it still only reflects that moment. That one lesson that went well, or didn't. How much better to build a culture where discussions about learning are happening regularly? A culture built on trust, mutual respect and responsibility. Where professionalism is cherished and autonomy seen as a force for excellence.

It's time to pause.

Reflection

- Are my performance reviews supportive?
- How do I feel about observations in my setting?
- Who observes me?
- How often am I observed?
- How long are my observations?
- How do I feel in the lead up to an observation?

- What are my experiences post observation?
- Do I find the observation process helpful and supportive?

Get autonomy back

In the classroom:

- Remember that teachers have legal protections; if you feel your performance reviews are biased or discriminatory, then you are able to challenge them.
- Speak honestly and openly in your reviews and where it is necessary, ask to have your review with another person – this is for teachers who feel that being vulnerable is too risky.
- If your appraisal process is lacking in support, then use the "model appraisal and accountability letter" on the NEU website (see references) to suggest changes to your headteacher (NEU, 2025).
- Avoid doing anything special for observational purposes – allow your SLT to *really* see what is happening in your classroom – they will only see challenges if we allow them to see the average hour in your class.
- If you do not receive feedback, then ask for it – I wouldn't expect to wait longer than 24 hours for general observation feedback.
- If the feedback isn't helpful, then ask SLT the following questions:
  1. What are my strengths?
  2. How can I work with the challenges I have?
  3. What are your plans to support me with my next steps?
- Finally, if the observation process isn't providing a safe space to grow, then approach your SLT or mental health and wellbeing lead – perhaps a reflection on the process can be the start of bigger change in your setting.

For senior leaders:

- Reflect (with your staff) on your appraisal process – does it offer a safe and collaborative space for growth?
- Remove performance-related pay (PRP).
- Reflect upon your current observation process and the use of the word "observation" – I personally prefer accompanying rather than observing – it suggests you are *with them* rather than watching them. Find a word that works for you.
- If your observation process is being done *to* staff, then change it – gather your team and talk about how a new approach might support and develop the whole staff team.
- Think about really being there for your teachers – dropping in and being present regularly so that they feel supported rather than watched.
- If you are continuing with the standard observation model ensure you give feedback within 24 hours to avoid staff anxiety developing.
- Ensure you take into account the context of each class and the moments that you were in their class.

For government officials:

- Make performance-related pay a thing of the past by removing it as an option for schools.
- Protect our teachers – make it so that academies and MATs have to follow the same Pay and Conditions document.
- Give schools more training on collaborative and formative observation models.
- Speak and work with those on the ground to find ways to support schools in their skills development.
- Utilise support from local authorities who are more aware of the contexts and challenges individual schools are experiencing.
- Provide time and space to share good practice within local authorities.
- Slim down the curriculum so that teachers do not feel they need to meet unrealistic demands adding to the pressure during observations.

Final thought on observations

I am not a fan of observations, and I think Ben Levinson OBE has proven that they are not a necessity. Checking up on teachers is adding to the pressure cooker that teachers find themselves in. It is time to come together, share and utilise our individual success and challenges – SLT cannot provide all of the answers. It's important to draw upon the passions and expertise of the *entire* workforce, not just a few at the top – let's invite individual educators' experiences, personalities and perspectives.

Data

> *We have forgotten that "data" means "information" not test scores. We have forgotten that "assessment" means "to sit beside" not entering data into a spreadsheet. We have forgotten that the most precious parts of our system are living, breathing humans who want to flourish but can't.*
>
> (Tina Farr. Schools as Organic Systems. 2025)

Having recently filled out the government curriculum review survey, one of the recurring themes about the packed and outdated curriculum was the fact that its subject focus is imbalanced. This is undoubtedly down to the selective data collection that takes place at certain points in a child's education journey. This data is often required only for maths and literacy (because we all know – that's all that matters). The assessments take place in reception (the start of schooling), year 1 (phonics screening), year 2 (Standard Assessment Tests (SATs) – now opted in by schools), year 4 (multiplication tests) and year 6 (SATs). In primary school, children are not tested in years 3 and 5, thank you very much for that!

This data is supposed to give us an overview of progress, but having administered these tests, they are at best an unreliable tool to check on *children's* learning, and in reality, they are yet *another* way to check on teacher's commitment to the cause. Testing is damaging our children's learning experiences and masking potential (more on this in **Chapter 4**). If a teacher's cohort data comes in poor, this can be pretty damning. Ofsted will check data (albeit in any format that the school uses) during their inspections which can send schools into a panic as to the state of their data. With added pressures of falling birth rates and an exodus to the outskirts of cities, we are seeing a number of schools being closed down - good data, in this case, becomes extremely pivotal in the maintenance of the school community and staff jobs.

Testing

In primary education, children are tested in their first year of schooling. Children who are 4 and 5 years old take a baseline assessment in their sixth week of reception where a set of questions is scripted and lacklustre resources are provided. I have administered these baselines hundreds of times, and I can tell you there are a number of responses that you get from children taking part in these assessments; some children get bored and give up listening, looking around the environment for something more stimulating. Some will start out enthusiastic and then their attention will wane, and then you have the children who look completely bewildered by some of the questions which can be very unclear - these children try to second guess what the teacher is expecting of them as they acknowledge the pressure to "get it right". One of the literacy questions asks the child to order three images in a story you have previously told them. Any creative 4 or 5 years old or adult knows - stories can go in any order, there should be no rules. To think there's a wrong answer in storytelling at this age is utterly ludicrous. Based on these few stock responses the data becomes completely unreliable.

If teachers were not so focused on "getting good data" and were given the time and space to instead get to know each child, they would be more able to create and enjoy more personalised learning experiences for their classes. The focus on outcome is down to fear of not getting "*good* outcomes" and so there is a need to control. When we overcontrol, we lose out on individual teachers' personalities, the child's identity, creativity and fun learning experiences.

Summative and formative assessment

As an Early Years specialist (and fan) I have quite a passion for assessment and I do not mean the clipboard and iPad kind. We Early Years people love getting to know our children and we do know them - inside out. This is because our curriculum recognises that personal, social and emotional development (PSED) is a prime area of learning, in other words, it's a core subject for us in the younger years and so it should be. Despite the current trickling down of formal learning and narrowing of the curriculum from key stage 1 to the Early Years, the practitioners know that personal and social learning is pivotal to learning the rest. We find ways to respond to children whatever it is they bring to us - we meet them where they are and recognise that every interaction with all children is a learning experience. We build strong relationships with families - the early years are notorious for parent/carer stay and plays, home visits, settling-in periods which means we really know our families. In my opinion, many schools should get their EYFS teams to develop their parent/home communication systems and success will be had all year round! One of the many reasons I choose to stay in the early years (I have tried all other primary years) is the fact that I have more say over the direction I take, more freedom to really *see* the children, respond to their interests and know that the curriculum backs me up. For all play fans out there - protect your early years, avoid allowing leaders, LAs and government to get their hands on our child-led, PSED-focused approach because once they do, it's hard to go back. They are on our case, adding pressure to focus more on maths and literacy, requesting that children sit still for longer periods, expecting dreaded worksheets and less time outdoors.

Be aware that notions like being "school ready" are attempting to take over the meaningful and organic interactions we create – stay strong.

Summative assessment provides unreliable data and informs us of how well the child has passed a test. As I explored earlier, the reception baseline is highly dependent on language, focus and personality – it tells me very little about what the child can actually do. Teachers must trust themselves – they know what their children can do through formative assessment – spending time with children, enjoying playing with them as opposed to marking tests. Give them experiences where they can show you what they know, rather than giving them papers to write down what they can do. Boredom and anxiety (both of which can be prevalent during test time) can have a profound effect on how we perform. In my experience, I gave up before I even started my tests at school – I was not academically "successful" and so checked out before I had even signed in. I put my head down on the table and felt bad about myself. What does this tell the person marking this test? Not that I am unable, but that the education system has failed me.

An effective way to note where children are and create further learning experiences for them would be by allowing teachers to choose how they collect information/data in a way they see fit. This could range from notebooks and a Google Doc to post-its and a folder for those who preferred. Whatever it is – it shouldn't matter – do your teachers know their children? I would trust that they do if you allow them the time to properly interact with them.

Planning

For more detail on planning formats, you can read **Chapter 2**, but it certainly does deserve a mention here when discussing accountability. The pressure to tick planning boxes is real, and micromanagement in this area can lead to over-detailed, over-checked and overwhelmed planning. The planning is, of course, tightly linked to assessment as assessment should inform your planning; however, if you are expected to cover certain topics, fit in test preparation and "cultural capital" (trips and visitors, etc.), you will find you are lacking in time and space to organically respond to individual learning and life experiences. For example, if a child in your class unexpectedly suffers a bereavement, you should be able to dedicate some time to explore this with them – the time you dedicate to this will ensure the child is held and able to engage in further learning. Without this time we cannot respond with humanity, in our natural way. The child is then left to experience this challenge alone. There is so much learning to be done in the whole of school life, not in discrete lessons but in our interactions. Organic interactions can't take place with such high-stakes accountability at play.

Educator experience – Data

Anon. Primary School Teacher.

Although I understood the school's emphasis on core subject teaching to equip and support the children (many with an EAL background), this negatively impacted their overall school experience, often making it an uninspiring time for them. The push for measurable outcomes and uniform teaching methods did not allow for a creative and innovative approach.

> Before teaching, I worked as an actor and regularly used these skills within my teaching, but I found there was very little encouragement or opportunity to promote Drama at the school I was at. As an example, there seemed to be no history of having class assemblies. I believe these kinds of presentations are fantastic for unifying children, combining areas of learning in a memorable and meaningful way and valuing life skills such as cooperation, self-confidence and empathy.
>
> I am fairly certain that the "shadow of OFSTED" is partly responsible for an overall lack of creativity, but having taught for nearly 20 years, I also believe we now have a culture in which many teachers, educators and (increasingly) children view education as a results-driven activity. Many colleagues seem immersed in the need to improve core subject statistics often at the expense of other important areas of school life. I have experienced pressure to meet percentage targets, which have been used as the sole indicator of my teaching standards, rather than being judged on other aspects of my practice, which I feel are no less important.
>
> It seems clear to me, especially after recent lockdown times, that we must place more emphasis on activities that encourage the wellbeing of both children and those who work with them. These will not necessarily be easily measured and objectively assessed, but they are necessary for the happiness and wellbeing of us all.

It's time to pause.

Reflection

- How well do I know the individuals in my class?
- Do I have time to respond to children's learning experiences?
- Do I feel pressured to cover topics, leaving children behind when they are not ready to move on?
- Do I feel trusted to make decisions to stay on a topic for longer or leave it sooner?
- Do I find my assessment and planning tools helpful?

Get autonomy back

In the classroom:

- Let's get rid of testing. Speak out on social media and join forces with organisations like Square Peg and More Than a Score.
- Question data you are being asked to provide - are you cutting and pasting or doubling up on work, and how does this data actually help you?
- Try to remember why you got into teaching - if you are teaching to the test then think again.
- Listen to and interact with your children - get to know them and show your human side.
- Bring your expertise, passions and hobbies into class with you - show the children who you are - it gives permission for them to do the same.

For senior leaders:

- Spend time discovering ways to ignite excitement and curiosity through fun and experiential learning experiences rather than getting good data.
- Let's get rid of testing. Speak out on social media and join forces with organisations like Square Peg and More Than a Score.
- If you are requesting data from your teachers, question whether this data is necessary and how it is going to help.
- Listen to teachers when they question the data requested. Reflect together on its pertinence.

For government officials:

- Reduce the amount of testing on children – I would suggest starting with the reception baseline and phonics screening and then reflect on the big time eaters like SATs. How sad that in the final year of primary school, children are subjected to teaching that is as dull as the test they complete at the end of the year.
- Slim down the curriculum (there it is again). This will ease pressures to tick off content and allow for responsive and relevant teaching.

Final thought on data

An obsession with product in terms of data and analysis is putting unnecessary pressure on education staff and starving our children of exciting and relevant learning experiences. The quality of the process has been forgotten, and we are teaching children a wealth of facts and figures and how to pass tests. Data forces teachers to impart knowledge and then requests that the children prove that they have remembered it via testing and mundane writing tasks. With trust we can take risks and have some fun!

Stakeholders

> We cannot make assumptions that because school is plentiful it is benign. The system has become more and more rigid. It forces parents to question themselves and their children, as they resist change they continue to deflect on us.
>
> (Eliza Fricker. 8:12 am Jan 15 2025. X)

Parents

I will not get caught up in parent bashing in this next section of the book. Parent blaming seems to be a trend right now – with comments about parents working from home causing the attendance crisis (thank you for that anecdotal contribution, Sir Michael Wilshaw) to the "Moments Matter, Attendance Counts" government campaign – parents are getting the wrap for something that, is the fault of bad policy and dated systems. A vital part of running a school is working effectively and compassionately with families, genuinely acknowledging and listening to them and creating a cohesive school community that trusts its educators and parents alike. Part of this is the ability for all involved to show vulnerability and have an open and honest conversation. Learning together is key. One of the biggest arguments to keep Ofsted reports is for parent clarity - parents need a transparent place to learn about the school possibilities for their children. I understand. As a parent myself when it came to choosing a primary school I felt extremely lucky that I had a sound knowledge of what I was and wasn't looking for. Searching for a school is an individual process; all parents will have a different focus (e.g. some parents focus on academic outcomes, while for others personal and social development is a priority). Recognising that not all parents want the same thing is the obstacle that schools need to manage - doing anything to please *all* parents is time wasted. This is why any staff team must find (a) their own individual ethos, (b) a team objective and approach. It is important that the team believes in this spirit so that it can develop into a strong school culture. When the parents choose a school, they choose the school culture that comes with it. That is not to say that it can't adapt and change over time, nor should it mean that parents stay quiet and put up with *all* a school has to offer. Parents should be part of the journey recognising that the adults working in their child's school are professionals and have been trained in child development with teachers recognising that parents are the experts on their child.

Ofsted reports have helped many parents make decisions on schools - most of my parent friends looked at the Ofsted report of the schools they contemplated for their children. This does not mean, however, that Ofsted is working well. Parents do not currently have any other way of exploring (not judging) a school, other than to visit (I always think this is the best bet - you just get a feel for a place). Parents are entitled to transparency when they are looking for and choosing a school for their child but not to the detriment of teacher wellbeing and autonomy and that is currently the trade-off. I would much prefer my children's teachers did not have to feel the stress of an upcoming Ofsted inspection than for me to be able to read that handwriting is their next school step. My child's teacher's wellbeing is paramount to their own and as a parent that is immeasurable.

Teacher autonomy cannot thrive in an environment where parents are hostile and dismissive of the professionals in school in the same way that parents cannot support us if we shut down their input. Mutual respect is required for a successful relationship between school and family. I spotted a question on Headteacher Chat that asked Can a Parent Request the Attendance Record of Their Child's Teachers? (Coy, Headteacher Chat). The answer is no they cannot, but it did get me thinking about entitlement within state education. The very fact that it is appropriately available to all can sometimes give the impression that teachers are public property. This can cause problematic relationships between parents and schools that the media tends to exacerbate by pitting us against one another. If we were able to work together and allow enough space for all of our professional and personal input, we would get a much better outcome.

Governors

Governors are mainly responsible for ensuring "that the vision, ethos and strategic direction of the school are clearly defined, ..." (Effective governance - Government guidance. 2024).

Whilst their role is vital in ensuring smooth running and holding leaders accountable, they are also *another* addition to many accountability systems in education that add to teacher workload. The level of bureaucracy involved in reporting to governors will vary between schools but for teaching and learning responsibilities (TLR) it is common for TLR holders to have to write a report, attend a meeting and share action plans and data with their link governors to prove the impact of their work in schools. TLR holders very rarely get given extra time for their role. Workload includes action plans for the academic year, displays, assemblies, meetings, arranging visitors, ordering resources, organising events, learning walks and supporting teachers. Imagine being asked to do these tasks with little to no time added to complete them. Then add proving yourself to governors in the form of reports, meetings and learning walks and you have a problem on your hands. When the workload becomes unmanageable, this is when creativity takes a nosedive. Exhaustion and stress remove the ability for teachers to be patient, understanding, responsive and compassionate. They also become unable to take risks and try out new and innovative ideas.

Governance is important, but the interaction between governors and teachers needs a rethink – a more consistently present and supportive model would be conducive to teachers having the space and time to be autonomous. As it currently stands, we have little to do with governors other than when being held accountable which does not allow the space for collaborative cultures to develop.

Local authority

Rarely have I felt judged by a visitor from LA. In my experience as a teacher, the main interactions I have had with people from the LA have been positive (sometimes linked to repetitive and unnecessary training, but that comes down to problems with SLT not finding time to check in with staff professional learning needs), but overall, in my experience they have been supportive, kind and practical. I am aware this may not be the experience for all teachers in other boroughs. The one problem I have is the amount of mocksteds, learning walks and audits that come from the LA without coordination with class teachers. We should be speaking to teachers and recognising where they feel support is needed and in what format. Usually booked in or agreed with the SLT, these visits add to the workload and pressure on teachers and can feel disconnected from their needs. The LA could be a really positive direction for formative and developmental accountability models (when not added onto a list of other accountability measures mentioned in this chapter). The borough has a good understanding of context, can build strong relationships with staff teams and provide relevant support and training to realise creative ideas and changes, linked to long-term school improvement. Local authority visits should happen as a result of conversation with staff teams as opposed to being done to them.

Parent experience – Stakeholders

Kiera Godfrey. Parent. Inner London Primary School.

Choosing your child's school in the area I live in is very noisy. Everyone has advice and everyone has an opinion. In reality, no school is perfect and no school is the perfect fit. Any teacher or website that promises a utopia is a big red flag. Good is what I'm looking for. I don't love Ofsted – I think it is just a tiny snapshot of what a school can do – but it is the system we have, and so I found it hard to ignore. I'd prefer a Good school as my first choice, rather than an Outstanding one. I think that is a sign that the school cares more about the kids and staff than the Ofsted result, and so hasn't spent months

> prepping, turning itself inside out and upside down to perform. That approach is not really about the children as individuals, but more about the school as an institution.
>
> If teachers are approachable and engaged when I tour a school, they know children's names in the hallway and what they are up to… or should be up to, then everything instantly feels more human. If at parents' evening the teachers are clearly in the know about my child and their learning, that means so much more to me than any details in a report. If I were looking for a primary school place now, I'd like to know if a school is able to cater to different learners within the same class space, if they do art lessons every week, if there are any women in the PE department and if they go crazy over SATs revision. All those things are still important to me when looking at secondary schools, but now I would like to know when they have to start choosing GCSE options, how many languages students can choose from, whether they have to choose between arts or sports, or if they can do both. Some of the answers might not be ideal, so you have to make the best possible choice for who your child is right now, but clarity and transparency are the key.
>
> I guess most of these things come down to flexibility – within reason, what works best for your child and if something is not working can the school help you find a solution. And the only way to know that is through good communication. If staff are open and honest about what a school can offer, I feel much more trust in them than if they were telling me their school was perfect.

It's time to pause.

Reflection

- How many people/processes hold me accountable?
- How much time do I think these processes take, over the course of a term?
- Are all of the processes helpful – do they provide me with essential tools to do my job properly?
- Do I find the processes collaborative, supportive and developmental?

Get autonomy back

In the classroom:

- Find a way to present any requested evidence in a document suitable for all audiences; this will save doubling up on work.
- Speak up – when you are requested to provide a report or prove that your work is making an impact – ask for time to complete this task.
- If you are a TLR holder, then request additional PPA time.
- There may be some evidence requests that you think are unreasonable – be open and honest about this where possible or contact your NEU rep for further advice.
- Make use of the NEU or your mental health and wellbeing lead where possible.

For senior leaders:

- Keep a list of the evidence and report requests you make of your staff teams - this will ensure the list doesn't become gigantic without your realising.
- Give TLR holders extra time to complete their additional work and don't make them ask for it.
- If you are adding another accountability measure, then get rid of one to balance it out - it is unreasonable to just keep adding to the workload.
- Reflect on impact - if something seems redundant, then do not be afraid to get rid of the process altogether.
- Be the voice of your staff - if the governors or LA are requesting evidence for something and you think it is unreasonable, or an ineffective use of your staff team's time, then speak up.

For government officials:

- Introduce workload limits including tasks that are set by LAs, parents and governors.
- Slim down the curriculum - make space for reflection and improvement.
- Introduce statutory training for teachers on establishing effective parent-school relationships.
- Support the building of community links - schools working alongside community organisations and parent groups to develop positive working relationships.
- Support flexible parent involvement - this could include online parent meetings or later parent evenings for those who work during the day. This should come with a reduction in workload elsewhere so as not to add to the teacher's working day.

Final thought on stakeholders

There are so many parties teachers are answerable to. I would advocate for a more streamlined approach to accountability - with the LA being the centre point of a formative and supportive accountability model. The collaboration developed between the school and LA can provide information that can be effectively shared with other stakeholders, such as parents and governors. A collaborative model provides information for all rather than having several different strands and preparation periods.

THE BIG IDEA - Accountability and Motivation

Andrew Cowley. Wellbeing Consultant, Speaker and Author, Coach for Designated Mental Health Leads and School Mental Health Award.

In literature and film, teachers are revered, from Miss Jean Brodie to Mr Chips, Dumbledore to John Keating. Health and safety requirements would prevent any of us from leaping on tables to proclaim "carpe diem" or "O Captain! My captain!" but would teachers in the 2020s share the same motivation? The intrinsic motivation portrayed by Robin Williams in "Dead Poets Society" was one of enjoyment and expression.

Is this the motivation of the modern teacher? Or are they driven by extrinsic motivation, of pay scales and promotion, or of the avoidance of criticism and negativity?

In my final teaching practice I was given the topic "Life Cycles" and little else other than "Look at level 2 and 3" in what were the early days of the National Curriculum. No schemes of work, no flipcharts (interactive white boards came years later) and no booklets. The motivation was to create meaningful, sequential learning, and even as a trainee I had the same degree of autonomy as the experienced staff.

Autonomy, however, is offset by accountability. SATs, league tables, performance management, Ofsted and the cultures that have been absorbed into schools as a result of high-stakes accountability have impacted teacher autonomy and the standing of the profession to the point that collective and individual criticism has become normalised both outside and within schools.

Take, for example, the culture created by lesson observation. Even though Ofsted stopped grading lessons many years ago, lesson observations are still common in schools, creating a sense of fear. One consequence of this has been lessons written merely for an observation, one often repeated for the next observation cycle. A more worrisome consequence though has been around feedback, particularly around points for development or "Even Better If" which automatically triggers a feeling of what has been done incorrectly. Such a model has implications for the future, as those young teachers who have been observed take the same practice into observations they make when they take on leadership opportunities. The primary motivation becomes one not of the love of learning, but of the avoidance of negativity.

This does lie within the experience of many long-serving teachers, myself included. I was teaching during the first round of Ofsted inspections, which lasted a week and included a lay inspector. Our lay inspector spent three days picking holes in everything, including teacher cupboards and the width of display borders, to the point where the Head complained to the lead inspector who delivered a sharp dressing down to our relief. Fast forward 30 years, lay inspectors are a historical blip, but the culture of micromanagement still exists in many school environments.

What has happened to teacher motivation during this time? The erosion of the inexperienced teacher workforce in the first 3-5 years, mirrored by the departure of much of the experienced end of the profession, has left a void of skill and enthusiasm. The answer to some seems to lie in scripted lessons, learning booklets, set sequences, agreed flipcharts and cold calling. Does this suit every child, every class or every context?

Is the prime motivation for teachers getting the job done with a hard-nosed approach to avoid negativity, or are there still passionate educators driven by a love of learning, a knowledge of the whole child and the desire to create responsible young citizens? Which one of these would you want teaching your own children?

Contributors

1. Frances. Former Primary Headteacher.
2. Ben Levinson OBE. Director for School and Trust Development and Executive Headteacher. Kensington Primary School. Newham. London.
3. Anon. Primary School Teacher.
4. Andrew Cowley. Wellbeing Consultant, Speaker and Author, Coach for Designated Mental Health Leads and School Mental Health Award.

References

Appraisal and Accountability Bargaining Toolkit. 14 Jan 2025. NEU. https://neu.org.uk/advice/your-rights-work/performance-management/appraisal-and-accountability-bargaining-toolkit

Clare-Martin, A. 10 Dec 2023. The Independent. Ruth Perry: Ten More Headteachers Left Suicidal in Wake of Ofsted Inspections, Former Inspector Reveals. https://www.independent.co.uk/news/uk/home-news/ten-suicidal-headteachers-ofsted-ruth-perry-b2459393.html

Connor, H. 2023. Inquest into Death of Ruth Perry – Conclusions (redacted).

Coy, J. Mar 2025. Headteacher Chat: Can a Parent Request the Attendance Record of Their Child's Teachers? https://headteacherchat.com/blogs/can-a-parent-request-the-attendance-record-of-their-childs-teachers-uronx

Cumiskey, L. 1 Dec 2024. Schools Week. Unions Urge Schools Still Using Performance-Related Pay to Ditch It. https://schoolsweek.co.uk/unions-urge-schools-still-using-performance-related-pay-to-ditch-it/

Cutmore, C. 24 Mar 2023. The Guardian. As Caversham Parents, Ruth Perry's Death Has Opened Our Eyes to the Realities of Ofsted Inspections. https://www.theguardian.com/education/2023/mar/24/caversham-primary-school-parents-ruth-perry-death-realities-ofsted-inspections

Effective governance. Government guidance. 7 March 2024. https://www.gov.uk/guidance/governance-in-maintained-schools/1-effective-governance

Farr, T. 1 Mar 2025. Schools as Organic Systems.

Ford, N. and Warren, J. 16 Apr 2025. 'If My School Closes, I May Not See Friends Again'. BBC News. https://www.bbc.co.uk/news/articles/c9857r973xgo

Fricker, E. 8.12 am. 15 Jan. 2025. X. https://x.com/_MissingTheMark/status/1879441505590685792?t=vXAQM4in2LNstAUr59rp6A&s=03

Jeffreys, B. and George, S. 7 Dec 2023. BBC News. I.N.A.D.E.Q.U.A.T.E - Ruth Perry's Despair in Handwritten Notes. https://www.bbc.co.uk/news/education-67612233

McMullen, R. and Grimshaw, JP. 4 Feb 2025. Missed the Opportunity: Making Matters Worse. Headrest. https://www.headrestuk.co.uk/blog/missed-opportunity-making-matters-worse?s=03

Model Appraisal and Accountability Letter. 14 Jan 2025. NEU. https://neu.org.uk/latest/library/model-appraisal-and-accountability-letter

Muller, K. 2005. London Tonight. https://www.youtube.com/watch?v=NmvvlaIA4G0)

NEU. Why should Performance Related Pay be abolished? 25 July 2022. https://neu.org.uk/latest/library/why-should-performance-related-pay-be-abolished

Perry, R. 2019. Pilot Inspection Report Letter. Caversham Primary.

Pink, D. 2009. P. 106. The Surprising Truth About What Motivates Us. Canongate Books.

Teacher Appraisal - Guidance for Schools. July 2024. P. 3. https://assets.publishing.service.gov.uk/media/66a253b20808eaf43b50d742/Teacher_Appraisal_-_guidance_for_schools_July_2024.pdf

Teacher Tapp. 21 Jan 2025. Graded Observations, Modular Exams and Teacher Improvements. https://teachertapp.com/uk/articles/graded-observations-modular-exams-and-teacher-improvements/)

Teacher Tapp. 11 Feb 2025. ECTs, social media rules and calling in sick. https://teachertapp.com/uk/articles/ects-social-media-rules-and-calling-in-sick/

Waters, J. 5 Apr 2024. The Guardian. "Sister of Ruth Perry Urges Teachers Thinking of Suicide to Seek Help". https://www.theguardian.com/education/2024/apr/05/ruth-perry-sister-julia-waters-teachers-neu-conference

Waters, S. 2023. Written Evidence Submitted by Professor Sarah Waters. https://committees.parliament.uk/writtenevidence/122191/pdf/

Waters, S. 16.49 pm 18 July 2023. X. https://x.com/teachwellall/status/1681330465536352257?t=WFgYRmWUgukIntbs3fSbIg&s=03

Woodhead, C. 23 June 2015. The Telegraph. Obituary. https://www.telegraph.co.uk/news/obituaries/11693238/Sir-Chris-Woodhead-Ofsted-chief-obituary.html

Worth, J. and Van den Brande, J. 29 January 2020. P. 13 Teacher Autonomy: How Does It Relate to Job Satisfaction and Retention?. NFER. https://www.nfer.ac.uk/publications/teacher-autonomy-how-does-it-relate-to-job-satisfaction-and-retention/

4 The children

If children aren't coping with the system you have, you have to change the system because you don't get to swap the children you've got for some other ones.

(Sue Cowley. X. 4 May 2024)

> **Chapter 4 outline**
>
> In this chapter, we will explore:
>
> - the escalation of controlled education.
> - the current status of child mental health.
> - the current attendance crisis.
> - how a lack of teacher autonomy might contribute to the decline in engagement in education.
> - the increase in home-schooling.
> - the status of the Children's Wellbeing and Schools Bill.
> - play and the freedom to learn.
> - how autonomy can create the perfect grounds for developing genuine connection and belonging.
> - how, with trust, the teacher may be able to redress the balance on the current academic focus.

Children and autonomy

That's it – change the system, not the children. Author and trainer Dr Sue Allingham once said to me, "Gove and Gibb have a lot to answer for!" and she wasn't wrong. Remember the King James Bible? If the title is causing a nightmarish flash back, then it is likely you were teaching in the Gove and Gibb era. With a desire for an education system that echoes that of a Victorian classroom, Gove believed that children had been failed by "left-wing ideology" and dictated (he never asked the profession and acted with incredible speed) a return to learning facts including those about what he called our "rich island history". With his focus on how perfect the education landscape *used to be,* he attempted to bring back the past for children whose future would be far from anything *he* could ever imagine. His reintroduction of role models who were mainly white and male (with a token female, Jane Austen) (Meikle, 2012) and his inability to see children as humans rather than data caused damage that will take decades to repair. His actions resulted in a relationship breakdown between educators and government, with many feeling that they had to toe the line for fear of a "telling off" in the form of a bad Ofsted inspection and being at the bottom of school league tables. Gove is the reason that we moved backwards and not forwards. Gibb is the reason we have a phonics approach that is relentless and lacking in joy (despite Gibb *claiming* to recognise the importance of reading for pleasure).

The connection between the lack of autonomy and the Gove and Gibb era is that the conversation was brought to an abrupt end. Suddenly, teachers and children's voices didn't matter anymore, and we were expected to just "pass the test". The pressure has mounted ever since and due to an increasing fear of getting it wrong, (e.g. an Ofsted fail) schools have enforced standards. This has led to an evaporation of personality, exploration and creativity. We are now robots, feeling ignored and devalued. As stated in The Guardian back when Gove left his post as education secretary, "You've got teachers and heads now so obsessed with compliance that they are unable to work with the autonomy he's given us" (Tickle and Ratcliffe. 22 July 2014). Let's now explore how this stealing of autonomy has impacted, and continues to impact, the *children* in our schools.

Mental health

> *School is too much pressure.*
> **(Dr Maddi Popoola, Dr Sarah Sivers, Rebecca Hooper & Anila Ahad.**
> **A report on Young Peoples' Views on Mental Health)**

Teachers know what is going on - we are aware of the problems. The misjudged decisions, the decline in self-esteem and the behaviour for communication. We are witnessing the special educational needs and disabilities (SEND) crisis unfold, the desperate lack of the creative arts and time to respond to children who need us. We observe it every day and it is exhausting. Even more exhausting though is the lack of control we have as we watch it all transcend into chaos. Very rarely do we feel trusted enough to stand up, speak up and offer ideas for revised approaches. Every now and then, you work for a senior leadership team (SLT) that listens, that asks, that sees it too, and when they claim they *can't* see it you can't blame them - they feel the pressure to perform too.

When teachers have autonomy, children are more likely to be heard and when children are heard, we can respond effectively. Children are communicating with us - all is not as it should be. The mental health, SEND and attendance crises are all ways that children are letting us know that systemic change is needed urgently.

The Children's Society states that "1 in 6 children aged 5-16 are likely to have a mental health problem" and "in the last three years, the likelihood of young people having a mental health problem has increased by 50%". The Good Childhood Report 2024 states that having a sense of belonging in schools in the UK is ranked "fifth from the bottom out of 27 countries..." (The Children's Society, 2024). With mental health and wellbeing being high on the agenda and top topic for conversation in education, how are we getting it so wrong?

The heavy focus on mental health has become a source of debate, with many stating that it is *encouraging* rumination. Author and social scientist, Matilda Gosling, states that "... scratching the surface reveals a generation who may be identifying with their feelings to an unhealthy degree..." (Gosling, 2025. P. 120). I am not entirely sure how I feel about this statement. However, reflecting on my own experiences with depression, I've noticed that "dwelling on" a state can sometimes deepen the struggle or worsen the mental state. Following my first ever mindfulness course, I began my journey into a deep depression – some may argue that this was a coincidence, others may say that there were unresolved issues that had been pushed aside and that needed to come to the surface. Either way with teenagers being prone to ruminate (the emotional part of their brain is on overdrive), it seems feasible that an unhealthy obsession with mental health could exacerbate problems. I also believe that schools (in a bid to support children) offer interventions that are flimsy or unsubstantiated. Only time will tell us more about this, and it's something worth contemplating when deciding on your setting's approach to mental health and wellbeing. Research-led pedagogy is key. The current approach to mental health support in schools is missing the point entirely – mental health professionals are simply attempting to tidy the mess that the school systems are creating. To deal with the crisis, we need to look at the root cause – *the school system itself*.

The growing mental health crisis in our young people and the increasing persistent absence is a reminder that (a) children are not feeling motivated or enjoying their education, and (b) parents are starting to understand why. If you are consistently demotivated and unable to meet expectations, then self-esteem becomes damaged which will eventually lead to a "checking out".

As mentioned by Andrew Cowley "To be supportive of mental health, schools need to develop a culture in which children and adults alike are able to feel comfortable in discussing how they feel" (Cowley, 2021. P. 23). The important word here is *culture* – we cannot add in the odd mental health assembly but continue with punitive and outdated behaviour policies – if we are going to take care of mental health, we need to reflect this in our entire approach and make revolutionary and systemic change.

Social and emotional development

Autonomy is integral to a child's social and emotional learning. Children are more able to develop and apply these skills through exploratory and self-directed learning opportunities. The British Psychological Society states that children and young people need more autonomy to "...discover their strengths and weaknesses... while allowing them to start distinguishing their unique values and preferences for the future" (Khawaja and Bagley, 2024).

The Department for Education's Character Education guidance suggests that there are a number of "character traits which can improve educational attainment" (Department for Education, 2019. P. 7). These include traits such as self-belief, motivation, coping well and self-control.

There are several areas of social and emotional learning that develop and/or rely on autonomy;

- Self-awareness – when children can direct their own learning, they are able to openly explore their strengths, weaknesses and interests.
- Being independent – when a child is trusted to try out ideas and make mistakes, they learn to manage the outcome. This helps to develop their self-belief and self-esteem.

86 *Teacher Autonomy*

- Collaboration – developing their ability to work alongside a diverse range of ideas and people, understanding that when we work together, we can succeed. This also helps children develop their empathy and compassion for others.
- Instilling a growth mindset – supporting children to understand that we are always growing and developing and that people are not born with success and that we work towards our goals.
- Expression – helping a child develop their sense of value in the world.
- Confidence – when ideas are successful they can feel a sense of pride, developing their confidence to give things a go in the future.
- Emotional regulation – responding to challenges with an understanding that the journey is not always simple and straightforward – that we may find the road difficult and that it will pass and add to our rich life experience.
- Anxiety reduction – having the freedom to make choices and decisions gives children a sense of control over their lives leading to a reduction in anxiety and an increase in motivation.

From an evolutionary perspective and specifically a hunter-gatherer point of view, it didn't make sense to tell each other what to do, but instead share skills and ideas in an effort to

Figure 4.1 Freedom to choose fosters freedom to grow. Photograph by Sophie Smith-Tong, 2023

stay alive. In our current hierarchical education system, the teacher delivers the curriculum content to the children in the form of a "ready-made meal" rather than allowing them to work in the kitchen alongside them – ultimately, we are missing out on the voice of the child. The "sausage factory" structure seeks to provide all children with the same educational experience leading to disappointment and frustration on all parts – the teacher becomes exhausted with the challenge of making the impossible happen, the child feels like a failure because they cannot meet those expectations and the parents become frustrated with their child who lacks motivation for school.

Play

In the words of Peter Gray, "One thing we know for sure about anxiety and depression is that they correlate strongly with people's sense of control or lack of control over their own lives" (Gray, 2013. P. 16). Children currently have less freedom in school and now, from a younger age. We discussed the curriculum in depth earlier on in the book (**Chapter 2**) but to put it simply – our curriculum is cramped and leaves very little room for autonomy for both educator and child.

Play is motivating by nature. It is a journey where we get to choose the sequence of experiences. Choosing our route in the moment and with varied intentions – to find comfort, flow, challenge or all of the above – it's our call. It can be really hard to get this across to headteachers and senior leaders who have often had little experience in the early years. The Early Years Foundation Stage (EYFS) can be viewed as the bit of the school that nobody wants to head into – in my many years in early years classrooms I have had the odd visitor from the upper key stages – usually to borrow a cup of sand for their science experiment or a car and ramp for a year one "forces" lesson. When they enter, they always comment on "how cute it is down here" or "how little everything is". These comments always provoke a strong reaction in me – they speak volumes – we are not taken seriously. Early years practitioners can often be misunderstood when, in actual fact, we could support a lot of staff on how to adapt their practice, respond compassionately and work with families – this is the stuff we are really good at. Instead of us being able to spread our practice to the upper years, their practice is forcing its way into ours, meaning that the EYFS practice is narrowing. There's been a noticeable shift towards more carpet times and teacher-led talk, leaving less room for play – a significant loss for everyone involved. Those who do not understand play, fear it but as Michael Rosen succinctly reminds us, "Play is serious" (Bradbury et al., 2025. P. 3).

We are seeing more adults in education trying to take control of a child's play experiences – usually with an iPad in hand and interrogating them to see what they understand. There is a lack of trust in play itself, so the educator feels compelled to jot down notes and prove that the child is learning. Julie Fisher states that "for many young learners, the problem comes in nurseries or classrooms where the adults' agenda matters more than their own" (Fisher, 2016). Are we scared to just let play be? I cannot tell you how many times I have been asked "where is the learning?". The learning is in every interaction, conversation, individual and group moment – we should question any adult who attempts to "mark" these experiences.

88 *Teacher Autonomy*

Figure 4.2 Play is an act of autonomy. Photograph by Sophie Smith-Tong, 2021

If we begin to interfere, the children are no longer autonomous and then they lose flow and motivation. A decline in play is a decline in autonomy and a decline in both will mark a rise in struggle with emotional wellbeing.

*A note on "The play people"

I must mention Greg Bottrill and his movement to mobilise "The Play People". If you are a school that is concerned about removing schemes and structure in your Reception and Key Stage 1 classrooms, then Greg's *Play Projects* and *Drawing Club* are a fantastic way to adopt a structure without actually having to adopt one at all. These approaches give permission for teachers in schools who find it impossible to be trusted to find freedom and discover play within their classroom teaching. Both *Drawing Club* and *Play Projects* provide guidance, not prescription and facilitate the relearning of how to play for grown-ups who need that extra support. Both approaches allow children the ability to express themselves through art, mark making and writing in a way that will inspire and support your rediscovery of joy. Through these projects, Greg Bottrill cleverly gives you an autonomy super pass when you think it's impossible – I urge you to check them out at www.canigoandplaynow.com.

Educator experience – Play and autonomy

Peter Gray. Research Professor of Psychology and Neuroscience at Boston College.

The Biology of Education

Children come into the world biologically designed to educate themselves through self-chosen, self-directed activities. They are born with what I call educative instincts. These include:

1. **Curiosity** – the drive to understand. Children are extraordinarily curious. Newborns look more at novel objects than at those they have already seen. As they gain mobility, they explore ever-larger realms of their environment. Curiosity is nature's way of ensuring that children seek and acquire an understanding of the world around them.
2. **Playfulness** – the drive to practice and create. While curiosity motivates children to seek new knowledge and understanding, playfulness motivates them to practice new skills. When children have ample opportunity to play, they play at all the skills that are essential for healthy mental and physical development.
    - They play in physical ways, chasing, wrestling, leaping, climbing, etc., and that is how they develop strong bodies and graceful movements.
    - They play with language, and that is how they become proficient with language.
    - They play at building things, and that is how they become skilled at building.
    - They play games with rules, and that is how they learn to create and follow rules.
    - They play make-believe, and that is how they learn to use imagination and think hypothetically.
    - Perhaps most important, they play socially, with other children, and that is how they learn to negotiate, compromise, cooperate and empathize.
3. **Sociability** – including the drive to share knowledge with peers. Children are drawn to other children in large part so they can learn from one another. When children play and explore in groups, each child's discovery becomes the discovery of all.
4. **Willfulness** – the drive to take charge of one's own life. From as early as age two, children strive to make their own decisions and do things themselves to the degree possible. This may annoy adults, but children know, in their DNA, that this is how they grow up, how they move towards independent adulthood.
5. **Planfulness** – the drive to plan for the future. This develops gradually and appears first in play. When children play, they plan what they are playing and carry out that plan. With practice, children learn to plan ever further ahead. By the time they are teenagers, if they have had much experience planning for shorter terms, they may be prepared to make and carry out plans leading to a desired career.

My research in radically alternative educational settings convinces me that when children are free to follow these natural drives, in a supportive and caring environment,

> they educate themselves beautifully. Sadly, in our conventional schools, all these drives are suppressed. Go back over the list and think about how school quashes each. Good teachers, when free, can allow these drives to manifest themselves to at least some degree in conventional schools. But when governments dictate the contents of lessons and tests and hold teachers to them, this becomes difficult or impossible. I'm convinced that loss of kids' freedom, resulting in part from loss of teachers' freedom, is a major reason why kids are suffering at such high levels today and not learning enough that is relevant to their real lives.

It's time to pause.

Reflection

- How is personal, social and emotional learning threaded through school life in your setting?
- How does your setting teach emotional literacy?
- Are personal social health education (PSHE)/relationship sex education (RSE) lessons considered important?
- How much of your day is dedicated to free play?
- Do you only play in your EYFS? If so, why is this? (I am asking this question of secondary schools too!)
- Do you have role-play areas in all classrooms? (and yes, secondary schools could certainly use drama and role-play as an option to explore many topics including maths and science)
- Do you understand play, or do you fear it?
- Do you feel well equipped to facilitate play in your setting for all-aged children?

Get autonomy back

In the classroom:

- Avoid filling your timetable with carpet times and table work.
- Create opportunities for experiential learning where children can take control – e.g. if you are teaching push and pull, get a *real* bike into the classroom and investigate!
- If you are in the EYFS, push back against the formal learning model.
- If you feel fearful of allowing children to play for long periods of time, then request training. A fear of play is down to a lack of understanding of play.
- Ask your children – hear their voice.

For senior leaders:

- Make sure you learn about play and its power.
- Embed personal, social and emotional learning into the whole school ethos and culture.

- Think big change but accept it's a long-term goal – changing things overnight is unsettling and unrealistic.
- Engage parents with your ethos. Use research to sell your idea.
- Trust and value your EYFS teams and get them to share their approach with the rest of the school.
- Train up your whole staff team (not just EYFS) on the importance of play.
- Encourage your team to think creatively and avoid worksheets (this is better for the environment and budgets too!).

For government officials:

- Add a play module to the teacher training content for all ages.
- Reduce curriculum content so that we have time to learn through play.
- Make PSHE a statutory requirement and offer support and training to deliver high-quality learning in this area.
- Protect play – make play statutory for the EYFS and Key Stage 1 (KS1).
- Increase and protect outdoor play times for all ages.

Final thought on mental health

We are working with humans, not data. The situations we are managing are full of nuance and are unpredictable. In our classrooms we are best placed to see what challenges our young people are facing, yet we are rarely given the chance to speak out, collaborate or respond to these challenges. Instead, we are told how the government intends to fix these problems with initiatives that offer sticking plaster solutions. With the problems we face being so complex we need to be able to come together – revolutionise our education offering and begin to work on dealing with the deeper-rooted problems.

Personalised learning

> *You cannot force a person to learn. It is a deeply personal act and has to be personalised to be fully effective.*
>
> *(Ken and Kate Robinson. 2022. Imagine If...)*

When sitting around a table in a pupil progress meeting, looking at charts and tables, we can easily forget that each child is a human. As teachers we can get stuck, valuing the simplified child model:

- The extrovert.
- The extrovert that knows when to be quiet.
- The child that is still.
- The child that is at ease.
- The one that follows instructions first time.
- The individual that looks at you in the eye when you speak to them.
- The child who contributes (but only if they put their hand up and do not talk for too long).

What has become "successful" to us has to fit into a tight criterion. It does not take a professional to notice that these expectations hold no true value and that each child requires a personalised learning journey, as Ken and Kate so succinctly put it in the quote above. Large class sizes (now between 30 and 32 in the average UK primary) provide teachers with extensive challenges.

To celebrate each individual in our class we need time (and we know why we don't have enough - curriculum content overload and bureaucracy) but we also need to be trusted to respond and interact genuinely with compassion. The frustration felt by teachers can often be wrongly directed at the children but really it's about the unachievable expectations of the curriculum and timetable. Wouldn't it be amazing if when your class needed (or wanted) more time to explore a topic that you would have the autonomy to decide that you spend another week (or two!) on it. It is not uncommon to hear of children wishing they could choose to spend longer on an area but instead when their teacher discovers that they have understood something they desperately charge on to "challenge" or "extend them". We are always looking ahead because we have no time to look back, or more importantly to be present.

Each cohort will organically have what Andrew Cowley refers to as "Classroom Culture" (Cowley, 2021). This is a naturally developing classroom with no two classroom cultures the same - each one is a unique blend of children and adults. As most teachers will recognise, it only takes the absence of one child to completely alter the experience of your cohort. Our job as professionals is to respond to the very unique makeup of children that we have at any given time to create the perfect learning environment. Sensitive and perceptive responding can only happen with trust from SLT and those at the top. With the National Foundation for Educational Research (NFER) data showing that teachers have "…low levels of autonomy over curriculum content in their phase or subject (26%) (Worth and Van den Brande, 2020. P. 12), we do not find ourselves in an influential position (more on curriculum content in **Chapter 2**). There are many ways we could offer more autonomy, which would in turn provide more personalised learning journeys. "We must allow teachers more flexibility on content and subject" (Knight, J. Lord's debate, 2024).

Environment and resources

Tina Farr, headteacher of St. Ebbes in Oxford (see THE BIG IDEA at the end of this chapter for her amazing contribution), is making small changes (with huge impact) to the way children are taught in primary education. Aside from recognising the significance of the creative subjects, a focus on personal, social and emotional learning, the importance of play (even in year 2) and outdoor experiences, children in her year 5 class are now able to choose how they sit when they complete their work. Tina replaced half of her tables in a year 5 classroom with bean bags, comfortable chairs, and lap trays and created 37 seating options for 25 children (Farr, 2025).

The children have been given the chance to choose how they are most comfortable when learning - this may change daily. It may depend on mood, physical comfort, fatigue levels, their day so far amongst many other factors. Tina's approach causes us to question - why do we need to control how children sit? The environment we learn in is an important factor contributing to our focus and retention of information. If I am a child who fidgets and finds a

Figure 4.3 "This isn't about furniture—it's about autonomy". Photograph by Tina Farr, 2025

hard chair uncomfortable, this may be all I can focus on for the next 45 minutes, but instead I could choose to sit on a bean bag or cushion and *really* absorb the learning.

Resources are also an important part of the experience – for learners who best learn via concrete and tactile objects (which is most children in primary and many in secondary), we should have a wide range of toys and manipulatives for children to choose from at any given moment to complement and consolidate their experiences. Quite often we might add resources to the middle of a table that *we* feel best suits the learning, but why not ask the children what resources they might like to use too? There is a need for us to introduce ways to use resources, of course, but asking for their contribution means they can begin to develop an understanding of their own requirements to support their learning of abstract concepts. We may also ask ourselves about the ages we deem suitable to no longer offer these concrete resources (I quite often see year 6 classes with little or no access to complementary resources). I am 41 and would still prefer to have a resource in front of me to learn and develop an understanding of a mathematical concept. We need to open it up to the children and make fewer decisions on their behalf – instead offering ideas and facilitating their understanding of their own needs.

Could we trust children to sit with their friends more and foster a sense of collaboration as opposed to developing a fear of copying or lacking in focus? "We have to be silent in everything, I wish I didn't have to be", a year 1 child once shared with me. What happens to collaboration when we are silenced? We need to be honest with children – we cannot be strong in all areas, but we *can* seek support from the range of strengths in the room – let's talk and learn as opposed to expecting children to work isolated from others to prove their individual worth. It is time we stop attempting to control and allow thriving learning environments to develop – ones with personality and buzz. Teachers fear that allowing noise in their classrooms symbolises chaos. Whether it be for their own sense of control or for the members of SLT walking by – we need to question – who is it for?

Uniform

The Education Endowment Foundation's (EEF) research highlighted that uniforms did not seem to affect learning despite many believing non-school uniforms can act as a distraction. My only experience of this distraction is with the novelty of children being able to wear what they want – I am sure this would calm down if it became a permanent fixture (Education Endowment Foundation). In terms of feeling like yourself, what you wear can be important to adults and children. An article exploring uniforms in American schools stated that "uniforms deny students personal autonomy, which often causes feelings of discomfort. Clothing can be a sensitive choice for many people, especially teenagers" (Ali, 2023). My daughter is a good example of this – she feels uncomfortable in her school uniform and enjoys expressing herself through her clothes. She likes to dress herself and feel in control of this small part of her day. The morning can be fraught with sensory discomfort and a reminder that she is heading to school – a place she currently associates with anxiety. She struggles with a sense of identity, and so clothes help her to achieve this. As a teacher I also enjoy "being myself" in an outfit that I have chosen. In my first years of teaching, I had to adhere to a strict uniform policy which meant I was in clothes that were uncomfortable and misaligned.

In terms of budget – uniforms are expensive and can cause parents anxiety, especially in the earlier years when children are more likely to get dirty and need it washed for the next day – buying more than one set can be impossible for parents. The new Labour government, as part of the Children's Wellbeing and Schools Bill, is reducing the number of branded items to protect parents from costs. Alongside costs it is also worth thinking about your staff uniform policy and questioning why you have certain rules in place – comfort should be key in play-based areas of the school (I would argue that this should be everywhere!). In previous teaching jobs, I was not allowed to wear trainers, and I was working in a Nursery – totally impractical and uncomfortable. It also meant I could not fully get into my role and facilitate the children's play in the way I could with trainers on. Rules like no jeans, no trainers, no tattoos and brightly coloured hair should be heavily questioned – ask yourself why you have these rules and reflect upon the outcomes if you change them. I've encountered certain rules

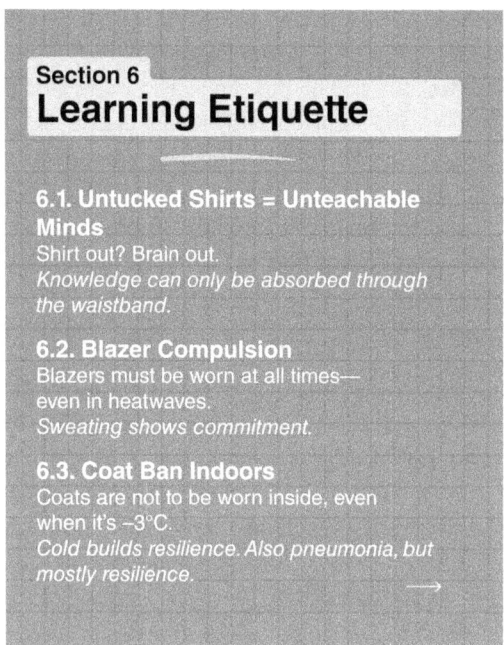

Figure 4.4 Is learning really linked to how we dress, or have we just been told it is? Learning Etiquette. Sally Michaels, 2025

that make complete sense to me, such as no short skirts, low-cut tops, or open-toed shoes, as they align with the practical demands of the job. However, boundaries that seem to be imposed without a clear rationale should be questioned.

Teacher-pupil relationships

Building trust is a process; it takes time. We cannot expect children to enter our classrooms and be ready to pledge allegiance. To connect we have to show them part of ourselves and be vulnerable – that way they know it is a safe space to do the same. I always find it fascinating and extremely telling that a member of staff at my children's school (who they have never had as a class teacher) is one of their "favourites". She makes an effort to be herself, to see them for who they are and find genuine connection with them.

As a child, I have fond memories of finding out who my new teacher was going to be in the next academic year. This excitement was born from seeing who they were as an individual, and I was excited to get to do things in a new way. There was the prospect of trying out new routines, learning new facts, getting to know a whole new human being – it was exciting! That's not to say that the teachers that we have now are all robots, but with growing prescriptions and scripts perhaps we are edging closer. Increased autonomy allows teachers to develop deeper, more meaningful relationships with their children, benefiting both in an academic and personal sense. It is important to mention that we also need to be mindful of transition and change challenges for some children – which can also be managed by trusting a teacher to respond appropriately to the individuals in their class.

In the early years we spend a good portion of the first term getting to know and connecting with our children and families (this is becoming harder to do with pressures for more carpet times and academic outcomes). Developing this connection works best when threaded throughout your time with the children and not necessarily taught discretely. The more time you carve out to have *real* conversation with your children, the more they invest in what you have to say. Children are really good at sniffing out disingenuous people. Unfortunately, the system we have is no longer conducive to building genuine and strong relationships – it *can* be done, but it's hard work when you are swimming against the tide and so I judge nobody for losing sight of this.

Connection and belonging

A connection is not necessarily tied to a formal role or hierarchy. To develop a connection there needs to be a level playing field, time, space and comfort. The right conditions for developing connections are not currently found in our schools. Hierarchical structures, an absence of democracy, mutual respect and a two-way conversation are lacking. Education is being done *to* children rather than being shaped *by* them. Choosing to make space and time for this connection currently comes at a cost – in some schools this would mean the difference between good and bad observation outcomes, pay increases and performance management (more on this in **Chapter 6**), Ofsted outcomes and school league tables. When allowing time to make connections with your class, whether this be following a child's interest or going off on a curriculum tangent, something else has to give. In years where children are assessed (e.g. standard assessment tests [SATs] or multiplication tests), this can mean the difference between data showing you are doing your job well and data that suggests you are not.

Without connection the children are separate from us – their experience of school is dictated *by* us. When we feel disconnected, we lack care and motivation and without this our mental health and wellbeing suffer and we find ourselves back in that cycle, trapped by the system.

Child experience – Connection

Woody. Year 6 Child. Inner London Primary.

I think it is important that I know about a teacher's personality because it means I can relate to their hobbies, opinions and ideas. It also makes me feel like I know them better. This comes across in my work because if I know them more and I am more likely to listen to what they are saying in the same way you listen to your friends and family. I am also more likely to put my hand up and contribute more since I feel more comfortable talking to them. As well as helping my learning, it also helps me talk to them if something is wrong. For example, if I felt like someone was bullying me and I was scared that if I told someone I would get bullied more, I would be more likely to tell a teacher if I knew them better. Like, if I knew that they had also been bullied at school because they had told me about their childhood. I would think they would know what to do in this situation. Another teacher might have also been bullied at school but they did not feel the right to tell their class. I would not be as likely to tell that teacher rather than the one who expressed their life experiences.

It's time to pause.

Reflection

- Do I feel able to connect with the children in my class?
- Am I given the space and time to gel with my cohort at the beginning of a new school year?
- What about when somebody new joins my class – adult or child?
- Do I know what makes each child special?
- Am I able to give time to celebrate these special traits?
- Am I given the opportunity to share parts of my own personality with the children?
- Are the children in my care supported on a pastoral level?

Get autonomy back

In the classroom:

- Next time you attempt to control, ask yourself the reason – is it for you or for the children?
- Try Tina Farr's seating autonomy – be patient, change takes time to embed.
- Introduce more child autonomy when it comes to learning aids and support materials.
- Trial collaboration rather than isolation – start small and understand that this is a skill that will need to be given time to develop – it might feel chaotic at first.
- Make time to connect as a cohort and really get to know one another – share appropriate anecdotes that humanise and allow space for the children to do the same.

For senior leaders:

- Allow flexibility within your classrooms – flexible timetabling and curriculum coverage.
- Recognise the importance of free time within the curriculum – an opportunity for teachers to connect and respond to children as individuals.
- Invest in a range of resources for all ages to grasp and consolidate concepts within their learning.
- Get to know your staff – this will ensure you know how each member of staff can add value to your class cohorts.
- Read Ben Levinson's contribution in **chapter 3** and learn about flexible timetables and trust in staff.
- Encourage a collaborative approach to creating policy and curriculum content (more on this in **Chapters 2** and **3**).

For government officials:

- Slim down the curriculum.
- Explore and research the use of schemes and the infiltration of standardised learning.
- Support schools in implementing play, promoting approaches suited to their school community and the removal of the one-size-fits-all strategy.

Final thought on personalised learning

The level of nuance we navigate in schools requires something other than harsh behaviour policies or "putting our foot down". We must begin to trust that love and compassion will take us to a place where real learning can happen. Our work is challenging and the behaviour for communication is telling us that we are not currently getting it right. Rather than place a plaster over it (because what is underneath is too complex to deal with), we must avoid fearing the individuals that walk into our classrooms every day and instead welcome them in with open arms.

Attendance

> ...self-withdrawal is evidence of a contractual breakdown. The contract being one where the young person attends and complies at school, and in return the school offers a "safe environment, meaningful and relevant learning, opportunities for association with friends, and dignified and respectful treatment" (2006: 208); the contractual breakdown therefore occurs when a young person does not feel safe, protected, respected or dignified.
>
> *(Beth Bodycote, 2023. Square Pegs)*

The attendance crisis was brought into the media spotlight by the pandemic and continues to dominate headlines, with the push back from parents and many educators gaining momentum. As I write, the data on the government website states that "across 2023/24, the overall absence rate was 7.1%, higher than prepandemic rates (4.7% in 2018/19)" (Department for Education, 2025). Are we sending children to school who are both physically and mentally unwell because it's considered the best place for them to be?

The increase in prepandemic levels is telling. Following the pandemic, the attendance crisis continued to spiral and with this came the same old pack of sticking plasters. This time they included "attendance hubs", "the recovery curriculum", "the national tutoring programme" and cancelled exams. It became quite clear that we were headed for disaster when Sir Kevan Collins (he recommended significant investment in education recovery) resigned in protest at the lack of funding provided by the Conservative government in 2021.

Reactionary behaviourist approaches, the SEND and staff retention crises are placing anxiety and a lack of faith at the heart of our education system - is it any wonder children do not want to be there. As I taught online in the pandemic I was struck by the amount of parents who contacted me to share:

- that they were surprised by the content we teach children.
- that their children seemed to be happier and less anxious learning at home.
- that parents were feeling the pressure to meet school demands.
- that they found forcing children to complete work that was both irrelevant and, in a timescale, designed by others quite impossible and unsettling.

The meltdowns they were witnessing were shocking to them, but not to me - I had often seen a variety of behaviours used as communication in our classrooms. The children were telling us that they could no longer meet our demands and were now telling their parents. By July 2022, the organisation *Not Fine in School* (an organisation for families with children experiencing school attendance barriers) had gained nearly 30,000 members and currently has a staggering 72.5K members. (Not Fine in School, 2025).

The government attendance campaign in 2024 suggested that school attendance was important not just for a child's learning, but also for their overall wellbeing. But what happens when school attendance causes anxiety so bad that your child begins to self-harm, suffer from severe tics or a fear of leaving the house? These are real-life symptoms of burnout shared by families whose children have been let down by a school system that forces them to conceal their true selves – creating a sense of shame that is both neglectful and damaging. When we can't be ourselves or control the direction of our daily lives, we start to suffer from poor mental and physical health.

Schools make matters worse when they respond to government and local authority attendance pressure by ramping up the stakes. Attendance certificates and prizes leave children and families feeling shame on top of their already anxious states. Their parents carry guilt when they receive phone calls and letters saying their child needs to be in school but receive no tailored support – our lack of autonomy and time to respond to families individually creates barriers between teachers and families. Ineffective blanket responses such as "they are fine when they are in school" or "they are best placed in school" leave families feeling frustrated and silenced. Responding to a child with school attendance anxiety does not require a quick fix, such as the introduction of the Zones of Regulation or a bit more time to enter the classroom in the morning (these might help short term or could make matters worse). Long term we must look at the *cause* of the anxiety – when I speak to children (including my own) about their anxieties around school, there is no sign of irrational or disordered thinking – it makes sense. They are attempting to learn in adverse conditions; their anxieties are a product of a system that is attempting to tightly control.

The attendance crisis needs to be met with less policy and rigour and more love and understanding. It also needs to recognise that the root cause of the attendance crisis comes not from parents or the current generation's lack of resilience but instead is born from a lack of child autonomy; they have been removed from their own learning experiences.

Children's Wellbeing and Schools Bill

As I write, the Children's Wellbeing and Schools Bill is in the House of Lords for its second reading (Department for Education, 2024). The bill has received varied responses – both a welcoming of a bill that explores child mental health and a feeling that it misses the mark in terms of the specifics it offers, including a home school register and qualified teacher status (QTS) required for those who teach. The CEO at Anna Freud responded, "we also want to see a statutory duty to establish a whole-school approach to mental health and wellbeing to help ensure children and young people flourish not just academically, but socially and emotionally" (Freud, 2025). Along with an announcement that mental health support teams will be in all schools by 2029/30, it seems there is currently a lot of firefighting going on. Education officials are recognising the signs of ill mental health but not necessarily noting that its old and irrelevant systems and content may be the problem. Many parents are also concerned that the home-school register is just another way to remove parent and child autonomy – especially when those that home-school their children are often families that have experienced firsthand the damage that the unnecessarily controlling system can do in the first place.

Home-School

The number of children being electively home educated (EHE) in England as of the autumn term 2024 is 111,700. This is an increase from 92,000 in the previous autumn (Department for Education, 2024/2025). This statistic does not include children on an education otherwise than at school (EOTAS) package, for children who cannot attend school. I found comfort in home-schooling my two children during the pandemic, despite the stress of it being alongside my responsibilities of whole school pastoral care. I felt lucky to be able to give my children the opportunity to learn autonomously at no financial cost. It was a huge relief to be able to educate them in a holistic and play-based way. My children were 2 and 5 when the pandemic hit – our learning included topics such as Glastonbury Week (we took several weeks to create our own Glastonbury model using photos and our own memories of the festival to recreate the model) and we even added in a WaterAid tap and sent it to the charity who used it to market their campaign. We built a language website to learn Spanish and made a film called *Little Lockdown* directed and created by the children exploring their experiences of the pandemic. All of these learning experiences were facilitated by me and led by the children – if they lost interest then we didn't do it. Home-schooling will look different for everyone, and there really aren't many wrongs and rights, but the freedom you have when choosing to school at home is what makes it truly special. Autonomy is the key to long-term learning – when the children

Figure 4.5 Home-school during lockdown 2020. The beginnings of a 2-week-long Glastonbury Project. Photograph by Sophie Smith-Tong

> ## Young person experience – Attendance
>
> **Livia. Year 11. Inner London Secondary.**
>
> Throughout my time in secondary, particularly in year 9 and year 10, I struggled to go to school. I went to a primary school where there were a variety of extracurriculars to get involved with, friendly people and a safe environment. At my secondary school, extracurriculars didn't exist. There were no sports teams or drama clubs (that wasn't even offered as a subject).
>
> I have always loved drama and acting, so going to a school where that culture didn't exist was extremely hard because nothing appealed to me. It was boring. I struggled to get up in the morning most days for a number of different reasons including friendship struggles, an unkind environment and other aspects outside of school. There was one point where I didn't go to school for almost a month. My mum received the routine text message every morning saying, "Liv did not register for school today". Other than that, nothing was done. No one questioned why a student like myself, who rarely got into trouble and attained good grades suddenly "dropped off the face of the planet" (as one teacher said to me at parents' evening).
>
> Not one person from the school called my mum and asked her why I wasn't there or if I was okay, which I really wasn't at the time. Although I managed to "play the game" and get on with my education, grinning and bearing the environment I hated, not everyone can do that. Needs haven't been met. Over 10 children in my year were permanently excluded from my school over a 5-year period. This was for being "too difficult" and not fitting the mould of the system. I think that if there were more opportunities to do the things that I loved at school, I would've struggled less. Anyone who was different was shunned, anyone who was enthusiastic had their confidence destroyed and anyone who spoke out was given detention. This is a cliche that most kids will say about school, but for me, it was like prison.

are invested, they will remember it. If we had this kind of freedom in schools, imagine the learning experiences that could take place.

It's time to pause.

Reflection

- What is the attendance story in my setting?
- Does my school use a carrot-and-stick attendance approach?
- What impact is this having on my school community's wellbeing?
- How might my setting improve the way it supports families struggling with attendance?
- Does my school offer a flexi-schooling programme for those who cannot attend school full-time?
- What are my current views on home-schooling, and can I challenge these views either way?

Get autonomy back

In the classroom:

- Avoid using rewards and punitive measures to manage attendance.
- Remember that *children* are rarely responsible for lateness and absence.
- Read *Can't Not Won't* by Eliza Fricker – get to know the reasons behind many attendance challenges.
- Avoid humiliation techniques when a child enters your classroom late or following an absence.
- Remember that attendance problems are a communication tool – be curious and find out what is happening for that child/family.

For senior leaders:

- Ditch attendance assemblies and prizes.
- Instead create a compassionate and restorative attendance policy that includes conversation, support and compassion.
- Be open to flexible schooling that supports children who find full-time too much.
- Be supportive and avoid being judgmental.

For government officials:

- Speak to the families of those who are finding attendance impossible and begin to recognise and develop the support needed.
- Avoid blaming parents.
- Stop sticking plasters over problems – delve deeper, do the harder work and revolutionise our education offering in the form of a more democratic and compassionate model.

Final thought on attendance

My youngest child never wants to go to school and has never been ok leaving me or her father at the school gates. It breaks my heart every time I wave goodbye to her, crying and waving at the door. For some families, this escalates over time with children experiencing burnout – signs and symptoms can include a refusal to leave their house, self-harm, tics and a mental shutdown. The pressure the government is currently putting on families to attend, despite these issues, shows a lack of trust in parents and educators. It also conveys an ignorance of the outdated and irrelevant schooling that is currently taking place. Let's be bold and offer them autonomy in their learning and give them a reason to come to school each day.

Defining success

> *Despite the astronomical changes in circumstances between the Industrial Revolution and the twenty-first century, formal systems of education by and large remain structurally the same.*
> **(Ken and Kate Robinson. 2022. Imagine If...)**

So, here we are, with children and families voting with their feet. Why are the kids voting with their feet?

Srinivasa Ramanujan (you can find out more about his interesting life on Wikipedia or in the book and film made about him) was a mathematical genius who received a scholarship to go to the Government Arts College in Kumbakonam, India. He failed all of his other exams because of his dedication to maths. His story made me question - what would have happened to Srinivasa if we made *maths* a less significant or valued part of our learning - imagine we gave drama an hour slot every day and maths we did every other week - what would have happened to Srinivasa? It is likely that his self-esteem and enjoyment of learning would have been slowly eroded over time. His teacher may not have discovered his skills and he may not have been emotionally secure enough to approach learning in the way that he did. This is what we are doing to children whose expertise and passions lie in subjects other than what the curriculum document deems important (e.g. maths and english).

In a letter to Amanda Spielman (former Chief Inspector of Education for Ofsted), States of Mind (a self-development organisation led by young people and psychologists) shared that "we feel that instead of gaining valuable knowledge which we are able to apply towards our future, the education system promotes the continuous memorisation of facts and the "cramming" of content from textbooks to be regurgitated - and forgotten soon after". (StatesofMind.org, 2016). Schools are in a rush to jam as much information into our children as possible - like stuffing a Build-a-Bear without the variety - consisting mainly of maths and literacy bears and every now and then we get a limited edition - an opportunity for child to experience their passion in the form of a drama or art lesson. The production line is far from inspiring and now with the addition of learning objectives, success criteria and plenaries, it has all gotten a bit too heavy.

Academic achievement

To really absorb what we are learning, we need to be in a place of safety and comfort. Children start out knowing that they are more than just grades, but if teachers don't believe that, a child's belief will quickly begin to waver. Children are losing faith in our systems earlier and earlier - years 1 and 2 seem to be a big turning point as this is when the formal learning model now takes hold. The expectation for children to sit still and listen for long periods of time to get results quicker is eroding their self-belief as they just can't meet the expectations. Our trust in them and appreciation of them as individuals, and not just on the data they provide, is crucial.

My own school experience was a journey that went something like this: first, I failed to meet the system's expectations, that then grew into a fear of making mistakes, which eventually led me to avoid trying anything at all, so I switched off. I was not mentally or physically able to put myself into what I deemed a risky situation. Leisa Rea was my drama teacher when I entered year 8. As I entered her classroom (a crumbling portacabin, not fit for purpose thanks to school budgets), I could feel the difference. Leisa had transformed the classroom into a police station fit for detectives. Set up with missing people photos, clues and evidence Leisa captured our imaginations, got us motivated and set me free of my fear-based limitations. Not only was the lesson creative, but it was also full to the brim with her - her personality, her creativity, her identity. I believed in it because it was real, a genuine effort.

It then required us to bring what we had to move it forward; she made space for our unique offering to take the lesson to the next step. In this situation both teacher and children had autonomy (read Leisa's contribution in the final section of this book).

It was from here that I began to develop self-belief. I gained confidence and slowly began to try new challenges (this came in my late 20s, the damage was deep). I still lacked belief and checked out in maths lessons. I felt unable to access much of the academic learning but at least I now had a period a week where I was doing something I enjoyed and felt good at. Over time this enabled me to develop my self-esteem across the curriculum (had drama been timetabled more maybe the process of recovery would have worked quicker). At age 26 I retook my maths General Certificate of Secondary Education – I originally got an E and at 26 received an A. This proved to me that I was capable but the environment I had been in had made learning impossible.

I do not deny the importance of academic attainment, but it's essential to note the current unfortunate separating of academic attainment from creativity, pastoral and holistic care. They need each other and should not be detached. We need leaders who genuinely see and believe this – without their belief bad habits are born in our staff teams. In the past I have received feedback from staff on wellbeing initiatives to tell me that the focus on mental health was taking away from other lessons or SLT members telling me to cancel the one art lesson I have in the week for a booster maths session – we need to develop an understanding of the intrinsic link between both academic and creative approaches.

Creativity

When I was at school I wasn't naturally gifted at the "academic subjects". My secondary school was in the middle of a transition – an "inadequate" label meant lots of change, cracking down and reinforcing rules and rigour. No blazers off in the sweltering heat and maths and literacy were at the very top of the subject hierarchy. In year 9, my SATs results in maths were low – they used these results to stream us and so I got "moved down" a class. This was both humiliating and upsetting. I was lucky that in my new "lower class" I found my people, friends that would turn out to be lifelong allies. Despite my strong friendships I never really got over the humiliation of being moved down a class and my self-esteem took a hit that would barely recover; I am still working on it.

The curriculum's narrow focus on success means that a lot of us are failing in its eyes. It fails to notice the individual talents – the budding illustrator who is obsessed with doodling on their book, the child who enjoys reading graphic novels and yes, *only* graphic novels, the year 6 child who struggles with writing but who has no role-play area to consolidate their learning in a way suitable for them. Teachers are under too much pressure to strictly follow directives, rather than allowing children the freedom to explore their interests and develop their creative strengths.

It isn't about adding another hour of drama in – it is about a shift in perspective – a rebalancing – a genuine realisation that drama *is* just as important as maths. I am not a strong mathematician, for many reasons – it did not come to me naturally and my teachers gave up on me quite early on – I gave them no reason (good data perhaps) for them to stick with me. Having to retake my maths GCSE at 26 tells us everything about the importance of self-esteem. At 26, I had begun to do some of the much-needed work on self-belief through the creative arts. It was then that I could fully apply myself to this academic subject.

If we continue with the heavy focus on a very limited number of subjects, then we will continue to fail thousands of children. As Sir Jim Knight said in the Lord's debate

> "…this narrow focus is failing at least a third of our children and disproportionately the disadvantaged" (Knight, J. Lord's debate, 2024).

Flexibility and innovation

When teachers have autonomy, we feel better equipped to share it with the children. To facilitate the flourishing of autonomy we need to learn to be flexible. This is not something that comes easy when we have been trained to follow policy and systems rigidly. Being mindful as to how and why we are responding in any given moment in education really helps to develop the ability to challenge our own thinking.

Let's list the things a child might currently find difficult to do freely in many schools:

- Move around/fidget
- Daydream
- Sit up on their knees during carpet time
- Go to the toilet
- Wear comfortable clothes
- Be outside
- Find space and quiet
- Speak
- Collaborate
- Drink water
- Use a pen (pen licenses are a solid no-go for me!)
- Ask questions
- Sit with their friends
- Take breaks

If a child fidgets on the carpet, what is your response? Do you trust that they need to move and give them the autonomy over their own movement, or do you shut it down as quickly as possible? After all, you have that rule up on the board showing that they need to sit still (and it's laminated, so you can't go back on it!?) Do you get children to walk silently in perfect lines throughout the setting because that's in your school policy? It's what you have always done, so you continue with more of the same. Or do you allow some sensible movement that doesn't always look completely neat, but it's safe and harmless? Do you allow some quiet chatting in the corridor as you recognise the importance of social connection? Recognition that even as adults when we are moving around the setting will chat to one another - it's only natural right?

We must start to question our inflexibilities and wonder who they are serving? If it's for any of the following reasons, then perhaps it's time to shake things up:

- Your own sense of control.
- You have always done it that way.
- Your policy states that it should be done that way.

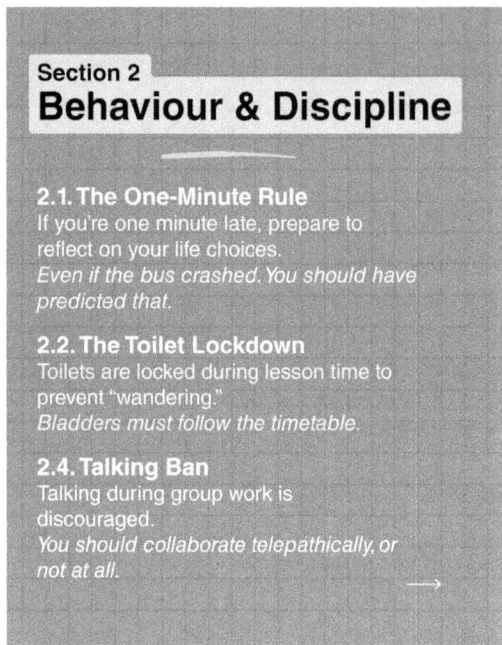

Figure 4.6 Are your rules helping or holding you all back? Behaviour and Discipline. Sally Michaels

It's time to allow the children the autonomy to decide what *they need* at any given moment – whether that be needing the toilet, a sip from their water bottle, a fidget on their bottom or to whisper to their friend in front of them in the line – with this trust comes respect and a real connection.

Be bold, brave and innovative – it could really pay off in the long term and offer real solutions for a lack of school engagement and attendance and instil a love of being in a safe and mutually respectful environment, one where children feel heard, valued and trusted.

Democratic schools

Democratic schools are institutions that offer children and staff the opportunity to exercise autonomy and self-directed learning. Together the pupils and staff make decisions on how the school is run and the content of the teaching and learning. One of the more well-known democratic schools is The Awen Project, founded by singer Charlotte Church. Charlotte founded The Awen Project in a bid to "transform education" (TheAwenProject.com). The Awen Project states "We do not follow any exam curriculum for traditional subjects, however if students decide that they would like to study for a GCSE or other qualification then they will be supported as part of self-directed learning". The videos on their website show children speaking of being heard, understood and being prepared for flexibility and creativity, required in later life (TheAwenProject.com).

Another democratic school is SML Brighton – a college for self-managed learning developed to respond to the frustrations of mainstream schooling. This school "encourages curiosity and inquisitiveness and helps students learn how to manage their time, stay focused, and explore in greater detail the areas that they are passionate about" (SMLCollege.org.uk).

Although there are many children who get through mainstream education with minor scrapes, there are also a great deal of children who are disengaged and unhappy at school. Schools that require long hours, a timetable decided by others, a hierarchical structure and a behaviourist approach – the pressurised environment is just too much.

Democratic schools lie somewhere in between home and mainstream schooling – offering the structure and social benefits of traditional education but providing the freedom, flexibility and self-direction of home-schooling. Unfortunately, there is not a wealth of democratic schools in the UK. Perhaps utilising the skills of democratic school staff teams and employing the democratic school set-up and structure in our state education system could help us to make progress towards a more successful and autonomous learning model.

Behaviour

When teachers are under pressure they are less likely to be able to show patience, understanding and compassion. With limits on time and a packed curriculum, teachers can feel there is no time to coach the behaviour for communication that comes up regularly, especially after a break or lunch time. Following a lunch break, you find you are surrounded by many children sharing a range of conflicts and challenges they have faced during their 45 minutes in the playground. Teachers become aware of the ticking clock and the lesson content they need to cover – it feels impossible to be compassionate and thorough at this moment. This does not mean teachers are intentionally being neglectful, but the pressures of the system are stealing what could be valuable emotional learning opportunities.

Mossbourne Academy in Hackney has come under scrutiny for its dated and punitive behaviour techniques – it is "accused of bullying and damaging children's mental health as local authority asked to step in" with teachers having been accused of shouting and humiliating children. One parent stated, "There is this cookie-cutter mentality. They don't care if it destroys your child" (Fazackerley, 2024). Having previously written a blog piece on my visits to secondary schools for my son, that received a lot of attention and feedback, it seems this kind of damaging behaviourist approach is commonplace. Problems such as not being able to go to the toilet and the use of isolation booths in response to "high fiving" in the corridor show us that we are reacting to behaviour rather than asking why. Rather than ban going to the toilet, why not make the lessons engaging enough that children don't want to leave (and if they actually *do* need to go, then let's let them go). Rather than stop "high fiving" in the corridor – let's learn about consent and boundaries and when it is appropriate to "high five". Utilising autonomy, rather than putting in place blanket rules and policies, would enable us to respond to each conflict individually, case-by-case. Let's not forget the biggest barrier here – time (let's slim down that curriculum!).

Behaviour and Education Specialist, Adele Bates, says that "What they want is the autonomy to use the right tool in the right context, something they can't do in an intransigent system, one that is fuelled by the fear of adults and children alike" (Bates, 2023. P. 210). When I work with parents on the challenging behaviour they are experiencing at home, I always ask them about the outcome that they are hoping for. Do they want their children to do what they say, or do they want their children to connect with them, feel safe and develop their emotional literacy, taking these skills into their adulthood? With a punitive and rewards-driven motivation, life can be pretty straightforward - we are in control, and we can scare children into doing what we want them to do. The other option is harder, but it helps shape a person who can self-regulate, understands and embraces their emotions, is resilient, can take risks without fear of failure, develop self-compassion, and has respect for others and a readiness to learn.

Educator experience - Creativity

Berrin S. Bates. Art Teacher and Art Therapist. Inner London Primary.

After 30 years of teaching art and working as an Art Therapist, I've seen it all. And let me tell you, our education system desperately needs a complete overhaul. I'm not just concerned - I'm deeply worried about the future of our children, especially those who are neurodivergent. We're failing them, and it's time we acknowledge it and do something about it!

The magic of arts and creativity

I've witnessed firsthand the transformative power of the arts in education. It's not just about painting pretty pictures - it's about giving children a voice, a way to express themselves when words fail them. Visual arts, music, drama - these aren't luxuries, they're necessities! They build confidence, spark joy, and offer a lifeline to children who might otherwise feel lost in the system. I've seen quiet, struggling students blossom into confident individuals through the power of creativity. It's nothing short of magical!

Breaking out of the box

For heaven's sake, why are we still trying to fit all children into the same mould? It's madness! We're seeing more children than ever starting school with attention deficit hyperactivity disorder (ADHD), autism spectrum disorder, anxiety and developmental delays. And what do we do? We try to squeeze them into a system that wasn't designed for them. It's like trying to force a square peg into a round hole - it's frustrating for everyone and damaging to the child. Schools are not factories, and children are not products on an assembly line!

Teachers need freedom!

Our teachers are amazing, but they're being stifled. The curriculum is like a straitjacket, limiting their ability to adapt and be creative. I've been incredibly lucky in my career - OFSTED left me alone once they saw the incredible artwork my students produced. But not every teacher has that freedom. We're burning out our best educators by micromanaging them. Give them autonomy, give them support and watch them work wonders!

The neurodiversity crisis

I am extremely concerned – no, I'm honestly heartbroken – about what's happening to our neurodiverse children. They're being pushed aside, their families are struggling and help is scarce. As an Art Therapist, I see these children's needs going unaddressed in schools. It's not the fault of headteachers or teachers – it's a systemic failure. We need to embrace neurodiversity, not try to "fix" it. These children have incredible gifts if only we'd take the time to understand and nurture them!

Confidence is everything!

I can't stress this enough – confidence is the key to everything in life! How can we expect children to achieve anything if they don't believe in themselves? And how can they gain confidence if they're constantly reminded that they're not "good enough" by our rigid education system? It's a recipe for failure and lifelong struggles. We need to build children up, not tear them down!

The power of expression

Visual arts, music, drama – these aren't just subjects, they're lifelines! They give children a chance to express themselves in different ways, to find their strengths, to shine! I've seen shy children come alive on stage, troubled kids find peace with a paintbrush and struggling students excel in music. These experiences are priceless – they build confidence, self-esteem, and a love for learning that lasts a lifetime.

A call for radical change

We need to change our education system entirely – and I mean entirely! We need to:

1. embrace creativity and arts across all subjects.
2. celebrate neurodiversity instead of trying to "correct" it.
3. give teachers the freedom and support they desperately need.
4. focus on building confidence and emotional well-being in every child.
5. recognise that each child is unique and valuable, not a problem to be solved.

I am passionate about children's emotional well-being because they are our future. It's not just a nice idea – it's crucial for the survival and success of our society. We need to treat each child as the most important thing in the world because, guess what? They are!

It's time for a revolution in education. We need to create schools where every child can thrive, where creativity is celebrated, where teachers are empowered and where the joy of learning is at the heart of everything we do. Our children deserve nothing less. Let's make it happen!

It's time to pause.

Reflection

- Do I have a flexible timetable?
- Do I believe the creative subjects have equal weighting in my school?
- Are the creative and foundation subjects always the first to be cancelled when something else needs a space?
- Do I always teach maths and english in the morning?
- Am I able to listen to my children and follow their interests?
- How am I currently managing behaviour for communication?
- Do I use a restorative and compassionate behaviour model?

Get autonomy back

In the classroom:

- Try to get more creativity into your lessons - question the need for worksheets and "book work" - can you get the children up and experiencing their learning more often?
- Move away from slides when you can, get the children up and moving!
- Request relevant professional learning.
- Show the children that you have genuine care for the creative and foundation subjects by placing them in different parts of your day including the morning.
- Within a comfortable window try to instil a flexible approach to your learning and timetable - if a child wants to learn more about Rosa Parks, why can't you spend a bit longer on her?
- Avoid a punitive and rewards-based behaviour system - red cards, clouds, rainbows, traffic lights give the wrong message when a child is trying to communicate their feelings.

For senior leaders:

- Allow your staff the flexibility within their planning and timetables to get creative.
- Ensure you model, develop and embed an equal respect for the foundation and creative subjects. This can be done through timetabling, resourcing, partnerships and professional learning. It is also communicated through TLR pay scales - paying your maths and literacy leads more than your art and wellbeing leads speaks volumes!
- Reflect on your current behaviour policy and training for staff. Does it react to behaviour or seek to understand the feelings behind it?

For government officials:

- Slim down the curriculum.
- Remove all the testing on maths and literacy - this will make space for a broad, balanced and interesting curriculum.

- Find funding for more democratic schools or bring more of this model into mainstream schools.
- Ensure that teacher training includes a module on a relational approach to behaviour so that we can remove the current "luck of the draw" behaviour policies.

Final thought on defining success

For all of my childhood and most of my 20s, I was defined by my failure to meet the academic expectations of my school years. I managed to scrape through, but it was painful and exhausting. Many will not scrape through, leaving them with little to no self-esteem and when given the chance to be autonomous, unable to grasp it. Much of the school day is directed towards outcomes rather than process – pen licences, spelling tests, mock SATs and assessments, writing in books to summarise what children have learned, worksheets and homework. Proving yourself has become the education model for children and staff. It is time we gave back control to the kids and had some fun!

THE BIG IDEA - Impacts on Children

Tina Farr. Headteacher. St. Ebbes Primary. Oxford.

> *All I wanted was to be trusted. It's palpable in your communication that you trust us. It's rare I think.*
>
> *(St. Ebbe's Teacher)*

Teachers at St. Ebbe's feel autonomous and they can't help but flourish. The skill of shaping the learning in response to the young people in front of them is the very essence of being a teacher. When we create cultures of fear of being "told off" for non-compliance, we strip teachers of their very essence. I have seen teachers, through no fault of their own, bring this fearful state to the classroom environment, jumping up if a senior leader enters the room and negatively impacting the way children feel about school and their own creativity and imagination.

When teachers sense deep trust, they can't help but bring this to the children in their classrooms. Teachers at St. Ebbe's are seen, heard and loved by our leadership team; they replicate this in their classrooms. Often in schools, the answer is "no" to curious questions or ideas from staff and children; we work in a rigid way, stemming from control, which stifles creativity. At St. Ebbe's, the answer is "yes" or "let's try it and see", unless what is requested absolutely can't be. Our minds are open to new possibilities, and the atmosphere is one of aliveness and growth, of generating learning together.

Each of our projects has an overarching philosophical question that encompasses the different subject areas: how do our beliefs shape our actions? Is success the same for everyone? Spending time engaging with these questions gives teachers and children the opportunity to share, generate and accept different viewpoints. The floor is open for discussion, and no one yet knows what they will learn from and about each other. These questions work because our teachers have the autonomy to shape the projects in

> response to the children's contributions. For example, our Stone Age Project, Do we need art and why? prompted such moving and varied responses from the children that their teacher shaped her teaching of writing around them, abandoning her previous plan. The National Curriculum objectives she'd intended were still covered, but everyone was way more invested in the process than they would have been if she'd stuck rigidly to her original idea. She didn't need to check with me either. The writing outcomes were out of this world. Had she been delivering a pre-written scheme of work for English, this option wouldn't have been available, and the magic of this writing would have been lost.
>
> When a curriculum is tightly planned by someone else, teachers become only conveyors of knowledge. The joy that is possible in a classroom is lost because the pressure is on to stick rigidly to the scheme of work. Schemes of work are by their very nature, generic. They do have useful bits for us to pick and choose from and may provide a coherent structure for long-term coverage of the National Curriculum, but they should not dictate all of the content.
>
> When there is space for the teacher to shape the learning in response to the curiosities of the young people in front of them, they begin to learn with the children. They move from "knower" to fellow "learner". Information is exchanged and built on. Excitement is palpable, and the room comes alive with the joy of discovery.

Contributors

1. Peter Gray. Research Professor of Psychology and Neuroscience at Boston College.
2. Woody. Year 6 Child. Inner London Primary.
3. Livia. Year 11 Child. Inner London Secondary.
4. Berrin S. Bates. Art Teacher and Art Therapist. Inner London Primary.
5. Tina Farr. Headteacher. St. Ebbes Primary. Oxford.

References

Ali, M. 2023. School Uniforms: A Ploy for Conformity. The Manor. https://scadmanor.com/school-uniforms-a-ploy-for-conformity/

Bates, A. 2023. P. 210. Square Pegs. Crown House.

Bodycote, B. 2023. P. 38. Square Pegs. Crown House Publishing.

Bradbury, A. et al. Mar 2025. Play Matters. Early Years Reviews. https://www.early-years-reviews.com/_files/ugd/c871c5_37c8d65a5d6c4f6a981edbb3a0e6310b.pdf

Cowley, A. 2021. P. 23. The Wellbeing Curriculum. Bloomsbury.

Cowley, A. 2021. P. 137. The Wellbeing Curriculum. Bloomsbury.

Cowley, S.X. 4 May 2024. https://x.com/Sue_Cowley/status/1786846208708813212?t=_pfT_sdTWgvvDxtVRuKaFA&s=19

Department for Education. Nov 2019. P. 7. Character Education Framework Guidance. https://assets.publishing.service.gov.uk/media/5f20087fe90e07456b18abfc/Character_Education_Framework_Guidance.pdf

Department for Education. 2024. Children's Wellbeing and Schools Bill 2024: Policy Summary. https://www.gov.uk/government/publications/childrens-wellbeing-and-schools-bill-2024-policy-summary

Department for Education. Autumn 2024/25. Elective Home Education. https://explore-education-statistics.service.gov.uk/find-statistics/elective-home-education

Department for Education. 2025. Pupil Attendance in Schools. https://explore-education-statistics.service.gov.uk/find-statistics/pupil-attendance-in-schools/2025-week-12

Education Endowment Foundation. July 2021. School Uniform. Unclear Impact for Very Low Cost Based on Insufficient Evidence. https://educationendowmentfoundation.org.uk/education-evidence/teaching-learning-toolkit/school-uniform

Farr, T. 2025. LinkedIn. https://www.linkedin.com/posts/tina-farr-8667952bb_childhood-education-autonomy-activity-7312157699729698816-CMbj?utm_source=share&utm_medium=member_desktop&rcm=ACoAADSiNDcBj6IHrVTzfMCqlFDtXZiC7GP959s

Fazackerley, A. 2024. Teachers at Top Academy in Hackney 'Screamed at' and Humiliated Pupils, Say Angry Parents. The Guardian. https://www.theguardian.com/education/2024/nov/23/teachers-at-mossbourne-academy-in-hackney-screamed-at-and-humiliated-pupils-say-angry-parents?s=09

Fisher, J. 2 May 2016. Nursery World. EYFS Best Practice - All about...interactions.

Freud, A. 10 January 2025. Our response to the new Children's Wellbeing and Schools Bill. https://www.annafreud.org/news/our-response-to-the-new-childrens-wellbeing-and-schools-bill/

Gosling, M. 2025. P. 120. Teenagers: The Evidence Base. Swift Press.

Gray, P. 2013. P. 16. Free to Learn. Basic Books.

Khawaja, J and Bagley, C. 8 November 2024. Breaking the Silence. https://www.bps.org.uk/psychologist/breaking-silence

Knight, J. 2024. Lords debate. https://www.linkedin.com/posts/jimpknight_today-i-enjoyed-taking-part-in-the-lords-activity-7222605013171249154-oTD2?utm_source=share&utm_medium=member_desktop)

Meikle, J. 27 February 2012. The Guardian. https://www.theguardian.com/education/2012/feb/27/gove-schools-history-revamp

Not Fine in School. 2025. Facebook. https://www.facebook.com/groups/NFISFamilySupport/

Popoola, M., Sivers, S., Hooper, R. and Ahad, A. 2023. Young Peoples' Views on Mental Health. A Report. https://drive.google.com/file/d/1vdxravNG6MVNzhD_M3b4GMbJjRIvwWCZ/view

Ramanujan, S. https://en.wikipedia.org/wiki/Srinivasa_Ramanujan

Robinson, K. and Robinson, K. 2022. P. 57. Imagine If... Penguin.

SML College. Brighton https://smlcollege.org.uk/

States of Mind. September 2016. Reimagining Education by Breaking the Silence. https://www.statesofmind.org/journal/2020/09/16/students-ofsted-open-letter.html

The Awen Project. Founded by Charlotte Church. https://www.theawenproject.com/

The Children's Society. 2024. P. 52. The Good Childhood Report. https://www.childrenssociety.org.uk/what-we-do/our-work/well-being/mental-health-statistics

Tickle, L. and Ratcliffe, R. 22 July 2014. The Guardian. https://www.theguardian.com/education/2014/jul/22/michael-gove-legacy-education-secretary

Worth, J. and Van den Brande, J. 29 January 2020. P. 12. Teacher Autonomy: How Does It Relate to Job Satisfaction and Retention? NFER. https://www.nfer.ac.uk/publications/teacher-autonomy-how-does-it-relate-to-job-satisfaction-and-retention/

5 Digital autonomy

If men learn this (writing), it will implant forgetfulness in their souls; they will cease to exercise memory because they rely on that which is written, calling things to remembrance no longer from within themselves, but by means of external marks.

(Plato. Phaedrus. Page 275. 370 BC)

Chapter 5 outline

In this chapter, we will explore:

- Artificial Intelligence (AI) in teaching and think about how we navigate both trust and autonomy in our use of AI.
- AI and efficiency – how we might use it to save time.
- how using AI may be the cause of further workload.
- educator use of social media.
- phone use in the classroom for educators and children.
- the use of smart boards in education.
- creativity and technology.

The digital age and autonomy

Isn't it funny that Plato had the above view on the introduction of writing? It mirrors the fear many feel about technology. In the early stages of writing this book, ChatGPT entered our lives and with it, a whole new chapter was born (not written by AI, I promise!). This chapter dips into autonomy in our digital worlds as educators. My own personal shortfalls with technology and the speed at which it moves mean that this chapter is just an introduction to a complex but necessary topic – brief but hopefully thought-provoking, it aims to facilitate further reflection and conversation in this area, perhaps providing more questions than solutions at this point.

Now, as you now know, I am a fan of autonomy, but handing over autonomy within technology scares me a little. This is likely down to my awkwardness around it and the media's obsession with the damage it might do. I am not anti-tech, nor do I believe that it should be used with complete freedom. I am aware that it can be detrimental to a person's mental health when misused. Being a Millennial parent of Gen Alpha children, I suffer from anxieties around my children's use of tech. I do not take decisions around tech use in the home or at school lightly - research is still very much incoming so I always err on the side of caution and try to read as much as I can when making decisions. I decided not to allow my children to have their own iPads, or a computer console in their early years. We have recently invested in a games console (they are currently 8 and 11), but with an agreement that we drew up together as a family stipulating its use. My children do not currently have access to social media. It is important to me to hear their voice, and I value their input as to how our family approaches technology, after all, my experience of it will differ greatly from theirs. The decisions we have made as a family are, of course, personal decisions and ever evolving. I would not expect every family to do the same. As parents we feel judged on our digital decisions - everyone has a strong opinion on how bad or good technology (and in particular screens) is without having reams of longitudinal research to back it up. It is important that children do not develop a fear of technology which can be instigated by a "clamping down" without conversation. Schools and families must try to listen to one another rather than dictate rules and boundaries (within safeguarding parameters). Autonomy in this area is as important as autonomy anywhere else.

In the early years human connection is of particular importance - during a talk with a large group of Key Stage 2 (KS2) children, when asked which communities they belonged to they continuously referred to online gaming and social media communities - they found it near impossible to share in-person communities that they were part of (despite school being one of the most obvious). Building online relationships is a huge part of our children's lives but in my mind for every minute spent on a screen there is a minute of human connection lost. On the other hand, for those who find socialising challenging and therefore are isolated, every minute spent online can be a minute more of connection.

This chapter hasn't been written to advise people on their child's screen use or to contemplate how the education system should tackle the technology challenges we face. It instead seeks to explore and ask questions on a topic that we currently have very little understanding of. How much autonomy do we currently have over our use of technology in schools, and what do we predict for the future freedoms in this area? It is much more complex than previous chapters as it navigates a whole safeguarding and wellbeing protection issue. How do we balance autonomy and our duty of care?

It is likely that by the time this book is released, technology and the educational landscape will have changed yet again with the Department for Education (DfE) stating that they will "take up this great new technological era to modernise our education system, back our teachers and deliver for our children" (DfE, 2025). Modernising our education system is what is required but how does this integrate technology, and will it make space for autonomy?

AI in education

AI has been in our lives for a while now - in the form of AI-powered machines, systems that check our spelling and grammar, voice assistants and biometrics but the introduction of generative AI is groundbreaking and has the potential to change educator's lives and offer unique experiences for children's learning. In August 2024, Teacher Tapp noted an increase in AI use with more than half of teachers using a chatbot for schoolwork, and more than one in ten as a tool in a lesson (Teacher Tapp, 2024). The Department for Education is dedicating one million pounds to create and develop AI tools to support teachers in their daily tasks, such as assessment and marking (DfE, 2025).

Schools are still very much in the exploratory phase of AI use with little to no training and existing policy around its use – the arrival of topical publications being inevitable with the rollout of a new curriculum. Depending on an individual's personal experiences with AI, staff will use it in a variety of ways with some not even knowing it exists at all. I currently use a chatbot tool for a few of my teacher tasks – writing a section of the school newsletter has become a task that takes 10/15 minutes instead of 30/40 minutes – after all the school newsletter isn't a vehicle to prove my creative writing skills, it is merely a way to hand over information to parent/carers – something that AI can do a lot more efficiently and clearly than I can. Using AI to write reports is now a commonly available tool with big education publishing houses and organisations offering this service/feature. The government Education Hub states that "teachers can use AI to help with things like planning lessons, creating resources, marking work, giving feedback and handling administrative tasks. But they need to use their professional judgement and check that anything AI generates is accurate and appropriate– the final responsibility always rests with them and their school" (DfE, 2025). The freedom to use it as we see fit is welcomed but autonomy cannot thrive in conditions where staff are ill-equipped – letting us "get on with it" without the necessary training is irresponsible, unfair and sets us up to fail. Using AI to help with workload should be an option for everyone, and training would ensure equity of opportunity.

With unregulated and unsupported use, we may stumble across some problems. Author Laura Bates states that AI is "regurgitating the harms and inequalities inherent within the material they have gobbled – vomiting our racism and sexism and class inequality back at us" (Bates, 2025). AI has been trained on information that already exists, and what exists is inevitably biased. This becomes problematic when you are using it to inform your teaching or for children using it in their learning. However, the solutions may lie in AI itself with the option of additional chatbot prompts to consider potential biases – the opportunities seem endless. Schools must reflect upon whether

a) their staff are trained in utilising AI effectively and safely, and
b) they have assigned a computing lead to keep up and share the ever-changing landscape of AI.

There has been an influx of AI consultants who will provide schools with the knowledge and skills they require to use it effectively and in time. I expect policy on AI technology to become more detailed and robust. With technology being a specialist topic, teacher training may need to do more to equip teachers with the right tools in order that they are given autonomy in this area. This has the potential to cause fear which may result in tightening controls.

Despite there being many predictions about the future of AI, nobody *really* knows what lies ahead. As it currently stands, AI requires input from humans but at some point, AI will be able to gain context from what it can hear and see and help us *without* our input. How might that look? Imagine that you are wearing a pair of glasses that can guide you through interactions

The UK education system—"THE FINEST IN THE WORLD" (snort) is GRINDING young people through a machine that was built for a world that no longer exists. Industrial revolution thinking in a POST-HUMAN INTELLIGENCE world. The Victorian classroom still lives – except now it has interactive whiteboards and 50-page safeguarding audits.

STILL BASICALLY THIS but now with Chromebooks. BUILD STUFF, DAMMIT!!

This cow is more future-ready. That's the bar

Kids are more likely to learn REAL-WORLD AI SKILLS from TikTok hacks or YouTube speed-runs of ChatGPT prompts than from the curriculum. We still havent given teachers the time or trust to redesign learning around curiosity, autonomy, OR PLAY. We talk about future jobs, but we don't LET THEM PRACTISE BEING FUTURE HUMANS.

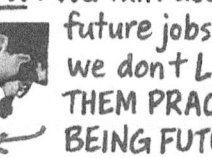

65% of today's students will work in jobs that don't yet exist.

Do they look ready to shape the future or just survive it.

COOL. SO WHY ARE WE TEACHING THEM LIKE 1993?

WE'VE GOT IT BACKWARDS.
- Real AI readiness is about ethics.
- About learning how to learn.
- Asking better questions.
- About building tools, not just them.
- About knowing when NOT to auto-
- About being more human, not less.

TEACH WONDER.
TEACH POWER.
TEACH NOW.

Until we STOP.CLINGING TO THE PAST like it's some holy script and START DESIGNING FOR THE FUTURE THAT'S ALREADY HERE, we're

Figure 5.1 "ChatGPT – Write a monologue of your real thoughts on the current UK education system and how it is preparing young people for future careers in an AI world." Words and image from Chris Goodall on LinkedIn. 2025

in the classroom; AI can signal that a child is showing signs of dysregulation and reminds you of effective strategies you have previously used with this individual. From 2025, mandatory training will be in place for teachers on how to use assistive technology to support children with special educational needs and disabilities (SEND). In terms of supporting inclusive teaching practice, AI could really help - it has the ability to make adaptations on all of the lessons it (or you) creates and not just three ways but 30 ways, and pretty effortlessly. I do however worry about the loss of heart in teaching - if it wasn't for the current pressures, accountability measures and bureaucracy, would we even need AI? I like to think that without the unachievable expectations we would be teaching from the heart - with compassion, humility and empathy. Will AI just make room for more work, or will it make room for the soul?

> **Educator experience - Autonomy, technology and the future of work in education**
>
> **Lucy Lewin. Founder of The Profitable Nursery Academy.**
>
> There's a shift happening and it's louder than many want to admit. I see it in my own children, in the teams I lead, and in the early years leaders I coach. Younger generations are no longer content with "just doing the job". They crave meaning, certainty and impact, and they are willing to walk away if they do not get it.
>
> This is not laziness or entitlement. I believe it is clarity. A generation raised with dopamine loops and instant access to information has a low tolerance for poor leadership, outdated systems or doing something simply because "that's how it's always been". They challenge the status quo, speak truth to power and value alignment over obligation. It is not that they won't work hard, it's that they won't work pointlessly.
>
> In contrast, many early years leaders are burnt out. They are firefighting daily, mistaking being busy for being productive. Pride is lost in the chaos. Autonomy fades when the job becomes about surviving, not leading. And leadership, especially in education, can feel deeply lonely. There is often a conflict between head and heart, between what we believe matters and what the system demands. Fear of getting it wrong, of letting people down, of change itself keeps people stuck.
>
> This is where technology can be transformational. AI, automation and systems do not steal autonomy, they restore it. Just like tractors did not remove farmers, they changed how humans worked, technology gives us back time. It takes the weight of repetitive tasks and allows space for creativity, relationships and strategic thought. The gift is freedom if we are brave enough to accept it.
>
> This is where systems matter. Not bureaucracy, real systems. The kind that takes pressure off instead of piling it on. Systems give structure to autonomy. They hold the weight of the repetitive, the operational, the overwhelming so that people can show up as thinkers, leaders and learners. When designed well, systems do not constrain us, they free us.
>
> Yet the greatest barrier is not tech. It is our mindset. Finite thinking, where we need infinite thinking. Leaders who see the next generation as difficult rather than

> discerning. Institutions that fear change more than they fear irrelevance. If we want to prepare children for a future that's already here, we have to model autonomy, not just preach it.
>
> A human-first future is possible. One where people lead with purpose, supported by smart systems. Where autonomy is not earned through burnout, it is built and embedded by design. Where education, leadership and work feel like something to be proud of again.
>
> This is not a pipe dream. It is a pivot, and it starts with us.

It's time to pause.

Reflection

- Do I believe that AI could provide us with more autonomy?
- Have I thought about how AI could enhance my teaching and learning?
- What AI do I currently use in school?
- How do I feel about using AI?
- Do I want to learn more about using AI at work?
- Would I feel comfortable sharing my concerns about using AI?
- Do I shut down the use of AI due to fear of the unknown?
- How do I feel about the environmental impact of AI use?

Get autonomy back

In the classroom:

- Find freedom in your use of AI – learn about General Data Protection Regulation (GDPR) and how you can safely use AI without breaching data privacy and be mindful of biases when using AI to provide lesson plans and creative experiences.
- Ask for help – "I am bad with computers" is a common phrase in our workforce, and being honest about how uncomfortable you feel can be embarrassing – speak to someone you trust in your team and request training.
- Request collaboration on your school approach to AI to ensure you are being heard and able to present the challenges you face in the classroom.
- Avoid feeling pressured to use AI – it should be a choice.

For senior leaders:

- Assign a member of staff to lead and share technology advancements (and give them time to do so).
- Create a working group that has representatives from across your setting so that you get a detailed picture of experiences across the school.

- Encourage staff to share how they're using AI to help their daily working lives with one another.
- Protect your teacher's autonomy by being transparent with parents about your trust in your team, your approach, and the training you provide.
- Keep in touch with your staff members - do they need training to utilise AI effectively to manage workloads and complete tasks?
- Create an open and non-judgmental culture where staff members can be vulnerable and honest about their struggles with AI.
- Provide time for regular meetings and staff training to keep up with the constant changes in tech.
- Arrange for staff to visit schools that are experts in this area. Autonomy cannot thrive without confidence, knowledge and skills.
- Avoid "clamping down" on teacher autonomy in this area - seek to understand so that teachers can find their feet with AI.
- Be flexible - some staff members may not want to use AI. Be curious and hear them out.

For government officials:

- Broaden the training that trainee teachers receive - not just in assistive technologies but in AI use for daily teaching life too.
- Support parents in their technology learning - this will ensure the messages are consistent across school communities and we feel able to roam autonomously with protection in place.

Final thought on AI

Making space for reflecting on our intentions with AI is extremely important. AI has the potential to make many tasks easier, but easy isn't *always* the best way - we need to learn through facing challenges, making mistakes and having conversations. We must use our humility to scan and review if AI is being a useful tool or if it is replacing our humanness. I am also acutely aware that in education there is the potential for AI to increase workloads with senior leaders seeing it as a way to *squeeze more in*, but I prefer to think that AI will help us deliver on the education revolution - with it, we might finally find the time to get autonomy back.

Screens

> 69% of children spend more than two hours a day on a device.
> **(Hazel Shearing. BBC News. 10 April 2025)**

Screen use can take away from time interacting with others and for young children, this comes at a time when the brain is forming connections and making huge leaps which could be detrimental to their development. Scientists have found that children need real-life experiences to develop empathy, build focus and control impulses (UNICEF). With screen time research still incoming, teachers are not equipped to support and develop a child's autonomous use of tech with confidence.

As a teacher, I use a smartboard and sometimes we use it to watch relevant content such as Dough Disco for hand muscle development or the odd topical show, but I do not see it as my right to add to screen time unnecessarily when children are having long periods of time on screens at home. Approaches to screens are likely to vary between teachers; a strong school ethos will determine a consistent and research-led approach with an allowance for each teacher to respond with professional judgement.

Phones

I am not allowed to have my phone with me in class. There are not many jobs where this is the case, and it is a privilege not to be tied to my phone for a huge chunk of my day. It means I am focused on the present moment rather than looking for distraction. It means I connect with the children in my care. I do, however, know of schools that trust teachers to have their phones in the classroom with them, where they can read emails, contact colleagues in other rooms and take photos. I was surprised to learn that only "4% primary teachers and 1% of secondary teachers work in schools where mobile phones cannot be taken into the classroom and must be locked away during the day" (Teacher Tapp, 2025). Is this autonomy or a level of trust that places employees and children at risk?

As much as I advocate for autonomy, it is our duty to free children from devices during their school day unless it is enhancing a learning experience, which can only be decided by the adults and in certain circumstances the children they are working with. Children and young people will find the prevalence of peer pressure (and fixations) outweigh their understanding of the impacts of device use on their mental health and wellbeing. Headteachers have been given the autonomy to make decisions on phone use in schools in the UK with Dame Rachel de Souza stating that she would support any headteacher's choice as it would be "based on their knowledge of what's best for the children in their own classrooms, not a direction imposed nationally by the government"(Shearing, 2025). Many argue that a national ban would help to get parents on side and ensure consistency. I welcome Rachel De Souza's trust in headteachers and would advise all local authorities and senior leaders to speak to not only those working in class with the children but also the children themselves - what are their experiences? What support do they need? Teacher Tapp has done just that with educators and found that "70% of primary teachers in schools that allow phones say they'd prefer a complete ban" and "in secondary schools, that jumps to 82% who want phones banned altogether" (Teacher Tapp, 2025). I wonder what the data exploring children's opinions on this would suggest? Should we be asking them? I'm not sure if adults banning phones altogether aligns with child autonomy.

Social media

> 51% of primary schools and 53% of secondary schools now have a social media policy.
> **(Teacher Tapp, 2025)**

The recently published book, *The Anxious Generation* by Jonathan Haidt and the Netflix drama series *Adolescence* have both been catalysts for further exploration (and panic) regarding social media use. How much is too much? What age is the right age? Where should they be using their devices? Should it be allowed in school? The hysteria these relentless questions can cause often prompts reaction rather than considered response. The latest reaction being every teenager needing to watch Adolescence (Netflix has announced that the drama will be available to all UK secondary schools). Another sticking plaster rather than investigating and tackling deeper-rooted problems.

Staff social media guidelines are now usually part of a school's online policy and contract. Should teachers be told how they can and can't use their personal social media accounts? I have already spoken about teachers being mistakenly viewed as public property – does the freedom to use social media accounts unrestricted leave teachers vulnerable? Even when accounts are used for educational content, teachers can find themselves victim to silencing or judgement. It was only last year that independent education consultant, Ruth Swailes, went to media outlets following a subject access request (SAR) to the DfE. The SAR revealed that the DfE held information on all of her social media posts (which politely and professionally questioned the DfE's initiatives). The DfE then used this information to place barriers between Ruth and the work she was offered through her consultancy business (Dearden, 2024). If we choose to speak openly about our work on social media, will we be silenced?

When it comes to your personal life and the sharing of locations, nights out, relationships, etc. then in a protective vein, I think boundaries need to be collaboratively created. It should be a team effort to discuss and come up with reasonable ways to manage a teacher's social media use rather than a top-down instruction or shut down.

Television and smart boards

The whiteboard enables a teacher to share a screen with the whole class and can provide interactive learning experiences. The use of slides on an interactive whiteboard has grown with PowerPoint continuing "to dominate classroom teaching across all subjects and phases" (Teacher Tapp, 2022). It is a requirement in some schools that teachers use their digital presentations as planning records. This particular use of slides might be an effective use of time but it does assume their use for every lesson. Slideshows can be limiting and encourage the use of "flat lessons" rather than active experiences. This may limit a teacher's sense of autonomy in terms of structuring the lesson in a way that moves away from a smartboard altogether. I would also argue that persistant use of Powerpoints for young children seems ludicrous – I can barely sit through them as an adult!

Showing television shows as part of a child's school day depends on a school's approach and policy regarding screen use. I have worked in a school where this is not allowed at all unless you are watching a film on the last day of term. I have also worked where this decision has been left up to my own professional judgement. These decisions should be made following training that includes up-to-date research on screen use and child development. It is my opinion that teachers are more than capable of deciding on the effective use of screens if senior leaders provide enough guidance and training.

Figure 5.2 Screens do not need to mean passive learning. Making music with tech. Photograph by Sophie-Smith-Tong

Educator experience – Phones

Anon. Secondary School Teacher.

As a secondary school teacher, I understand why our school has implemented a ban on smartphones. Conflict on social media was the catalyst for a spate of real-world fights last year, in which staff members were hurt. On a less serious note, smartphones are distracting for students in the classroom. But even though I enforce the rule as part of our broader school culture, I often find myself questioning whether this all-or-nothing approach is actually helping the students manage their relationship to smartphones.

On the surface, the policy (no smartphones in the building, no excuses) is clearly working. Students are less likely to text each other under their desks or sneak glances at social media when they know there are consequences. But this doesn't mean the distraction is gone. It just goes underground. The impulse to check their notifications hasn't disappeared – it's just been pushed out of sight. Or sometimes not, when we see students wandering around with AirPods in or headphones on in the morning, which "they just like to wear". In one cover lesson, where a student was sleeping, the class clown exclaimed, "I would love to take a picture. If ONLY I had a phone on me!", to the amusement of everyone – including me.

> We do have a frustrating lack of autonomy in navigating this policy. There are moments when I genuinely believe a phone could be a useful tool - researching a topic, taking a photo of notes for my year 11 classes, or using classroom software like Kahoot. There are also times when they can be a useful way to connect with students - for example, asking the year 11s about their prom dresses or when a year 9 student has a new sibling and I'd love to see a picture of them holding the baby.
>
> However, this lack of autonomy is not limited to phones. It is across the school - earrings, other than a plain stud, and any other jewellery, if seen, should be confiscated. Blazers must be on, and we must remind them to do so. No homework or incomplete homework is a detention. A minute late to class - also a detention. Failing to implement these policies can result in a slap on the wrist from above, but also can result in dysregulated classrooms - students are incredibly used to the strict discipline of the school, and, as I learned the hard way in my training year, you risk being seen as "soft" if you don't follow the strict rules they have come to expect. We have very little autonomy in navigating the behaviour system as a whole, particularly in a MAT of my scale.
>
> Overall, I feel ambivalent about the ban. Teenagers are still learning self-regulation, and it's undeniable that social media companies prey on young people with incredibly addicting products - I've been intrigued by Jonathan Haidt's arguments in *The Anxious Generation*, that we should limit all smartphone use until 16. However, in our current world, where students all have smartphones and don't seem inclined to give them up any time soon, this feels unrealistic. I worry we are pushing the issue of students' relationships to the online world further out of sight.

It's time to pause.

Reflection

- Have I read my school's online policy?
- Is there an opportunity for me to contribute to it?
- Am I aware of the guidance around social media for staff?
- How do I feel about my school's social media guidance?
- Do I feel I have a say over how much technology I use in my teaching?
- Have I had the opportunity to develop my understanding of technology in education?
- Am I required to use slides in all of my lessons?

Get autonomy back

In the classroom:

- Request specific technology professional learning opportunities - knowledge is power.
- Model autonomy and then give children opportunities to use technology autonomously such as for a project or in cross-curricular activities.

- Provide space and time for children to share thoughts, feelings and ideas about specific topics and approaches to technology.

For senior leaders:

- Ensure that you provide regular and specific technology training for all staff - don't just deliver internet safety training, rather use training to support staff in finding new and exciting ways to use tech.
- Utilise your ECTs - now that assistive technology training is mandatory for trainee teachers you will have some skills in your schools that should be shared.
- Make sure that your staff feel supported, alongside being able to share their ideas and question current practice and approaches in a safe space.

For government officials:

- Broaden the training trainee teachers receive - not just in assistive technologies but in AI use, social media, screens and the link between technology and emotional and mental health.
- Support parents in their technology learning - this will ensure the messages are consistent across school communities and we feel able to roam autonomously within that.

Final thought on screens

As we learn more about the impact of screens, we can begin to formulate a plan that might shed some consistent light on our use of them. Schools should work in a way that reflects up-to-date research, data and a child's holistic health. If schools can continue to train their staff in up-to-date and progressive uses of tech and also share that with local communities, we can begin to find balance and personalisation in our use.

Creativity and tech

> Yes, we need AI skills. But we also need to leave space for the artists, the dreamers, the ones who bring beauty, emotion, and imagination into the world - qualities that are increasingly being sidelined.
> **(Helen Buzdugan. 6 May 2025. LinkedIn)**

Creativity can enhance autonomy - as discussed in previous chapters, it can develop problem-solving skills, the ability to self-express and promote independent thinking. Will technology render us useless, hinder our growth and prevent us from thinking and developing creatively? Many fear that technology will replace creativity or suppress the growth of imagination and human connection. The kind of fear that is similar to Plato's thoughts on writing at the start of this chapter, don't you think? Others argue that it will free up time that can then be used creatively.

In terms of equipment, schools generally have a basic stash of laptops or tablets available for whole-class teaching. There is usually a sense of dread precomputing lessons as you anticipate the difficulty in getting them all working, and children logged on all at the same time. By the time they are logged on the lesson is almost over. Teaching computing in schools does not fill me with excitement (there are a few beacon schools who are well-equipped to get creative with technology) but unless we have the training, computing in schools can certainly lack oomph, deriving from a discomfort, a lack of time and confidence.

I was once asked in a teacher focus group about preferences for a drama workshop - online videos versus in-person visits. Many teachers shared that the online videos were much more accessible to children as they were more attentive and focused. They found the in-person sessions triggered challenging behaviour. I began to reflect on this - are we attempting to remove any experience that provides challenge? Where is the learning if we remove the opportunity to build focus and self-expression? If children do not have the chance to build their levels of focus and practise those skills, then how do we expect them to have them at all? On the other hand, for those who are autistic or have ADHD, the screen workshops can help regulate in an environment that, when in person, can potentially be overwhelming. A teacher's choice on this needs to be well-informed - training and collaboration are key here.

Technology can be a scaffold for creative thinking giving us the tools to create - having a range of technological systems available means we can utilise autonomy and choose when and where to use them effectively. However, it does have the potential to make us lazy and prevent the development of focus, perseverance and critical thinking which are often needed for other enjoyable tasks in the classroom such as sharing a story book together. "Only 40% of parents with children aged 0 to 13 agreed that 'reading books to my child is fun' for them" (Creamer, 2025). Is the easy access to stimulation inhibiting the development of attention and determination? Utilising autonomy to choose how we "spend" our technology time should always factor in a child's wellbeing. As I mentioned in **Chapter 2** - the rigidity of schemes can render the teacher inflexible - we are at risk of the same happening with technology use. On the other hand, denying that technology can provide us with flexibility is also damaging - there are a lot of learning opportunities in technology. A strong school ethos agreed upon by staff teams (made up from representatives from across the setting) will ensure that there is safety, fun and exploration at the heart of our digital learning.

Tech capitalism in education

The decisions on what and how children learn should be made by those working with them and those who have had training in child development. This is not a job for tech giants and big organisations who have financial gain as their ultimate goal (it is my belief that capitalism has already taken hold of our education system); we need to prevent its expansion. Local authorities (LAs) would be well placed to filter through reputable companies, tech applications and resources to schools. By providing schools with a wealth of options and opportunities, they can then decide on what is best in their context. Sharing good practice within local cluster meetings could ensure coherence and experimentation in this area.

Digital literacy

Some of you will remember the TV being wheeled out from the TV cupboard every Friday, then there were the overhead projectors (that took up half of your desk space), audio recording buttons, BeeBots, desktops, laptops and tablets. I haven't had any training in

Figure 5.3 Getting creative with tech at the Tate Modern. Photograph by Sophie-Smith-Tong

the use of technology in my 15 years as a teacher, and I have found that it is often left to the computing teaching and learning responsibilities (TLR) holder to provide the answers to tech use in schools. It is my experience that schools can fall behind or lack creativity with technology for this reason; this can be down to tight budgets and time constraints resulting in little to no training and experimentation time. David White's theory notes that "individuals are all placed somewhere along a range of digital 'visitors' and 'residents'" (Joines, 2024). Our individual experiences of and confidence in technology will vary hugely amongst our staff teams. It is up to the school leadership team to provide training to create equity in autonomy. Much of what we do know in schools relies on being confident with computers – from online observation platforms in the early years to Google Classrooms in the later years – the pandemic ensured that we have moved towards a model more reliant on technology. Digital autonomy becomes impossible without targeted and tailored professional learning to ensure effective and appropriate use.

Digital homework

First and foremost – I do not believe in homework. The use of Google Classroom during the pandemic opened up the possibilities for online homework platforms and eradicated the job of sticking generic worksheets into homework books each week. Software applications such as DoodleMaths and Mathletics provide homework tailored to each individual (a child's activity on DoodleMaths is tailored to the outcome of that child's previous tasks on the application).

Decision-making on which platforms work best should be a collaborative process, a coming together of staff teams and a conversation about what works best with the cohort you have. With support from the computing TLR holder and the senior leadership team (SLT), teachers should feel they can speak up regarding homework platforms they deem intrusive of home life, passive or ineffective (please note - my argument would be that *all* homework, digital or otherwise, falls under these categories). Dictating which platforms that teachers use is ineffective, they must be given the space to try out software with their classes before committing and should have flexibility where possible. Teachers should not feel that they have to use a digital platform at all - a hands-on project would always be my preference!

An artist's experience - Creativity and AI

Lyle Perkins. Artist.

A learning model's success lies in the optimisation of a prompt and the strength of a question. This is the foundation for compelling art making.

Tools and technology have been part of an artist's practice for centuries. Science and art coexist. Where creativity dreams up the future, science makes it a reality. Inversely, it is often the experimentation with such instruments by creative thinkers where invention tends to thrive.

The act of creativity is predicated on a human desire to communicate, not primarily to drive efficiency (which appears to be the current motive for many corporations). People are predisposed to take the path of least resistance, so having access to predictive learning becomes an alluring prospect. There is something to be said for task-oriented work being handled by such systems for some of the heavy lifting but without that struggle for discovery, would those breakthroughs be as fulfilling?

It is important to distinguish, whilst we still can, that the act of creating is a pursuit on its own terms as each brush stroke informs the next, culminating in the author's vision. By allowing chance through expressive gestures or putting combinations together of things that do not usually belong can lead to happy accidents - in theory, this could be actionable through multiple prompts but somewhat obfuscates the visceral experience of creativity.

Until recently, our idiosyncrasies and schisms are bound up in the work making it a semblance of self. Now our enquiries can be harvested and used in training data that can cosplay whichever author is selected and happens to inhabit that model to become part of someone else's work. We are being exposed to countless examples in various art styles flexed by AI that initially appear impressive whilst simultaneously exacerbating concerns around artistic value - although due to the speed of AI development and algorithm-dependent trends the current iteration's longevity seems unlikely. A similar analogy against AI could be drawn from the sampling era of music production where whole genres were created out of the DNA from prerecorded performers without the creator's consent or financial benefit. Like sampling, plagiarism throughout the ages is nothing new and from which discoveries can (and have) been made.

> In an attempt to push the relationship between original creation and AI, ArtSensei was founded by Rob Colvin as a visual aid for practising artists; more info: https://artsensei.ai/
>
> This tool analyses and provides suggestions for works in development which can help resolve compositional problems. Rather than using AI to dream up entire completed works this app pertains to critique what an artist has already committed to, assisting individuals that may not have access to higher education or get feedback to help improve their practice.
>
> Perhaps the issue lies more with regulation as opposed to general intelligence itself and whether legislation will accommodate an individual's own copyright. Images made with AI cannot yet be copyrighted; however, the dataset using artists' original works to make those images are very difficult to decouple from that process. Maybe a digital watermark could be embedded, similar to minting an non-fungible token (NFT) where residuals are credited to the creator in a similar way that musicians receive royalties from their work being used by other producers. Having said this, it can be very tricky to link widespread fragments of copyrighted music samples back to the source.
>
> The potential impact of this technology is uncertain, and in some fields such as medicine, its application is proving very beneficial. However, within the context of creativity maybe we need to prepare to rethink what creativity is and looks like.

It's time to pause.

Reflection

- Am I scared of technology and where it is going?
- Does this fear come from a lack of understanding?
- Do I dread planning and delivering lessons that involve technology?
- Do I shut down tech use because I do not understand it?
- Do I have autonomy over how or if I use it in class?
- Have I thought about what applications I find effective and which I would like to move on from?

Get autonomy back

In the classroom:

- Speak up if you need training in how you can be more creative with your use of tech in the classroom.
- Give the children autonomy over technology – what would they like to learn, what could they teach others (including you!).
- Be part of the tech story in your school – request time to come together to talk through what works and what doesn't.

For senior leaders:

- Listen to your teachers – ask them how they are finding the technology used in their classrooms.
- Put the feedback into action – value and hear your teachers and children by not just listening but responding.
- Assign someone to lead on collaboration efforts – maybe your computing lead would be best placed for this or maybe it's a role independent from this.

For government officials:

- Slim down the curriculum – make space for more creativity in our use of technology in the classroom.
- Deliver on a new approach to tech in our new curriculum.
- Add a module to teacher training that supports trainee teachers in using technology creatively.
- Encourage and fund LAs in becoming more involved in supporting schools in their use of technology.

Final thought on creativity and tech

Just as I talk about play being misunderstood and therefore feared, the same can happen with technology. Creativity is innate in us all but can be shut away by an educator's lack of time, money and resourcing. Instead of shutting down, we need to open up to tech and the possibilities and opportunities it holds in developing our creativity. We are currently in a battle for autonomy – could tech help us win that battle? It is certainly fathomable that it could support time saving, encourage creative thinking and resource our big ideas.

THE BIG IDEA – Digital autonomy

Bukky Yusuf. Senior Leader, Educational Consultant and Coach.

With the increased prevalence of technology in education (EdTech) during the last three decades, one interesting concept to consider is the idea of "digital autonomy". If we take the idea of autonomy as "our ability to choose and control how technology integrates in our lives" (Sandler, 2020), we can extend this to mean the ability of educators to choose the technology that can be deployed for teaching and learning.

Let's explore this concept on a number of levels.

If we take where we currently are with regard to AI in education, there are many tools/platforms that can be used. So many schools are in the exploration stage where teachers have the option to try out different AI tools (with due diligence around GDPR), review the impact upon specific aspects of teaching and learning and make suggestions on how they can be used within their subject area. This can be done as part of working groups such as digital working groups operating on a whole school basis or within faculties/departments.

When I think back to the time I led the whole school digital implementation and undertook EdTech reviews to capture which software different departments had, it was interesting to see how much was on the system from a whole school perspective. Many types of software/tools/programmes had been introduced and then forgotten about over the years, yet continued to take up a lot of digital storage.

It therefore makes sense during our current landscape of reduced school budgets, for careful considerations of digital tools that would form part of a school's digital ecosystem, and the considerations of these lying solely with those having responsibility for overseeing the whole school digital strategy.

However, there are ways in which teachers can still have choice and digital autonomy when it comes to teaching and learning.

The layers of onion model concept provide a clear framework with how this can be done (Department for Education, 2022).

The core of the onion represents core systems used by the whole school. Examples of these could be tools within Microsoft Education or Management Information Systems. In my previous EdTech role, our digital ecosystem was set up within Google Workspace for Education. Discussions and decisions around this were made with our IT providers.

The next layer within the onion represents technologies that have been reviewed (within or beyond the school) and shown to work well. I used iPad Champions to try out and review a number of iPad applications. These champions were a select group of colleagues who had complete autonomy around the tools they explored and in identifying the pedagogical impact on learning. The champions included staff teaching from core, practical and performance arts subjects. It allowed us to capture the various ways in which technology could be used to enhance teaching and learning. Staff in the classroom helped to provide fresh insights and perspectives with regard to the most up-to-date/relevant technologies. This helped to increase their levels of creativity, motivation and agency. When they presented their findings to the whole staff, it led to greater buy-in. The best practices of EdTech adoption, therefore, include time for the exploration phase.

The outermost layer relates to optional technology used on a small-scale basis, such as accessibility tools for a select number of SEND students. This part of the model provides teaching staff with the greatest potential for digital autonomy as they communicate with the digital lead/senior leader about technology they have identified that could help to address specific learning needs.

In the very best practices, there are clear protocols in place that provide opportunities for a teacher's digital autonomy even within "fixed" digital ecosystems.

Bukky Yusuf Reference:

Department for Education (2022). Implementation of education technology in schools and colleges. [online] Available at: https://assets.publishing.service.gov.uk/media/63355d2ee90e0772dc965174/Implementation_of_education_technology_in_schools__and_colleges.pdf. [Accessed September 2022]

Contributors

1. Lucy Lewin. Founder of The Profitable Nursery Academy.
2. Anon. Secondary School Teacher.
3. Lyle Perkins. Artist.
4. Bukky Yusuf. Senior Leader, Educational Consultant and Coach.

References

Bates, L. 2025. P. 228. The New Age of Sexism. Simon and Schuster UK Ltd.

Buzdugan, H. 6 May 2025. LinkedIn. https://www.linkedin.com/posts/helenbuzdugan_a-skills-pipeline-thats-how-the-government-activity-7325607821872365572--78v?utm_source=share&utm_medium=member_desktop&rcm=ACoAADSiNDcBj6IHrVTzfMCqlFDtXZiC7GP959s

Creamer, E. 30 Apr 2025. The Guardian. Most Parents Don't Enjoy Reading to Their Children, Survey Suggests. https://www.theguardian.com/books/2025/apr/30/most-parents-dont-enjoy-reading-to-their-children-survey-suggests

Dearden, L. 29 Dec 2024. The Guardian. 'Authoritarian and Heavy-Handed': Call for Investigation into Vetting of Experts by UK Civil Servants. https://www.theguardian.com/world/2024/dec/29/authoritarian-and-heavy-handed-call-for-investigation-into-vetting-of-experts-by-uk-civil-servants

Department for Education. 13 Jan 2025. AI Teacher Tools Set To Break Down Barriers to Opportunity. https://www.gov.uk/government/news/ai-teacher-tools-set-to-break-down-barriers-to-opportunity

Department for Education. 22 Jan 2025. Education Secretary Outlines Plans to Modernise Education Sector. https://www.gov.uk/government/news/education-secretary-outlines-plans-to-modernise-education-sector

Department for Education. 31 Mar 2025. The Education Hub. https://educationhub.blog.gov.uk/2025/03/artificial-intelligence-in-schools-everything-you-need-to-know/

Joines, F. Dec 2024. P. 1. Ready to Have a Go. https://www.fionajoines.co.uk/wp-content/uploads/2025/02/Ready-to-have-a-go-NW-part-2-2.pdf

Plato. Phaedrus. 370 BC. P. 275. https://www.goodreads.com/quotes/259062-if-men-learn-this-it-will-implant-forgetfulness-in-their

Sandler, K. 2020. Karen Sandler talks 'Digital Autonomy' in advance of her OpenUK Healthcare keynote in London on 6 February - OpenUK. [online] OpenUK. Available at: https://openuk.uk/digital-autonomy-our-ability-to-choose-and-control-how-technology-integrates-in-our-lives-has-never-been-more-important-it-also-has-never-been-more-fragile/

Shearing, H. 10 Apr 2025. BBC News. Leave School Phone Bans to Head Teachers, Children's Commissioner Says. https://www.bbc.co.uk/news/articles/cly1127Onpeo

Teacher Tapp. 15 Mar 2022. Is School Enjoyable, PowerPoint or Textbooks, Seating Plans and an Experiment! https://teachertapp.com/uk/articles/is-school-enjoyable-powerpoint-or-textbooks-seating-plans-and-an-experiment/

Teacher Tapp. 28 Aug 2024. AI Teachers, School Exclusions and Cutting Workload. https://teachertapp.com/uk/articles/ai-teachers-school-exclusions-and-cutting-workload/

Teacher Tapp. 11 Feb 2025. ECTs, Social Media Rules and Calling in Sick. https://teachertapp.com/uk/articles/ects-social-media-rules-and-calling-in-sick/

Teacher Tapp. 20 May 2025. Teacher Tapp Dials in on Mobile Phones. https://teachertapp.com/uk/articles/teacher-tapp-dials-in-on-mobile-phones/

Thomson, H. 19 Apr 2025. The Guardian. 'Don't Ask What AI Can Do for Us, Ask What It Is Doing to Us': Are ChatGPT and Co Harming Human Intelligence? https://www.theguardian.com/technology/2025/apr/19/dont-ask-what-ai-can-do-for-us-ask-what-it-is-doing-to-us-are-chatgpt-and-co-harming-human-intelligence

Unicef. Babies Need Humans, Not Screens. https://www.unicef.org/parenting/child-development/babies-screen-time

6 Autonomy in action

We have an educational polycrisis on our hands. I believe it is now clear that a radical change of course is necessary. The question is: how should we approach this tangled web of interconnected issues?

(Dr. James Mannion. Confronting the Educational Polycrisis. Seven crises, one system – and a path forward. 3 May 2025)

> **Chapter 6 Outline**
>
> In this chapter, we will explore:
>
> - the practical embedding of autonomy.
> - an early career teacher's (ECT) experience of autonomy.
> - pay scales and their connection with autonomy.
> - autonomy and professional development.
> - autonomy and time allocation and use.
> - the role of school leaders and hierarchy in education.
> - how we assess the efficacy of leaders and hold them accountable.
> - diversity and inclusion and autonomy.

Autonomy in practice

All of the previous chapters prove the existence of the polycrisis that Dr James Mannion speaks of above – the problem is complex and one that has many layers. Decision-making, policy, interactions and systems either work towards enabling or disabling autonomy in education.

Settings that attempt to feign trust or disingenuously "care" for their school community will fail to give autonomy the respect it requires. A lack of autonomy can go unnoticed and unaddressed, making change seem overwhelming and unimaginable. In a conversation with a senior leader regarding my own personal pursuit for education change, they raised concerns about my regular publicly shared strong opinions on the current education system. They believed that it might be a "conflict of interest" with being a teacher in a school. I fundamentally disagree and see my own fight for change as a sign that I care passionately about the

DOI: 10.4324/9781003532729-7

sector I work in. That is not to say that teachers who choose not to speak up are apathetic – there are a variety of ways to show your passion for your work, this being mine. This interaction reminded me of the inherent danger educators (and in particular leaders) face when speaking up. The prospect of having to manage stakeholder reaction, challenging behaviour and losing face is just too daunting, and so they are silenced. Balancing this in addition to everything else can feel impossible – there is so much work involved when seeking change. To develop autonomy in schools we must deep dive into all of the ways that contribute to thriving autonomy – including those that may initially seem irrelevant.

Organisation and autonomy

> Despite lots of noise about PPA flexibility, the reality seems to be that there has been no big jump in the number of teachers allowed to work from home during their PPA hours.
> **(Teacher Tapp. PPA home or away? 24 September 2024)**

Professional entitlements such as planning, preparation and assessment (PPA) time, professional learning and pay scales are not peripheral but integral to our pursuit of professional autonomy and play a part in its success (or failure). They form the structural foundation upon which autonomy is built, enabling rather than distracting from it. Approaches to PPA and professional learning might seem like small components of a teacher's work life but in fact, a setting's approach to these factors sends strong messages about its feelings on autonomy and its level of trust.

Decisions about these facets should be made in consultation with representatives from all departments. Let's delve into some of these components to see how they are currently managed and explore how they might work better.

Early career teachers (ECT)

ECTs are a breath of fresh air – they bring a progressive way of thinking, refreshing approaches and energy to the classroom. A new reliance on schemes in schools is stunting the growth of our ECTs' creative freedoms and is also causing a feeling that there is little to no room for mistakes. An ECT's "roll of the dice" school placement means the levels of autonomy they experience will vary.

I spoke to several and one described having "lots of freedom" and felt trusted to use her "professional judgements" when it came to lesson planning, timetabling and assessments. She did, however, say that there were certain whole-school initiatives that she had to take part in that she felt were not beneficial, such as learning objectives (LOs). She believes that it "does not benefit" her learners and stated that "school policies such as writing LOs and our marking policy" do affect her sense of autonomy. "These are completed because they have to be, rather than because they help the learners. This can be frustrating. While I understand policies have to be in place, there cannot be a 'one size fits all'". This was mentioned several times with another ECT saying that "policies provide useful structure but sometimes feel restrictive, especially when a different approach might be more effective for certain students". Many were frustrated with facets of the system but felt unable to speak up about areas of teaching and learning that were not working for them for fear of the consequences. Other areas that were considered difficult to talk about included the use of plenaries and success criteria, marking policies and workload. There was a general feeling that a lack of experience to provide solutions meant they worried they would come across as problem focused.

ECTs also described senior leaders' emphasis on "consistency over creativity, which can feel limiting" with larger decision-making often needing "approval or must align with the school's overall curriculum structure". There is a real sense of frustration that "often an expectation to follow the scheme of work closely" was at odds with "freedom in curriculum planning and assessment choices to better fit the specific needs" of their children. It became clear from my conversations that in many settings "innovations are welcomed, while others are met with caution. There is often subtle pressure to stick to what's proven or expected".

What also surfaced is that in those early days of being a teacher, preplanned activities and predecided structures can feel hugely valuable with many believing that it enabled them to focus on "being a teacher". The National Foundation for Educational Research (NFER) states that "... too much autonomy for novices risks overwhelming them, as they are early in the process of establishing their competence and forming working relationships" (Worth and Van den Brande, 2020. P. 6). Some ECTs recognised that autonomy would become more important to them later on in their career with one ECT stating that if the freedom to bring their own ideas to the classroom wasn't later available to them, then leaving the school they were working in would be a preferred option. It was interesting to see that ECTs seem to feel they have to *earn* their autonomy – is this another example of the accountability culture with ECTs feeling they need to prove to others (and themselves) that they are capable of utilising autonomy;

- "As I have more experience, I grow in confidence and in my professional judgments. I am now more autonomous than at the start of my career".
- "Yes, it has improved slightly as I've become more confident and built trust with senior staff, but I still feel I need to "earn" the space to try new things".
- "I think I will want more autonomy as I grow in confidence".

The NFER states that "Teacher autonomy is lower among early career teachers and higher among senior leaders" (Worth and Van den Brande, 2020. P. 4). We should be making more of an effort to build a culture where mistakes are welcomed, enabling ECTs to take risks.

Schools, and in particular mentors, are in a position to support and empower ECTs in the form of a culture that welcomes risk taking and mistakes for learning. Even if it challenges all of the teaching norms and embedded practices – we want new teachers to bring new life to the classroom and we prevent education growth by not offering a safe space and encouraging autonomy in our trainee teachers.

Pay scales

80% of teachers said they would feel uncomfortable arguing for a higher salary (Teacher Tapp, 2023). As classroom teachers progress through the pay scales their levels of autonomy do not necessarily increase. However, those with leadership roles and advanced teaching posts (and therefore on the upper pay scale), carry more freedom over our curriculum, pedagogy and

Figure 6.1 Beth Ewin. ECT. T-shirt by Teachappy. Photograph by Sophie Smith-Tong

> **Educator experience – ECTs**
>
> **Beth Ewin. ECT. Reception Class Teacher. Inner London Primary School.**
>
> Being an ECT, in my first term I welcomed phonics and maths schemes. The planning was already done, and I could watch the "how to" videos of how to teach a lesson. This gave me more time to focus on getting to know my new class and resource the environment. As I reached spring term, I dreaded teaching these lessons. I felt like a robot and there was a huge disconnect with my class. I began to question if this is really what being a teacher is like? Are teachers not trusted enough to create their own lessons and teaching styles?

professional decisions (Worth and Van den Brande, 2020. P. 11). When pursuing a career that is undeniably rewarding, showing an interest in pay progression can be frowned upon – after all, we teach because we are passionate about it. But money is important, and when the pay reward is inconsistent and/or withheld this can cause a devaluing of a teacher's efforts.

Autonomy in Action 137

Despite performance-related pay no longer being a statutory requirement, some schools still choose to adopt it. Teachers are also protected by increasing annual payment scales which not only increase our pay year on year but also include bands for teaching and leadership responsibilities (TLR) which are added onto main scale salaries. Pay has not been in line with inflation for years, hence the strikes in 2023, but the most recent funded increase (2024/2025) has eased the pressure on the government. "Teachers' pay awards have improved recently, relatively speaking, but they have been behind those across the whole economy for most of the past 17 years" (NEU, 2025). A recent announcement of a 4.0% pay rise has been welcomed, but ramps up pressure on school heads who have been asked to partially fund the awards through "improved productivity and smarter spending" (Seddon, 2025).

Despite our pay being low compared to other professions, the comfort that comes with incremental pay increases can help to keep teachers in service – it's a small but well-deserved perk. In a job outside of teaching, perhaps in a healthy private sector, it is not uncommon for a team member to search for another job if they feel that they are not being fairly financially rewarded. Senior leaders know that they have room to hold back on pay increases when teachers find reward in their job outside of pay and may find it difficult to transition into a new career.

It is not unusual for teachers to be given extra responsibilities without being offered the TLR payments – it is also not unheard of that staff are not made aware of this financial add

Figure 6.2 NEU strike for better pay. March 2023. Photograph by Sophie Smith-Tong

on. Whose responsibility is it to ensure that teachers are aware of their entitlements? My gut says senior leaders/line managers should be – or perhaps it should become a statutory requirement that it's covered in teacher training. There is nothing like knowledge to empower those heading into the profession.

With tight budgets, education is rarely forthcoming with financial information. When it comes to money, schools keep increases and financial possibilities on the downlow. Leadership teams may fear that offering unrequested pay rises will instil complacency and have catastrophic effects on budgets. With that in mind, I shamefully share that I have only *just* learned that you do not have to be a member of the leadership team to apply for an upper pay scale (UPS)! I have been a teacher for 15+ years (and yes, you could blame my lack of research) but I am shocked that this has never been brought to my attention in my many supervision meetings throughout my career. Additionally, I was dismayed to hear about the hoops you have to jump through to apply for the UPS increase (including an "application", "associated information" and "evidence"), something I am put off by when my workload is already unmanageable.

"Applications are assessed using the following criteria:

a) that the teacher is highly competent in all elements of the relevant standards; and
b) that the teacher's achievements and contribution to an educational setting or settings are substantial and sustained."

(NEU. Moving to the UPR or UPS [threshold progression])

How is it that I can work as a teacher in a school alongside the leadership team (and be held accountable consistently) *and* then must further prove my worth to get a pay increase after making it to the M6 pay scale? There are several reasons why I deem this to be both unfair and demotivating;

o Teachers already have a huge emotional daily strain in the job they do – adding a requirement for a portfolio of evidence when we can see their input daily in person only adds to this. See **Chapter 3** for all the ways we are already held accountable.
o Leaders involved in the decision-making may have biases that will make the outcome skewed. This is also the case for strained relationships between educators and leaders.
o The criteria can be vague and open to interpretation – what might be deemed "highly competent" in one school may not be the same in the other.
o Some teachers interpret the guidelines around UPS as requiring them to go above and beyond. Should we be depriving pay progression from those who are unable to give on a wider scale but work hard daily and have done so for several years? What might this do to their motivation? It works based on rewarding those who comply and punishing those who challenge the expectations and workload. When you have to prove your worth through imposed measures, it removes the opportunity for self-directed development and reflects a lack of trust and autonomy.

Professional learning

Developing autonomy over professional development is an important part of motivating and retaining staff. Inset and training days can cause eye-rolling and yawns. Well intentioned consultants who have not worked in a classroom for years and deliver wellbeing training can be the hardest to stomach as you sit there wishing you had the time to do the tasks on your list which would *actually* contribute to your wellbeing. Very rarely are teachers given the opportunity to request tailored inset days. Supervisions and check-ins provide the perfect opportunity for your team to share ways in which they would like to pursue further development. It is vital that these conversations are noted and used to build your training programme for the year ahead – many teachers share their suggestions but find it rarely comes to fruition.

Ensuring your training is relevant to those attending is essential – nothing is more demotivating than that of content that you have recently covered or is irrelevant to you. This is commonplace in the early years, with teachers expected to attend school training that is irrelevant. When speaking to Adrian Bethune for the Autonomy Mini-Series podcast (Mindfulness for learning podcast, 2025), he mentions a school that hosts three different training sessions at one time on their inset days – this means that staff can choose the training which they feel is most relevant to their needs and interests. This is a great example of how to motivate, innovate and provide staff with the autonomy to choose the training best suited to them.

In my experience, local school "cluster meetings" have great potential but often fail in finding the right structure and purpose, with teachers often wanting to use the space to air challenges and find out how other schools are managing certain aspects of teaching – it is hard to stay on task. If we were to remove the focus in some of these meetings so that staff can just informally share and chat this might hand over the autonomy to those in the room rather than the cluster lead deciding on the agenda. These meetings usually offer a calm, considerate and safe space to explore development for those who find themselves in similar contexts.

Teachers get very little time to observe others, not only at other settings but also each other within their own schools. Heading into other teachers' classrooms could broaden their approach and enhance their understanding of new ideas, initiatives and research. Companies like Google allow their staff one day a week to work on a "passion project". Imagine the same story for education – with staff being given time to put in place new and creative ideas in their settings or that could be shared with an entire local authority (LA). One of the recommendations for the Department for Education from the NFER is that they "…should produce guidance around the Teacher CPD Standards to emphasise how teachers can be given greater involvement in designing content, processes and goals" (Worth and Van den Brande, 2020. P. 4). It's time we hand over the designing of our development landscapes to the people on the ground.

Time

Autonomy is meaningless without the time to practice it. Teachers want to be creative and plan for fun learning experiences with their children (if this isn't the case then maybe a career rethink is necessary). Teachers want more time and space to *really* think about how and what they teach and build deeper and more meaningful connections with their work and the community, but as it currently stands, it feels impossible. When time is so tightly controlled then so is autonomy – teachers rarely have time to play with. The NFER states that "The average teacher in England also reports a lower level of autonomy over what tasks they do, the order in which they carry out tasks, the pace at which they work and their working hours, compared to similar professionals" (Worth and Van den Brande, 2020. P. 4).

It is tokenistic to say that, as a setting, you value time when in actual fact your teachers are not given the time to utilise their autonomy. Training is chosen for us, meetings added into our working weeks, timetables decided upon and behaviour policies handed over without question. David Pink speaks of the high turnover of call centre employees who have very little autonomy over their daily working lives (Pink, 2011. P. 102). The job is quite different of course but these employees listen to customers and follow a script, their interactions are dictated (remind you of the scheme discussion in **Chapter 2** by any chance?). With a more collaborative approach to designing a teacher's use of time we may find creative doors open, increased staff motivation and therefore retention. We need to be given time and take back our control over it.

Preparation and planning and assessment time (PPA)

Making use of the time we are given is reliant on that time being used for what it was intended for and our levels of autonomy over how we manage it. An important part of a teacher's week is PPA. In some settings PPA is regularly cancelled or moved last minute and is rarely used to actually complete planning. It is common for other tasks to be added in throughout the week with no specific time allocated to complete them. PPA taken at home is becoming more common but again tentatively - "33% of primary teachers are allowed to do their PPA from home, up 2 percentage points from when we asked last academic year. Just 9% of secondary school teachers are allowed to do PPA from home, up one percentage point compared to last academic year" (Teacher Tapp, 2024).

Tokenistic offerings such as limiting PPA taken at home to...

- Only when requested
- With good reason
- With permission
- Once a month
- Once a term
- Once a year

prove just what little trust in teachers there really is. With Bridget Phillipson stating that the government will now make it clear that PPA *can* be taken at home - it will be interesting to see how many schools take up on that. As David H. Pink states, "management isn't about walking around and seeing if people are in their offices...it's about creating conditions for people to do their best work" (Pink, 2011. P. 86.) There is a fear that if we allow these freedoms that teachers will begin to take advantage of them. The research presented by David H. Pink proves differently.

Educator experience - PPA and professional autonomy

Hannah Grange. Manager of Secondary Training, Inspection and Improvement at Aldar Education HQ.

Across three schools - two in the UK and one internationally - I've experienced a range of approaches to PPA (planning, preparation and assessment) time, but the consistent thread has been a balancing act between flexibility, professional trust and institutional need.

> In my first school in the UK, as an NQT (now ECT) and later as Assistant Head of Department with responsibility for KS3, I felt genuinely empowered in how I used my PPA. Initially, I used this time to observe experienced colleagues and reflect on practice, which was incredibly valuable for my professional growth. As I moved into more senior responsibilities, PPA became a platform for curriculum innovation, literacy leadership across the curriculum and mentoring NQTs. I was also involved in leading parent workshops and designing and running a literacy summer school to support students transitioning from primary to secondary. The time wasn't policed – it was trusted. That trust fuelled creativity and a deep sense of professional purpose.
>
> My second UK school, where I served as Deputy Head of Department with a focus on KS4, had a more outcome-driven culture, especially around GCSE coursework. While my PPA was still respected, much of it was redirected (often willingly) into intervention work. I used this time for small group support sessions, coursework mentoring and data tracking. Though this wasn't always strictly "my" time, it still felt meaningful and student focused. But the line between directed time and PPA began to blur.
>
> Internationally, the experience has varied depending on the school. Some institutions offer non-contact time in addition to PPA but label a portion of it as potentially available for cover. This creates a two-tiered system where some time is genuinely protected, and other time is at risk. While this model theoretically offers flexibility, in practice, cover requirements, invigilation duties, revision boosters and ad hoc meetings often take priority. The message is clear: PPA is only yours if the school doesn't need it. That conditionality chips away at professional autonomy and planning reliability.
>
> The most significant impact of this shifting autonomy over PPA is felt in workload and wellbeing. When PPA is regularly interrupted or reclaimed, evenings and weekends become the catch-up zone. The sense of ownership over one's professional time erodes, and with it, some of the joy and creativity of teaching. Where PPA is trusted, not monitored or pre-emptively claimed, teachers feel more empowered to use their expertise well. That autonomy is energising and sustainable.
>
> The change I'd like to see is not necessarily more PPA but more protected and trusted PPA. School systems must treat it not as a bonus but as a non-negotiable foundation for quality teaching, self-directed CPD and assessment feedback (to inform planning and instruction).

It's time to pause.

Reflection

- How are ECTs supported in my setting?
- Is pay scale information readily available or volunteered?
- How does the professional learning offering/timetabling work in my setting?
- Do I feel that I have time to play with?
- Is the structure and timetable for PPA effective?

Get autonomy back

In the classroom:

- ECTs
  - you can do it! Make mistakes and learn from them and avoid relying too heavily on prescriptive learning styles, structures and timetables (but bite off a bit at a time, don't overwhelm yourself). Ultimately – make it work for you.
  - seek support when required – this will ensure you are able to utilise your autonomy.
  - be curious and ask questions. If it doesn't feel like it is working, then it probably isn't – trust your instinct and connection with the children you are working with. You may not have all the answers, but sharing your thoughts and ideas with others can help find solutions. Just because something has been done a certain way for a while doesn't mean that it's the best way.
- In your supervision meetings ask about pay progressions and additional pay available.
- Request professional learning opportunities that you enjoy and feel you need.
- Offer polite and constructive feedback on ineffective and time-wasting professional learning – until we speak up, we cannot expect change.
- If you do not have time for a given task, then ask the senior leadership team (SLT) for time.
- If PPA is cancelled regularly, is taken at a time that is inconvenient or must be taken in school then be curious, ask why and request the changes you require.

For senior leaders:

- Tell your ECTs that you trust them and that you are there for them. Encourage risk taking, creativity and play – it will work in your favour.
- Avoid judging and/or shutting down ideas and changes to current systems and structures – change can be hard but it can also be extremely effective and progressive.
- Offer pay information voluntarily and avoid expecting your staff to do more for no more. TLR holders should be given an immediate increase to reflect their efforts, and they should not have to request or chase it.
- Get organised – invite teachers to be involved in the PPA timetable and book in regular cover – make it work consistently for all.
- Trust your staff to decide where they take their PPA time – we teach children, we can be trusted to make the decision as to where we utilise our time.

For government officials:

- Incorporate PPA from home into the professional expectations and guidance.
- Make sharing pay scales, expectations and progressions a statutory part of supervision meetings.
- Ensure that student teachers are provided with the skills to approach difficult situations where they find they cannot express their own thoughts, ideas and feelings in a setting.
- Provide training for senior leaders/mentors that are hiring and supporting ECTs to encourage their risk-taking, making mistakes and growth.

Autonomy in Action

Final thought on organisation

The thread that runs through our working week consists of the components mentioned in this section. PPA, professional learning and pay are all holding up our daily access to autonomy and send a strong message as to how a school feels about us as a staff team. They strongly impact our ability to not only do our job but be motivated to do it *well*. Giving these components the time and consideration they deserve will make life much easier in the long term – providing strong foundations for teachers to build upon.

Collaboration as motivation

> *...it starts with bold leadership willing to admit that the current system isn't fit for purpose.*
> **(Victoria Bagnall. LinkedIn. March 2025)**

Autonomy is not independent but collaborative. For autonomy to be exercised fully we need to be working cooperatively with our communities, organisations, families, SLT, support staff and LAs. If there are persistent limits and a requirement to follow stringent rules and inflexible policies it becomes impossible to progress. Amongst staff teams there are a number of strengths to be discovered – there is a real lack of time dedicated to staff sharing. With a need for control and barriers between educators and their SLT, making changes to long-standing policies and systems and seizing opportunities to be bold can feel out of reach.

Chaos is not a product of autonomous working although that is often the fear. Autonomy is not a trade-off for consistency. For autonomy to work there needs to be a consideration of the bigger picture and the individuals within it. Without this consideration, chaos will ensue.

Senior leadership teams (SLT)

> *In general, teachers who stay in the classroom after their first five years do not experience increased autonomy as their careers progress and are likely to only if they enter leadership roles.*
> **(NFER. Teacher autonomy: how does it relate to job satisfaction and retention?**
> **Jack Worth and Jens Van den Brande. P. 4)**

It is up to SLT to empower teachers with autonomy genuinely, not just freedom in theory. Despite high-stakes accountability, SLT do have the power to grant autonomy to their staff teams and communities. Depending on a senior leader's experience they may not feel up for questioning the status quo and trying something new and challenging. As we have explored in the book some headteachers are pathing the way for others – showing us how we can begin to step outside the lines that have been drawn around us and find freedom and joy in teaching and learning. Read **Chapters 3** and **4** for more on this.

When speaking to headteacher, Tina Farr, on the Autonomy Mini-Series (Mindfulness for learning, 2025) mentions the ineffectiveness of pitting progressive and traditional learning models against each other – there is a balance we can find, utilising aspects of both learning models and coming together to make it work for any given context. With this balance and collaboration, we can discover work happiness with more ease – an embedding of flexible thinking will lead to autonomy.

SLT are working with many constraints and stakeholders including Ofsted, governing bodies, local authorities and parents/carers - we have to respect the pressure they are under and the choices they make with regard to how much more work they create for themselves. When we are inviting senior leaders to be bold, we must accept that they may not be in the mental headspace to be just that. It is at this point that we request others to take on the fight. I am in my 16th year of teaching, and dependent on what I have going on at work and in my own personal life there are times when I get tired of contesting the system - I know at this point that there are others who are continuing whilst I take a step back - there are enough of us to keep it going. It is important that, at times, we focus *only* on the daily running of operations - there is enough to be getting on with. This acknowledgement prevents burnout.

A top-down model is not the best way to develop an autonomous working space. Education works in a hierarchical structure. Naomi Fisher states, "...if a team is very hierarchical, then it can't really operate as a team because no one is free to say what they think" (Fisher and Fricker, 2024). Allowing a range of staff members to become involved in decision-making will ensure that all voices and perspectives are heard and valued. Leaders who allow others into their world and vice versa are more likely to get the most out of their teams.

How can we ensure that SLT are held accountable to an autonomous working model? We must not only encourage them to develop an autonomous working environment but also to model one - making use of the freedoms available to them to make decisions that help to develop that autonomous setting. If SLT consistently accepts and expects the unachievable expectations the system hands to us, then autonomy is never going to get off the ground. We must hold SLT to account by questioning them in a curious and non-judgemental way. Ask questions and encourage your team to do the same. Be supportive and respectful, but be well-informed with research, articles and schools that have made it work for any given area and invite them to see how it can work.

*A quick note on teaching and learning responsibility (TLR) holders

TLR holders are responsible for an entire area and usually alongside teaching a class. Within that space they are required to book in speakers and events, design initiatives, buy into curriculum support and communicate their ideas with the team and the school community. If SLT gives enough time for staff collaboration, then TLR holders will have a good understanding of the school ethos and purpose - there should be no need for micromanaging. If they do not have an in-depth understanding of this, then perhaps that's where the work is required. When TLR holders are required to have everything signed off by management it makes the job tiresome and ineffective. Headteachers should not hire someone and micromanage them - if they have been given the position then they should be trusted to do the job. Trying to move forward with anything when you are trying to get it signed off by a busy senior leader is impossible and eats into precious time. It's time we got comfortable with making mistakes. An end of term/year check in with your TLR holders will enable you to reflect upon areas of success and agree on where development/change is required for the coming year.

Educator experience - SLT

Ciara Rush. Head of Children's Centre. Inner London Children's Centre and Primary School.

There's no single factor that can predict a child's success in school or later life. However, passionate and valued teachers and practitioners make a significant impact on young children's lives. Given the current low recruitment and retention rates, coupled with the increasing demands and challenges posed by the English education system, it's crucial for leaders to prioritise staff mental health and wellbeing. Educator autonomy can significantly contribute to fostering good mental health and wellbeing. Giving staff more control over their work enhances morale, increases job satisfaction, retention and overall effectiveness, whilst reducing stress and workload.

That said, it isn't always straightforward, and other leaders I have spoken to often express concerns about autonomy for various reasons. In my first leadership role, I worried that without direct oversight, there was a risk that the curriculum and policies wouldn't be followed, leading to a decline in the quality of practice, performance issues and, ultimately, negatively impacting children's learning and development. However, as I grew in my role as a leader, I soon realised that this couldn't be any further from the truth!

Striking the right balance between autonomy and direction can be challenging, but I have found that embracing autonomy leads to a far more positive and productive working environment.

Here are my top tips for leaders on letting go of some control and giving educators more autonomy.

- Be clear in your own mind about what autonomy is and what it isn't, considering the context of your setting, the challenges it encounters, and the objectives you want to achieve. Autonomy doesn't give educators the freedom to do whatever they please but rather provide them with the space to utilise their skills and preferred practices that align with the setting's priorities, goals and vision.
- Collaborate with the team to establish a shared ethos and vision. Develop a curriculum that everyone can embrace, drawing upon the diverse experience and skills of the staff. Within the curriculum, clearly outline the sequence of learning, the specific skills, knowledge and vocabulary children should acquire, and a few fundamental principles. This will enable staff the freedom to respond and adapt the curriculum, whilst working within a framework.
- Take the time to get to know your team members beyond their roles. This will help you understand their motivations and the leadership style they respond best to. By understanding this, you can adjust your approach and determine when to step back and when to offer guidance.

- Provide regular half-termly check-ins with staff to understand their individual needs, challenges and progress towards goals. Provide thoughtful feedback or additional support as needed so that staff have what they need to succeed.
- Invest in high-quality professional development opportunities to help staff grow and stay up to date with best practices and current research. This includes subject-specific training, visits to other settings, peer-to-peer coaching, and reflective practice sessions.

And finally... trust your team. At the core of autonomy is trust. Believe that staff want to do the right thing and have faith they'll get their work done.

It's time to pause.

Reflection

- Do I feel heard in my setting?
- Do I have ideas that I want to share?
- Am I given space and time to share and collaborate?
- Is there an overpowering hierarchy preventing growth in my setting?
- Do I feel part of a team?

Get autonomy back

In the classroom:

- Write down and share your ideas – it's a good way to (a) contemplate what they are (b) develop them and (c) have them sent in writing to keep a record of ignored offerings and reminders to follow up.
- Introduce the idea of a slice team to your SLT (better still hand them the book *Making Change Stick* by Dr James Mannion). A slice team is a group of representatives from all areas in the school so that decisions get made with a variety of different perspectives and experiences.
- Be wary of a desire to do anything you want. Ensure that you are inviting a balance of independence and interdependence to streamline and maintain consistency.

For senior leaders:

- Invite your team to share their ideas – you can provide your values and ethos but don't expect that you can make it happen alone.
- Read *Making Change Stick* by Dr James Mannion – speak to your community and hear their voice.
- Be flexible – no employee will be the same or will have the same experiences and skill set.
- Show compassion to yourself – let go of full control and it will provide you with the space to be compassionate and patient with yourself and your team.

For government officials:

- Take the pressure off of SLT – get rid of Ofsted (more on this in **Chapter 3**).
- Give headteachers more training on how to move away from tools that schools have become so dependent on – schemes, data, league tables, worksheets, workbooks.
- Slim down the curriculum.
- Introduce the slice team model to school leadership teams.

Final thought on SLT

I have worked for a variety of settings and senior leaders – we all need to work alongside structures, people and policies that are not perfectly aligned with our own ethos and values. Perfection is not what we are after – respect is. We are professionals and are often not treated as such. I urge senior leaders to reflect upon their interactions with the adults in their schools – how are you speaking to your staff, are you making assumptions or shutting them down for fear of what you might find or what work might be created. Open the door and see what you find – my guess is that it will be passion, talent and joy.

The individual and autonomy

If our education system becomes more controlling (of both teachers and learners) and offers less in the way of agency and autonomy, then we really shouldn't be surprised if we see a fall in motivation and retention.

(Sue Cowley. 5 November 2024)

I had an Ofsted inspection recently, the inspector asked if every child leaves this school with the same qualities? I answered honestly, "no. Absolutely not, we are working with individuals not in a sausage factory. The one thing I can guarantee however is that each child will be met where they are and loved for who they are, as an individual". That is exactly where I find the love in teaching, in each and every child.

We are becoming more and more aware of the term "executive functioning". Victoria Bagnall is Co-Founder of Connections in Mind which is the first organisation to offer executive function coaching. At Connections in Mind they support learning about the brain and specifically how to develop our executive function skills. According to Connections in Mind, executive functions are a "family of top-down mental processes that make it possible to mentally play with ideas; approach unanticipated challenges with flexibility; take the time to think before acting; resist temptations, and to stay focused" (Connections in Mind).

For many neurodivergent people enabling executive function skills can be challenging, with many being labelled lazy, slow or unable to access daily learning opportunities in our current education system. It can also be the same experience for those working in education. It benefits us *all* to learn how to understand and develop these skills, but it is especially important for teachers who are working with many individual learners and employees day in and day out.

An exploration of our own experiences, trauma and preferences support our ability to shape our interactions and experiences at work. Greg Bottrill often refers to many educators holding ignored or unaddressed adversity and the damage that it may cause for the children we teach. I recently experienced a head belittling a secondary school child in front of a group of visiting parents on a tour, when looking around for my 11-year-old son. I wondered what experiences had shaped that headteacher's interaction? Without reflecting on or exploring past experiences it becomes impossible to create a positive learning environment for those that we teach. Self-reflection has to become part of the job we do in our settings (see **Chapter 1** for more on this). In other words, building a compassionate response can only happen when we learn to be compassionate to ourselves. Responding to the needs of every individual takes self-evaluation, vulnerability and deep exploratory work which can be painful. Without this exploration we can't figure out what we stand for, we have not spent time developing or understanding what we are passionate about, what motivates us, what makes us unique and therefore we are unable to do the same for others. How can we develop autonomy without an understanding of oneself?

Disruption

Disruption is central to the change I am advocating for in education – without it, education will remain as it is. In the insightful book, *The Caring Teacher*, secondary teacher Rob Potts states that policies and systems "are cast in stone and your job is to apply them as effectively (and consistently) as possible" (Potts, 2021). Of course, we can't just start ignoring the policies we have in place (as much as I would like to sometimes!) but what about *questioning* their effectiveness and functionality? When they are damaging children or hampering our efforts as educators, don't we need to be questioning them and disrupting the existing condition? As individuals this can be difficult and dependent on how safe you feel to do so, but where possible I urge you to speak up – individuals become a collective, then turn into an alliance – this is when change can *really* happen.

Diversity and inclusion

Our individual experiences can help to bring something new, a fresh perspective on how we approach teaching and learning in school. We must also be mindful of how limiting it can be to only focus on our individual experiences without collaboration. Bringing all of our own individual experiences together is where the magic happens. Where the staff team doesn't offer a diverse range of experiences then the work must be done – how can we trust that diversity and inclusion will be considered if we do not allow teachers to come together and make choices about:

- curriculum content.
- who to collaborate with to develop their understanding and approach.
- how to encourage and invite child autonomy.
- their own professional development.

Educator experience – Diversity and inclusion

Eva Long. Baby Room Lead. Inner London Children's Centre.

I think when considering diversity in the classroom there is a fine line between allowing teachers to be autonomous and having the trust it will be prioritised, whilst also ensuring there is a culture in the school of equality and diversity. There are lots of things to consider due to the potentially sensitive nature of equality and diversity. Ultimately, I think clear messages, guidelines and procedures need to be in place in schools. Teacher training needs to explicitly teach and equip students and in turn, newly qualified teachers will then feel able and empowered to be autonomous in their classroom approach to diversity. If we are not holding people accountable, will wrong views be challenged? Will they think they are doing enough? The work of equality, diversity and anti-racist practice is a never-ending journey on which we are constantly learning and evolving. Some other things worth considering

- Does the level of risk change depend on whether teachers are experienced or inexperienced, both professionally and in terms of lived experiences? I think there would be less risk from experienced teachers having more autonomy, but less-experienced teachers may need more direction.
- I wonder if autonomy impacts negatively on team working for example, strengths could potentially not be shared if all teachers are doing their own thing.
- Finally, the national curriculum and EYFS statutory guidance could be seen as quite prescriptive; autonomy could allow greater creativity and make teaching more enjoyable.

As an experienced early years practitioner, I welcome the opportunity to have a level of freedom which helps me respond to the uniqueness of the children and our particular cohort. However, I also feel a level of security in having some non-negotiables.

It's time to pause.

Reflection

- Do I value and acknowledge the individuals in my school?
- How can I reflect upon and explore my own personal experiences that have an impact on my interactions with my colleagues and the children I work with?
- What support might I need to reflect upon and develop my own ideas and passions within my work?
- Am I questioning what I am being asked to do in a healthy and constructive way?
- Am I relying on too much rigidity in school?
- Is a lack of cohesion causing an environment unfit for the development of autonomy?
- How do the current policies and practices empower staff and children from diverse backgrounds, including those with special educational needs and disabilities (SEND), to express their identities and participate fully without barriers?

Get autonomy back

In the classroom:

- Provide the perfect balance of flexibility and structure to create a safe environment for all. Make decisions about what balance works best for your cohort.
- Do not be afraid to make changes where things no longer work.
- Avoid responding to each individual in the same way – fairness is not giving everyone the same but giving each person what they need to succeed (colleagues and children).

For senior leaders:

- Ensure you ask staff what they need to feel supported.
- Have a bigger picture for your team to work towards – a shared goal.
- Invite your staff to contribute to the bigger picture in their own way.
- Do not expect all teachers to work in the same way; you provide the safe space/structure, and they can explore within it.
- Ensure your team collaborates on LGBTQ+, diversity and inclusion policy.

For government officials:

- Provide more space and time within the curriculum to explore.
- Allocate more time to diversity, inclusion, SEND and trauma-informed training for all trainee teachers.
- Encourage educators to explore their own experiences more deeply.
- Offer mindfulness training for educators to develop their ability to respond rather than react and to manage their fears and vulnerabilities within their work.

Final Thought on the individual

Collaboration is the coming together of a range of individuals – the magic that comes out of knowing, respecting and utilising everyone's experiences is what makes a school setting stand out. You can feel its pulse, see its identity, and hear its words. A school that respects the individual (staff, children and parents) is a hub of creativity and energy – a place where autonomy will thrive.

THE BIG IDEA – The power of real and human collaboration

Eliza Fricker. Missing the Mark. Parent, Illustrator and Author.

Is this a safe place to share?

My family's impactful experiences in educational settings began in nursery and continued until year 7 of secondary school and I have only a few professionals (teachers, educational psychologists, etc.) that I remember for their honesty. I remember them because there were so few, and it is not because other professionals I met were not kind or well-meaning (as most were), but there were so few that I felt were able to hold and reflect truly the experiences we were having as family. This honesty is something I think professionals feel worried about offering because I speak to families every week who say they too remember the "real deals", as there are so few.

Of course, over time we have all become sadly hardened to the local authority bureaucrats, who are unable to ever mention the protracted, often silent communication we face once we are trying to source support or funding. But those at the coal face in schools, meeting us and our children, often mean well. After all, we know them, we've met with each other many times.

However, as the support does not match or reflect the level of need, we, the parents/caregivers become attuned to seeing the worry in the eyes and the hesitancy in the words of the SENCO. As parents raising children who need other/different, we also have learnt to live with uncertainty, this need to think creatively, outside the box, ad hoc, how things can work one day and not the next. We do get it; we have every day of lived experience. And so, what we have learned that works is to remove hierarchical barriers to communication, to work together, to share that it is hard. Because holding steady with someone struggling, while it may seem like not doing much, is actually doing an awful lot. It is saying "I am here for you", "I am listening".

We need this because sharing the most difficult parts of our private lives about our children is exposing, it leaves us vulnerable, and we need to know that it is safe to do so. That you will offer clear, honest, gentle, supportive communication, so that we can work together and feel safe doing so.

Figure 6.3 Illustrated by Eliza Fricker for Teacher Autonomy. Where Has It Gone and Why We Need It Back, 2025.

Contributors

1. Beth Ewin. ECT Reception Class Teacher. Inner London Primary School.
2. Hannah Grange. Manager of Secondary Training, Inspection and Improvement at Aldar Education HQ.
3. Ciara Rush. Head of Children's Centre. Inner London Children's Centre and Primary School.
4. Eva Long. Baby Room Lead. Inner London Children's Centre.
5. Eliza Fricker. Sunday Times Bestseller. Illustrator and Author. Autism and Education.

References

Bagnall, V. Mar 2025. LinkedIn. https://www.linkedin.com/posts/victoria-bagnall-38204251_neuroinclusion-universaldesignforlearning-activity-7302357099471142914-_P_A?utm_source=share&utm_medium=member_desktop&rcm=ACoAADSiNDcBj6IHrVTzfMCqIFDtXZiC7GP959s

Connections in Mind. What Are Executive Functions? https://connectionsinmind.com/what-is-executive-function/

Cowley, S. 5 Nov 2024. X. https://x.com/Sue_Cowley/status/1853687967518191957

Department for Education. 2024. Children's Wellbeing and Schools Bill 2024: Policy Summary. https://www.gov.uk/government/publications/childrens-wellbeing-and-schools-bill-2024-policy-summary

Fisher, N and Fricker, E. 2024. P. 114. When the Naughty Step Makes Things Worse.

Mannion, J. 3 May 2025. Confronting the Educational Polycrisis. Seven Crises, One System – and a Path Forward.

Mannion, J. 2025. Making Change Stick. John Catt.

Mindfulness for learning. Jan 2025. Autonomy Mini-Series. https://open.spotify.com/episode/7cM6qInTjXRrdmFbNjIcOv?si=21cf256de9634733

NEU. Moving to the UPR or UPS (Threshold Progression) NEU. https://neu.org.uk/advice/your-rights-work/pay-advice/pay-progression/moving-upr-or-ups-threshold-progression

NEU. 1 Apr 2025. Teacher Pay Compares Poorly to Other Professions. https://neu.org.uk/press-releases/teacher-pay-compares-poorly-other-professions

Paul Seddon. 22 May 2025. BBC News. Teachers and Doctors in England Given 4% Pay Rise. https://www.bbc.co.uk/news/articles/clyv1vxkdjyo

Pink, D. 2011. P. 102. Drive. Canongate Books.

Pink, D. 2011. P. 86. Drive. Canongate Books.

Potts, R. 2021. P. 43. The Caring Teacher.

Teacher Tapp. 13 June 2023. Meetings & Money, Eyesight & Equity, Summer Holidays, Subject Knowledge - & Confessions! https://teachertapp.com/uk/articles/meetings-money-eyesight-and-equity-summer-holidays/#

Teacher Tapp. 24 Sep 2024. PPA Home or Away? https://teachertapp.com/uk/articles/ppa-smiling-teachers-and-classroom-disruptions/

Worth, J. and Van den Brande, J. 2020. P. 6. Teacher Autonomy: How Does It Relate to Job Satisfaction and Retention? National Foundation for Educational Research. https://www.nfer.ac.uk/publications/teacher-autonomy-how-does-it-relate-to-job-satisfaction-and-retention/

Worth, J. and Van den Brande, J. 2020. P. 4. Teacher Autonomy: How Does It Relate to Job Satisfaction and Retention? National Foundation for Educational Research. https://www.nfer.ac.uk/publications/teacher-autonomy-how-does-it-relate-to-job-satisfaction-and-retention/

Worth, J. and Van den Brande, J. 2020. P. 11. Teacher Autonomy: How Does It Relate to Job Satisfaction and Retention? National Foundation for Educational Research. https://www.nfer.ac.uk/publications/teacher-autonomy-how-does-it-relate-to-job-satisfaction-and-retention/

The future
The revolution begins here

> *The challenge is not to reform our systems but to transform them.*
> **(Ken and Kate Robinson. Imagine if... 2022)**

Transform - it's a powerful word that carries strength, hope and is especially powerful when compared to Becky Francis' persistent use of the very tame - "evolution". Evolution waits for change. We must try harder. We must do better. And with a sense of urgency.

On this writing journey, I have been back and forth with the idea of revolutionary change, questioning what is achievable in the space we have. During my conversations with Greg Bottrill, he used the phrase "we are not knocking down, we are building up". People become scared when they imagine the removal of something; they fear it will leave us with nothing, a vast empty space, a void. When we begin to build, we can start to see the possibilities and overwhelming potential. Building generates excitement, ignites energy and provides structure. It calls upon a team of experts, invites creative input and requires problem-solving. We must invite the children to support us in building an effective and sustainable way to empower and bring joy to them.

I arrived at the Institute of Education ready to speak to all of the trainee teachers on the day after the 2024 election results came in. Labour had won after 14 years of Conservative rule. When I was a student, the story was quite different. I trained under a Labour government but just before I entered the world of teaching, the Conservatives won. From the day I started teaching, I have found myself in battle, permanently in conflict with a system that is unfit for purpose. That morning, at the Institute of Education, I felt different. As I walked into the lecture theatre, there was a positive energy, a sense of relief; the tutors were bouncy, the students smiling. I mentioned the election and cheers filled the auditorium. This is a precious time that is calling out for change - could the moment really be here? Labour have set the wheels in motion but as time passes, we observe the change we had hoped for fade into the distance, yet again. It is clear that nobody is coming to save us. We cannot rely on anyone but ourselves to deliver the change we need.

There is a lot that is undecided in terms of the future of the Labour government's education agenda - we have had Ofsted under scrutiny (keep that up folks!), the curriculum and SEND review reports are expected. So much *could* change and yet, revolution or transformation seems too risky for the government, there is too much at stake for them. Therefore, we must spend *our* energy showing them exactly what is at stake if we remain as we are. A lost generation of children - a society educated by the past and sent off into the future.

It does not need to be this way.

I recognise that this book only scratches the surface of this topic and that much will change even before it is published, for the one thing that is consistent in education, is change. There is much more to discover, learn and write about – perhaps there is another book in here somewhere but for now I just ask that you imagine, imagine that we have the autonomy to;

- play more.
- connect more.
- be more flexible.
- choose love.
- learn more.

Then we would truly have an autonomous place in which to learn and we might just call that place school. Sounds exciting, doesn't it? I am hopeful; I hope you are too.

THE BIG IDEA - Autonomy

Leisa Rea. Creative Producer and Sophie's former Secondary Drama Teacher.

It was never my plan to be a teacher, and in truth, I had some reservations about becoming one. I was worried that schools were places where children were measured by ever-narrowing criteria. That schools might be missing important ways to value children, to value learning. That they might even (dare I say), be getting it wrong.

This unfavourable view of schools from the saddle of my high horse was in all ways coloured by my own experience as a child. After the freedom and creativity of my primary education, I struggled with the restrictive nature of my formal grammar school in the 1980s, with its draconian rules and single focus on examination results. The style of teaching I experienced supposed that the teacher had all the knowledge and the pupil was simply an empty vessel into which information could be poured. It was a one-way relationship, which left many children like me behind. I wasn't lazy or disruptive, I was filled with curiosity about all kinds of things and a hunger to learn, to ask my own questions. But in this context, I wasn't seen.

When I became a teacher in the mid-90s, I knew that learning must be reciprocal. I wanted children to feel seen and listened to. I tested the idea that if I could manage to nurture authentic, reciprocal trust in the classroom, with a spirit of non-judgement and openness, then children would know that they mattered (something that's important to them). They would feel safe enough to explore, ask questions, take risks and even more importantly, to make mistakes.

My experience is that "questions" are hugely underestimated and "answers" are hugely overrated. Even science is often based on "what we know so far". Questions unlock learning. They reflect the sorts of things children want to know and need to know and we should be prepared for such questions, verbal or non-verbal. What is being asked or thought about here? Questions show us that children are invested, curious, and sometimes, confused or lost. I remember a teaching colleague bemoaning the fact that my form group was wearing her out by asking too many questions. I couldn't have been prouder.

Successive Governments have and will meddle with the education system, responding to what they think children should know to fit in with current ideas about society or work. But perhaps it's not what we teach, but how we teach that really matters. Perhaps giving children the agency to make sense of their world and themselves is the best way to serve them.

This was at the heart of my approach to teaching. It meant a different power dynamic in the classroom. Shared equity. The right balance of freedom and safety. A place for curiosity to grow (and exams to be approached fearlessly). All teachers were once children, so we really have no excuse to forget that children must matter, be seen and listened to. We ignore that lesson at our peril.

INDEX

Note: Page numbers in *italics* refer to figures.

academic achievement 103-104
academic subjects 104
accountability 55; and autonomy 55; data 71-75; and motivation 79-80; observations 62-71; Ofsted 56-62; stakeholders 75-81
AI *see* artificial intelligence
Allingham, Sue 83
amygdala 20
anxiety 73; and developmental delays 108; parents 94
appraisals 65
artificial intelligence (AI) 39, 115-120
attendance 98-99, 101; children's wellbeing and schools bill 99; crisis 98; home-school 100-102
attention deficit hyperactivity disorder (ADHD) 108, 126
autism 108
autonomous working environments 9-10
autonomy 1-4, 10, 17, 154; and accountability 55; and curriculum 32-35; digital autonomy 130-131; overview 4; and poor retention 4-5; social and emotional learning 85-86; wellbeing and 8-9; *see also specific entries*
Awen Project 106

Bates, Adele 107
Bates, Berrin 108
Baylis, Lisa 21
behaviour 107-110
being independent 85
Bethune, Adrian 19, 25, 30, 38, 40, 47, 139

biology of education 89-90; curiosity 89; planfulness 89; playfulness 89; sociability 89; willfulness 89
boredom 73
Bottrill, Greg 24, 35, 88, 148, 153
boundaries 7
Bryce-Clegg, Alistair 49
Burgundy Book 67

Caring Teacher (Potts) 148
Charlotte Church 106
chatbot prompts 116
ChatGPT 114, *117*
child mental health illness 16
children and autonomy 83-84; attendance 98-102; mental health 84-91; personalised learning 91-98; success 102-112
Children's Society 84
Children's Wellbeing and Schools Bill 99
classroom 46-47; culture 92; environment research and professional development 48-51; learning environment 47; micromanagement or support 47-48
collaboration 86
collaboration as motivation 143; senior leadership teams (SLT) 143-144, 147; teaching and learning responsibility (TLR) holders 144-146
competence 1
confidence 86
conflict of interest 133
connection and belonging 96
continued professional development (CPD) 48, 134, 138-139

continuous provision 47
cookie-cutter mentality 107
Cowley, Andrew 15, 32, 36, 39, 79, 83, 85, 92
Cowley, Sue 33, 35, 147-148
CPD *see* continued professional development
creativity 84, 104-105, 108-110
creativity and tech 125-126; digital homework 127-130; digital literacy 126-127; tech capitalism in education 126
cultural capital 73
curiosity 89
curriculum 51-53; and assessment 33; and autonomy 32-35; review 33-35
curriculum content 92

data 71-72; planning 73-75; summative and formative assessment 72-73; testing 72
Deci, E. 1
decision-making 127
democratic schools 106-107
Department for Education (DfE) 35, 115
Department for Education's Character Education 85
DeSilva, Sarah 24, 44
digital age and autonomy 114-115; AI in education 115-120; creativity and tech 125-130; screens 120-125
digital autonomy 130-131
digital homework 127-130
digital literacy 126-127
Dixons Academy Trust 27
DoodleMaths 127
Dough Disco 121
Drawing Club 88
Drive: The Surprising Truth About What Motivates Us (Pink) 10

early career teachers (ECTs) 2, 11, 42, 134-135
Early Years Foundation Stage (EYFS) framework 4, 87
ECTs *see* early career teachers
Education Endowment Foundation (EEF) 94
education otherwise than at school (EOTAS) package 100
educators 2; autonomy, absence of 2; burnout 2; motivation 10
electively home educated (EHE) children 100
ELP (Effort, Learning and Presentation) 43
emotional literacy 108

emotional regulation 86
environment and resources 93-94
Equality Act 2010 24
Ewin, Beth 135-136
exhaustion 77
exploration 84
expression 86

family anxiety 16
Farquharson, Matt 27
Farr, Tina 9, 92, 111-112, 143
Fisher, Julie 87
Fisher, Naomi 27, 144
flexibility and innovation 105-106
flexible working 26-27
Francis, Becky 33-34, 153
Freud, Anna 99
Fricker, Eliza 27, 75, 150-151

Gen Alpha children 115
Geri Yoga 4
Ghey, Esther 20
Gibb, Nick 56, 83-84
Gibbs, Rachel 47-48
Glastonbury model 100
Godfrey, Kiera 77
Good Childhood Report 2024 84
Gosling, Jess 39
Gosling, Matilda 85
Gove, Michael 32, 56, 83-84
governance 77
government attendance campaign 99
governors 76-77
Grange, Hannah 140
Gray, Peter 87, 89

Hadow Report of 1933 2
headphones 123
high-stakes accountability 43
Hippocampus 20
home-school 100-102

identity 24, 28-30; flexible working 26-29; isolated thinking 25-26; religion 24-25
individual and autonomy 147-148, 150; disruption 148; diversity and inclusion 148-149
instilling a growth mindset 86

Johnson, Vickie 26

Kapoor, Annabelle 39, 51
Kell, Emma 12, 19
Key Stage 2 (KS2) children 114
King, Vanessa 37

LA *see* local authorities
Lakin, L. 1
learning objectives (LOs) 134
left-wing ideology 83
Levinson, Ben 9, 62-63
Lewin, Lucy 118
Little Lockdown 100
local authorities (LAs) 77-79, 126, 139

Making Change Stick (Mannion) 12
Malaguzzi, Loris 47
Mannion, James 12, 15, 133, 146
mastery 10
Maternity Teacher, Paternity Teacher (MTPT) 26
Mathletics 127
mental health 84-85, 91; play 87-88; social and emotional development 85-87; "the play people" 88-91
micromanagement 17
mindfulness 7, 20-21
mocksteds 57
Moffat, Andrew 24
Mossbourne Academy 107
Mother Pukka 27
motivation 10
multi-academy trusts (MATs) 56
multiplication tests 96

National Curriculum 32, 41, 52, 56, 59, 80, 112
National Education Union (NEU) 66, 70, 78, *137*, 138
National Foundation for Educational Research (NFER) 7, 59, 135; data 92
negative communication 47
newly qualified teacher (NQT) 2, 14
No Outsider programme 24

observations 62; performance reviews 65-66; school without observations 62-65; sickness and absence 67-71

Ofsted 2, 10-11, 38, 74-76, 84
openness and fairness 65
organisation and autonomy 134, 143; continued professional development (CPD) 138-139; early career teachers (ECT) 134-135; pay scales 135-138; preparation and planning and assessment time (PPA) 140-141; time 139-140

parents 75-76; anxiety 94
pay scales 135-138
performance-related pay (PRP) 10-11, 66
Perkins, Lyle 128
Perry, Ruth 56-58
personal, social and emotional development (PSED) 72
personalised learning 91-92, 98; connection and belonging 96-98; environment and resources 92-94; teacher-pupil relationships 95-96; uniform 94-95
personality 84
Phillipson, Bridget 140
phones 121
Pink, Daniel H. 10-11, 55
Pink, David H. 140
planfulness 89
planning 41-42, 44-46, 73-75; learning objectives and success criteria 43; legal and policy considerations 42-43; timing and pacing 43-44
planning, preparation and assessment (PPA) 134
play 87-91
playfulness 89
"the play people" 88-91
Play Projects 88
prefrontal cortex 20
Pre-Ofsted check-ups 57
preparation and planning and assessment time (PPA) 140-141
professionalism 13
psychological needs 1
purpose 10

qualified teacher status (QTS) 18, 99

Rachel de Souza, Dame 121
Ramanujan, Srinivasa 103
Rea, Leisa 154
real-life symptoms of burnout 99

relatedness 1
retention crisis 9; motivation, innovation and wellbeing 10-11; professionalism 13-16; workload and boundaries 12-13
rich island history 83
Rush, Ciara 145-146
Ryan, R. 1

"sausage factory" structure 87
schemes of work 35; and disconnect 36-37; hidden identity 37-38; inclusion, child development and schemes 39-41; phonics schemes 36; as support 38; and workload 38-39
screens 120-121; phones 121; social media 121-122; television and smart boards 122-125
self-awareness 85
self-care 7-9, 19-20, 22; mindfulness 20-21; stress management 21-23
Self-Compassion for Educators (Baylis) 21
self-determination theory (SDT) 1
self-esteem 18, 85, 103
self-expression 1
self-maintain 20
self-portraits in classrooms 48
self-withdrawal 98
senior leadership teams (SLT) 2-3, 7-9, 12-15, 19, 25, 30, 33-35, 42, 42-43, 46-49, 61-62, 64, 70-71, 77, 84, 92, 94, 104, 128, 142-147
sick days in education 67
Sir Kevan Collins Recovery Curriculum 35, 98
six-phase teaching programme 36
SLT *see* senior leadership teams; senior leadership teams (SLT)
smartboard 121
Smith, David 14
Smith-Tong, Sophie 8-9
sociability 89
social and emotional development 85-87
social and emotional learning 85-86
social media 115, 121-125
special educational needs and disabilities (SEND) 118; crisis 84
Spielman, Amanda 58, 103
stakeholders 75; governors 76-77; local authority 77-79; parents 75-76

standard assessment tests (SATs) 71, 96
standardising classrooms 49
stress 13, 20-23, 33, 57, 63, 64, 76, 77, 100, 145
stress management 21-23
success 102-103; academic achievement 103-104; behaviour 107-110; creativity 104-105; democratic schools 106-107; flexibility and innovation 105-106
summative and formative assessment 72-73
summative assessment 73

teacher burnout 33
teacher-pupil relationships 95-96
teacher-retention crisis 2
Teacher Talk Radio (TTR) 24
Teacher Tapp 1, 9, 36, 62, 66, 68, 116, 121, 134, 135, 140
Teacher Wellbeing Index 21
teaching and leadership responsibilities (TLR) 10-11, 76, 127, 137; holders 144-146
tech capitalism in education 126
television and smart boards 122-125
testing 72
Thatcher, Margaret 32
Thompson, Carol 41, 43
time 139-140
Times Education Supplement (TES) 41
TLR *see* teaching and leadership responsibilities
tokenistic offerings 140
trainee teacher 8, 11, 102, 125, 130, 135, 150, 153

Ultimate Guide to Lesson Planning, The (Thompson) 43
uniform 94-95

Waters, Sarah 58
wellbeing 8-9, 16, 30
wellbeing and autonomy 7-9
wellbeing in the workplace 16, 19; connections and relationships 17; self-esteem 17-19
Whitehouse, Anna 27
willfulness 89
Woodhead, Chris 57

For Product Safety Concerns and Information please contact our EU representative GPSR@taylorandfrancis.com
Taylor & Francis Verlag GmbH, Kaufingerstraße 24, 80331 München, Germany